Sports Illustrated

HOCKEY TALK

Sports Illustrated

HOCKEY TALK

FROM HAT TRICKS TO HEADSHOTS
AND EVERYTHING IN-BETWEEN

FOREWORD BY **KOSTYA KENNEDY**

FENN

M&S

Library and Archives Canada Cataloguing in Publication

Sports illustrated hockey talk : from hat tricks to headshots and everything in-between / the editors of Sports illustrated ; foreword by Kostya Kennedy

ISBN 978-0-7710-8322-8

1. Hockey–Miscellanea. 2. National Hockey League–Miscellanea. 3. Hockey players–Miscellanea.

GV847.S66 2011   796.962'64   C2011-905210-5

We acknowledge the financial support of the Government of Canada through the Book Publishing Industry Development Program and that of the Government of Ontario through the Ontario Media Development Corporation's Ontario Book Initiative. We further acknowledge the support of the Canada Council for the Arts and the Ontario Arts Council for our publishing program.

Published simultaneously in the United States of America by
McClelland & Stewart Ltd., P.O. Box 1030, Plattsburgh, New York 12901

Library of Congress Control Number: 2011937873

Typeset in Palatino by M&S, Toronto
Printed and bound in the United States of America

Fenn/McClelland & Stewart Ltd.
75 Sherbourne Street
Toronto, Ontario
M5A 2P9
www.mcclelland.com

1 2 3 4 5 15 14 13 12 11

CONTENTS

FOREWORD

THE ETHOS DOESN'T CHANGE. BACKYARD PONDS become Pee Wee rinks, then junior-league barns, and finally, glossy, 20,000-seat arenas. Years and generations pass. The NHL extends further and deeper into the international landscape. There's money to be made. And still hockey remains rooted in its hardiness and humility, in an appetite for hard work, a constancy of purpose, a willingness to absorb and play through pain, a determination, above all, to do whatever may be needed to help your team win. This is where the soul of the game resides.

Hockey's magnificent moments invariably come after a series of unseen and unglamorous ones. Sidney Crosby's Golden Goal – relived and freshly examined in Michael Farber's exquisite story *Eight Seconds* (page 2) – was not scored simply by dint of some isolated sleight of hand, but because of a sequence of decidedly blue-collar (if sophisticated) efforts. For Crosby, the praise that he gets around the rink is worth as much as the latest endorsement dollar. *No one works harder than Sidney,* any coach or teammate will tell you. And it takes only a short time watching him to see that this is true.

Bobby Orr had the ethos too, of course. For all his

spectacular skills, the rushes and weaves and feints that changed the sport forever, Orr's greatness was buttressed by the honored values of his craft: He could knock a guy flat. He could go into any corner against anyone (or even two of anyone) and come out with the puck on the blade of his stick. He played, and willed his team to victory, on knees that he could barely stand on. Those are the virtues that cling to Orr and that have made him – still elusive, still inscrutable (page 18) – a living legend.

The pinnacle Orr moment endures in part because it lives in black and white, the classic hockey photograph. Orr is soaring, horizontal to the ice, after scoring the winning goal of the 1970 Stanley Cup finals. The power of the photo is not just in the fact that he scored, nor in his apparent jubilation, but also in the knowledge that in the next frame Orr, who'd been tripped into the air by a Blues defenseman, will land hard on the Boston Garden ice.

In the most thrilling of hockey highlights, pain is just a breath away. In hockey, nothing comes for free.

WE WRITE ABOUT THE GREAT ONES OF COURSE. Crosby and Orr and Wayne Gretzky, Rocket Richard and Gordie Howe. They each elevated themselves by some mixture of, in the words of Herbert Warren Wind describing Richard (*Fire on Ice*, page 146), "his courage, his skill and that magical uncultivatable quality, true magnetism . . ."

Courage, it must be noted, comes first, the thing that unites not only the sport's immortal players but also all of the worthy foot soldiers; that quality (the ethos, again) that must attend a hockey player, lest he wind up left behind or banished to a coach's dreaded doghouse. Courage is needed because the threat of violence – legal or illegal, intentional or incidental – is always there.

In the fall of 2000 I wrote a story for SPORTS ILLUSTRATED on Marty McSorley, the aging NHL enforcer, then with the Bruins, who had just received the longest suspension ever mandated by the league. McSorley's crime (a provincial court ruled it to be exactly that) had been using his stick to club the Canucks tough guy Donald Brashear in the side of the head. It was a horrific act, awful to see (Brashear dropped like a bag of bones, and then lay convulsing on the ice) and unpardonable.

It was not, however, unique. The incident had given another glimpse into hockey's dark side. McSorley, Boston's primary fighter, was hoping to engage Brashear, the Canucks heavyweight, into combat. The blow had not simply been an outgrowth of that single game – Brashear and McSorley had fought in the first period and had circled one another throughout – but also of a career made essential by the nature of the professional game.

In his prime McSorley, best known as Gretzky's bodyguard with the Oilers and the Kings and a player who routinely finished near the top of the league in fights and penalty minutes, had made himself into an effective defenseman. Good for twenty-two minutes of ice time a night, smart with the puck, a plus-player. McSorley was no All-Star but was a solid top-four blue-liner, clearly something more than a goon.

And so I asked him, "Marty, do you think you would have made it to the NHL if you weren't such a good fighter?"

McSorley paused, and then he said: "I would not have made it to Junior A."

WHEN HE SWUNG HIS STICK AT BRASHEAR, McSORLEY crossed over the edge (far over) and broke hockey's do-and-don't code of violence. Jesse Boulerice crossed over as well – terribly, shockingly – when he raised his stick and battered Andrew Long in an OHL game (*Less Than Murder*, page 72). Such an event tends to burst into the public conversation, serve as a referendum on the sport.

Yet it is easy to parse. We abhor what Boulerice did and condemn it without restraint. *There is no place for that in hockey*, every observer, every player, every coach agrees. *Never was and never will be.*

But what about, say, the purposeful slash that Bobby Clarke, that revered and toothless Flyer, the rambunctious Canadian boy from Flin Flon, delivered to the great Russian forward Valery Kharlamov in the 1972 Summit Series? Kharlamov's ankle was fractured, his superb series finished, as Canada rallied in his absence to win the remaining games. How does the hockey purist regard Clarke's slash? Just a part of the sport? Over the line? Fair? Unsportsmanlike? Does that swing of the stick lift Clarke's legacy – and surely in many barroom conversations it has – or diminish it?

Fighting, that is, gloves-off and put 'em up fighting, has been part of North American hockey from its earliest age and remains close to the heart of the modern game – as evidenced in Farber's *Why Good Teams Fight* (page 102). Yet that particular form of violence, the clashing of enforcers away from the pulse of the game action, is something other than the slashes and cross-checks and high elbows that occur in mid-battle, and those are in turn something other than the body-rattling (but within the rules) hits and blows that pepper each shift and can define the environment of a game.

Hockey's beauty shows itself in many ways – the spectacular goals of Richard, the cerebral elegance of Gretzky, the dauntlessness of Howe, the tic-tac-toe of a power play tuned just right, the flash of a goalkeeper's glove. All of it takes place on a knife's edge: literally, on skate blades; figuratively, because at any moment on the ice, a collision may come, or a heavy check into the boards. And then things may unravel. Such ordinary run-ins, after all, are what concussed Crosby in the early of days of 2011, dizzying him and ending what had appeared destined to be another MVP season for the Kid.

Years ago in the Colorado Avalanche locker room I was talking with the NHL forward Dave Reid, who was then in the evensong of a nearly two-decade long professional career. Reid was raving about a young and energetic teammate, who, Reid said, "played every game, every shift, as if it might be his last." Smart, we agreed, because you never know if it would be.

That's the way the memorable players approach each night in the hockey rink, playing the game on some level as if it might be his last. "Leaving it all on the ice," so many players like to say. And, "Whatever it takes."

There it is again: the ethos, the soul of the game.

KOSTYA KENNEDY

Sports Illustrated

HOCKEY TALK

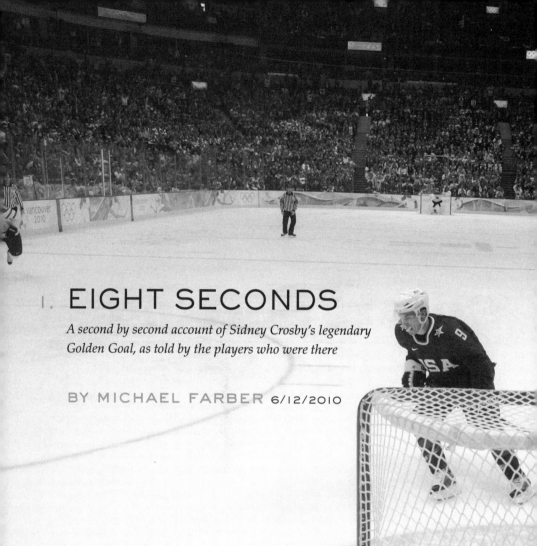

I. EIGHT SECONDS

A second by second account of Sidney Crosby's legendary
Golden Goal, as told by the players who were there

BY MICHAEL FARBER 6/12/2010

CONSIDER A MOMENT. NOW TAKE THAT MOMENT – maybe the most significant in sports in 2010 – and break it down frame by frame into 100 or so smaller moments. Hit STOP, REWIND, and PLAY. Now do it again. Follow the traveling puck, the dot that connects four men. Team Canada forwards Sidney Crosby and Jarome Iginla, American goalie Ryan Miller, and referee Bill McCreary. Seated in front of oversized plasmas or small laptops earlier this fall, clicking through a DVD, they watch adjustments, assumptions, decisions, and unadulterated dumb luck. No need for a spoiler alert. The climax never changes. Crosby scores with 12:20 left in overtime. Canada 3, USA 2. Olympic gold. These men know too well what will happen because they were there.

The golden goal in Vancouver is embroidered on the tapestry of hockey, part of a Crosby legacy that will one day veer into legend.

But what if Crosby had not scored to end the most significant game ever played on Canadian ice and an American like, say, Joe Pavelski, who had a credible chance seconds earlier, had?

The same people who still bask in the reflected glow of the goal light would be muttering about a hockey messiah who, other than a round-robin shootout winner, had experienced a middling Olympics.

Canadians would be lining their sackcloth with fur in anticipation of winter.

Hockey in the U.S. might have undergone a dramatic updraft that likely would have made Miller a breakout star, boosted

PREVIOUS PAGE: **Sidney Crosby seconds after scoring the Golden Goal at the 2010 Olympics.** *(Photograph by David E. Klutho)*

4

interest among hockey agnostics in NHL cities such as Atlanta and Columbus and maybe even prodded owners of the twenty-four American-based teams to look past their wallets and embrace participation in Sochi 2014 so Team USA could properly defend its gold medal.

"If we'd lost to the U.S.," Iginla says, his eyes dancing, "they'd've probably made another *Miracle* movie."

The four men met separately with SPORTS ILLUSTRATED and talked through the most memorable goal scored by a Canadian since 1972 and the most deflating one scored against the U.S. since, well, ever. Viewed through the prism of personal experience they deconstructed the kaleidoscopic twists of those last eight seconds, offering explanation but not excuse, hammering happenstance into narrative. As their tales eddied and flowed, it was clear they were not simply reliving how four men came to be in one quadrant of Olympic ice on the last day of February – but telling a universal story of how the regimented and the random blend to make history.

12:28

Crosby barrels into the high slot with the puck on his stick, trying to barge past defensemen Brian Rafalski and Ryan Suter. Their teammates, forwards Zach Parise and Jamie Langenbrunner, apply backside pressure, swallowing Crosby in a deep blue sea of U. S. and A. as the puck skitters ahead toward the American net. He is in jail. Crosby might be Superman, but unless he leaps defensemen in a single bound, his options are limited. The Americans are in control, which appeals to the man on the ice who most craves it.

Miller is a problem solver who likes to muse about the position he has played since age eight; he recognizes the egocentricity innate to goaltenders, wonders if the controlling nature of a goalie has psychosocial implications for a team. This is how he thinks. Sometimes this is how he talks. In any case he derives visceral pleasure from the challenge of denying shooters: Sid the Kid vs. Ryan the Id. During Miller's three years at Michigan State he would drop in at the basketball offices to visit Tom Izzo, not to have the coach help him think outside the box, but to expand that box. Izzo, NCAA champion, and Miller, Hobey Baker winner, often would talk about how to meet expectations.

Three hundred fifty-four minutes and fifty-nine seconds into his Olympic tournament, Miller has exceeded expectations. Those in the States who watch hockey once every four years reflexively attach themselves to goalies (Jim Craig in 1980, even Ray LeBlanc during a surprising run to the medal round in 1992) because it is the black-and-white position in a game with so many moving parts. The goalie stops the puck. Or he doesn't. Simple. And Miller has stopped it 138 times on 145 shots at the instant the puck dribbles toward him. In the past thirteen days a goalie who plays in the modest market of Buffalo has become a quasi-celebrity, one whose back story – he is dating an actress, he owns a chic clothing store in East Lansing – has become front-page material. He is accustomed to hockey being a cult sport to which people pay attention at their convenience, but now his game is the main attraction at the five-ring circus. The phrase "Miller-cle on Ice" is tweeted and retweeted. Four years after being left off the Olympic team because of a broken thumb, Miller is at the zenith of the position. The thing making him uneasy is having all the attention lavished on him rather than on his U.S. teammates.

Although Rafalski is deep into his shift, Miller, at the edge of his crease, backhands the loose puck toward the corner to his right.

12:27

McCreary is anticipating that Miller will freeze the puck – he guesses Rafalski is tired – and prepares to blow a quick whistle but then sees the goalie send the puck to the corner. Legs churning, Crosby pursues it as Suter and Rafalski, whose helmet has been knocked askew, sort out who will chase him and the play. Within one second, a benign one-on-four morphs into a one-on-one in the corner.

Iginla, who jumped onto the ice three seconds earlier, ponders his possibilities: He can position himself near the hash marks in anticipation of Crosby slinging the puck up the boards or he can switch positions with his center, allowing Crosby to skate back up the wing on the vacated ice. Judging the angle of Crosby's torso, Iginla is certain his center will keep walking up the wall.

Iginla is an optimist. He can no more help seeing the good in a situation than Miller can help analyzing it. Although his line has so far failed to produce the anticipated stream of goals – Crosby, Iginla, and Eric Staal have nine among them at this moment – he continually reassures them that they will get the Big One. He thinks he inherited his sunshine from his maternal grandfather. Rick Schuchard would drive Jarome to his youth hockey games and, if the team lost, on the ride home would say, "Oh, that other team sure got lucky." Once when Iginla's team finally scored near the end of a trouncing, Schuchard bellowed from the stands, "There goes the shutout!" He built the framework of his grandson's worldview one bromide at a time.

And Iginla pays it forward, at least once by credit card. During the 2002 Olympics, Iginla was introduced to four Flames fans who had driven from Calgary to Salt Lake City without tickets or a place to stay. When he learned they had been sleeping in their car in a hotel parking lot, he excused himself, made a few calls and booked them into the same hotel where his family was staying. Iginla later would score twice in the gold medal victory over Team USA, karmic proof there is a hockey god. (Crosby will ask only one player for an autographed stick in Vancouver – Iginla.)

As he skates toward the corner, Iginla figures if nothing develops for Crosby, the center might bounce the puck back to him so he will have a chance to roll for a shot.

12:26

Iginla is right. Crosby swivels his head and spots Iginla heading toward the corner, leaving him a path along the boards, a situation that is more ripe with promise than trying to manufacture a scoring chance from the extended goal line. Rafalski adjusts his helmet. Initially unsure whether Crosby or Iginla ultimately will wind up with the puck, McCreary must choose to stay along the boards or dart behind the net, a decision that will ultimately bring him more attention than his old-school mustache.

Some two and a half hours earlier McCreary had flipped the puck like a coin at midfield – the puck flip is the referee's signature; he started doing it fifteen years ago, as a way of saying hello to his five-year-old daughter, Melissa, who had suffered a stroke – and dropped it to start the match. This is McCreary's third Olympics, third gold medal game. (He called the 2002 final when Iginla scored twice.) NHL director of officiating Terry Gregson approvingly says McCreary "referees from the neck up." This means he knows how to control the flow of the game, understands when to intimidate players in order to lower the temperature of a match and realizes when he should swallow his whistle. McCreary is confident in his assessment of situations and players. Team USA general manager Brian Burke calls him "one of the best referees in the history of the NHL."

Still, McCreary is surprised to be here – in the final, in Vancouver at all, really. He is in the last year or two of his career, "past my time," and he is not certain the International Ice Hockey Federation is as enamored of him as his NHL bosses. He doesn't think he fits the IIHF "style." In a meeting before the medal-round games, an official from Finland tells him that he has to get off the boards and get to the net area more.

Two days before the gold medal game, McCreary learned he would be part of the most watched game in North America since the Miracle on Ice in 1980; another hallmark in a career brimming with them. (He also has worked in fifteen of the past sixteen Stanley Cup finals.) He will officiate with Dan O'Halloran, another well-regarded NHL referee. Like McCreary, O'Halloran is a Canadian. Even with experienced American-born NHL referees available, two Canadians are calling a Canada–USA final. This would not happen in any other Olympic sport – ever – but the IIHF and NHL make a daring assumption that professional referees are, well, professional.

Gregson who, with Konstantin Komissarov, the secretary of the IIHF's officiating committee, gave the game to McCreary and O'Halloran instead of force-feeding an American into the mix, is sensitive to the issue of neutrality; eleven years earlier he essentially had been labeled the worst thing a ref can be: a homer. Late in a scoreless Game 6 of the 1999 Maple Leafs–Flyers playoff series in Philadelphia, Gregson, who is from Ontario, called an elbowing penalty on Flyers star John LeClair. When Toronto scored on the ensuing power play to eliminate his team, Philadelphia chairman Ed Snider ranted in the home dressing room, assailing Gregson's impartiality while denouncing the call as "a disgrace to the game." When the referee supervisors and IIHF and NHL officials convene in Vancouver before the medal-round games, Gregson opens the meeting by saying, "Will we be using the best or are there political ramifications to our decisions?"

McCreary tries to make himself inconspicuous along the boards, trying to guess Crosby's next move.

12:25

Crosby crosses with Iginla, the center lugging the puck toward the hash marks and the right wing dropping to the goal line. There are now crevices in the American defense, a residue of Crosby's determined skating, but he fails to notice an avenue of clear ice from the boards to the middle in which he might have been able to squeeze a pass to Scott Niedermayer or Drew Doughty, the pinching defensemen. The opportunity vanishes. The puck rolls off the blade of Crosby's stick – he hasn't cupped it sufficiently – and ticks the front of his left skate, which pushes it toward the blue-line. McCreary thinks about jumping out of the path of the puck but stays planted because if he hops and holds on to the boards, he would hang in no man's land, unable to make it to the net quickly enough to rule on a goal.

In the three seconds since Crosby tried to bully his way past the defensemen, options have been weighed, choices made. Still nothing has alarmed Miller. Rafalski pressures Crosby. Good. Suter wanders to the corner to track Iginla. Well, fine. Parise, a left wing with a mature grasp of positioning, stands sentry outside the crease. In a perfect world Parise would chase the play and a defenseman would take the front of the net, but forwards and defensemen are free to make adjustments. Besides, hockey is an imperfect world.

The kaleidoscope turns. The one-on-four that evolved into a one-on-one is now a four-on-four.

12:24

The puck that glances off Crosby's left skate hits McCreary on the inside of the referee's right skate. (Stuff happens. The ref can be an impediment in any game. There are roughly 17,000 square feet of ice surface in Canada Hockey Place and the four officials – two referees and two linesmen – need to be somewhere.) Although McCreary has no idea it has struck his size eight, his skate has killed whatever momentum the puck had been carrying in the slushy residue along the boards. The puck sits there, inert as Monty Python's parrot.

Crosby overskates the dead puck. If an American corrals it – Rafalski appears to be in position to do so – the U.S. can counter three-on-two. Crosby senses the danger. He must make sure the puck does not slip past him. He must shovel it deep, toward Iginla in the corner, before Rafalski closes.

Crosby plants his left skate, unleashing a geyser of snowy spray that flies waist high – frozen testament to the immense power of his legs. The area along the boards looks as if someone has shaken a snow globe. With only his right hand on his stick, Crosby stabs at the puck.

12:23

The broken play is mended by Crosby's one-handed lunge, which propels the puck down along the boards to Iginla a foot in front of the extended goal line. Iginla originally thought the battle for the puck would be fifty-fifty, a coin toss, Crosby vs. Rafalski, but the situation turns up heads for Canada because Crosby chips the puck before the defenseman can nudge it in the opposite direction to Langenbrunner, who is about six feet up the boards.

This time, Miller will wryly note later, McCreary lifts his skates and the puck slides past.

Crosby notices Rafalski's momentum has carried him away from the changing flow. He sees Rafalski is flatfooted, which prompts. . . .

12:22

"IGGY!!!"

Iginla never especially liked the nickname Shane Doan gave him when they played junior hockey in Kamloops, B.C. He thought it sounded soft. Iggy. Like Eggy or something. Of course when your full name is Jarome Arthur-Leigh Adekunle Tij Junior Elvis Iginla, you shouldn't quibble. And if you object whenever a teammate uses a nickname that sounds as if it came from the comics section . . . well, that cements it, doesn't it?

Iginla has grown comfortable with his nickname through his thirteen years with the Flames. Iginla hears "Iggy" daily. Now he hears "IGGY!!!," ornamented with capital letters and exclamation points. He is planning to spin out of the corner and away from Suter, but the vehemence in Crosby's voice leads him to reconsider. Iginla certainly can differentiate degrees of urgency, and Crosby's yell is imbued with an unmistakable tone of, Get me the puck right now! Iginla's head is down. His eyes are on the puck. But the scream that drifts above the bedlam of 17,748 at Canada Hockey Place – "IGGY!!!" is clearly audible on the replay – demands he shift to a Plan B.

As Iginla suspects, Crosby, pushing off his left skate, has lost Rafalski.

When Crosby was thirteen and the best player his age in the world, he met Andy O'Brien, a strength and conditioning coach, at a hockey school in Prince Edward Island. When Crosby was fourteen, O'Brien moved his business to Halifax. Crosby was his only local client to start. For the past ten years O'Brien has worked with Crosby on building exceptional core strength. He has trained Crosby to develop hockey-related biomechanical and neurological efficiency. In three sessions over six hours on almost every summer day – 90 minutes on the track, 90 minutes of weights and 45 minutes of targeted muscle work interspersed with recovery periods – they nurtured the key elements of first-step speed: low center of gravity, shin forward, weight distribution on a single leg. They trained on unstable surfaces, like balance boards and Bosu balls, to enable Crosby to move his limbs dynamically while stabilizing his spine and pelvis. The result is Crosby's superb hockey haunches, what O'Brien calls his "massive ass." Crosby's obsession with angles (shin, torso, everything) is Euclidian; he forwards to O'Brien action photos of himself torn from magazines and newspapers and asks, "How do my angles look?" After 2,000 hours in O'Brien's company, and innumerable more hours of training on his own, no hockey player can accelerate from a dead stop to twenty-five miles per hour quite like the bowlegged Crosby.

Sometimes one moment is 2,000 hours in the making.

From his standing start, Crosby gains the edge of the face-off circle to Miller's right before Rafalski appreciably moves off the boards. He approaches the face-off dot before Rafalski gets to the edge of the circle.

The scoreboard clock still reads 12:22.

The recalcitrant puck is spinning, refusing to behave. Iginla struggles to retain control. He is wearing Suter like a size forty-two regular. And as Suter is about to check the off-balance Iginla to the ice, the winger flicks the puck across the face-off circle to Crosby, praying he has not reacted too late.

12:21

Miller, the Vezina Trophy–winner last season, plays for the Sabres, which means he faces Crosby, the Pittsburgh captain, four times a year in intraconference games. He knows Crosby usually looks at the net when he prepares to shoot. Crosby receives Iginla's pass on his backhand, tape to tape, then moves it to his forehand. Studying Crosby's posture, Miller concludes

Crosby is not contemplating a shot. Crosby generally releases the puck with his hands in front of his body, and they are now too far back. With the open lane – Parise is perhaps a step high but still in the play – the goalie expects Crosby to take another lateral stride to the front of the net, dip to his backhand and try to tuck the puck under the crossbar.

Miller shifts his hands on his stick, readying a poke check.

Because of his peripheral vision, Crosby knows Miller is relatively deep in his crease. In stories after the gold medal game, Miller's hands are identified as the factors that induce Crosby to shoot. In fact he never sees Miller move them. At first Crosby is not fully aware the goalie even has extended his stick. He rejects the lane to the front of the net not because of the incipient poke check but because he expects Parise to cut him off. Unsure of how Miller will play the situation – one pad down? butterfly? – Crosby decides to release a quick shot from the bottom of the circle, aiming low. Five hole or glove side. Either, really.

If Crosby holds the puck for a fraction of a second longer, Miller assumes he can salvage a deteriorating situation. The goalie, who has extended his stick like a man reaching with a broom for a quarter that has rolled under the sofa, thinks he can drop into his butterfly quickly enough to force Crosby to change his shooting angle.

"When he doesn't hold it," Miller says, turning from the computer, "now you know you're screwed."

12:20

Miller is late on his butterfly. Five hole. The puck is in the net. Pandemonium. Crosby flings his gloves skyward in a spasm of joy, an emotion that overwhelms rational thought. He is elated not for having scored a goal but for having won a game, even if the two are inextricable. Can you understand? If Crosby can detect the outlines of the big picture . . . well, that's all he can see in the blur of celebrating teammates. He knows this is about something larger than one player, no matter how prepared or how gifted. What's the cliché? There's no I in Canada.

Iginla hears rather than sees the goal. He is still on the ice, courtesy of a check by Suter that McCreary considered penalizing, but six months later, with the benefit of stop-rewind-click, knows was a legal play. The hike along the Olympic abyss has worn on Iginla – "We're winning games and everybody's asking, What about Sid? He didn't get a hat trick, he didn't get two goals," he says – but now a wave of relief washes over him. He is a sensitive man, aware of the wide world beyond the Olympic bubble. He knows that no matter what, the sun will rise Monday morning. He also knows that now it will shine that much brighter on a country whose identity is welded to the sport.

Miller, on his knees, hunches over the ice and bows his head.

EPILOGUE

On a brilliant September afternoon in New York City, after about a half hour of DVD to-and-fro, Miller is done. Really, he needed no video prompting. He played the game. Miller had stuffed it into the file cabinet of experience and moved on, although something in his eyes hints those eight seconds never will be far away.

"Right when [Crosby] did what I didn't think he would do,

I knew the puck was in," he says. "I didn't get angry. Just dis-appointed. [What I did] was in between what I should have done: held my net, the safe thing. But I played the whole tour-nament pretty aggressive. I just thought if he got in that area, that low, I would be on top of him by the time he figured things out. I probably only watched the replay once, until now. Why should I? I lived it. But history happens. Life goes on, and things unfold. You look back too much, you go crazy."

2. THE EVER ELUSIVE, ALWAYS INSCRUTIBLE, AND STILL INCOMPARABLE, BOBBY ORR

At sixty, he's been a player agent for longer than he ruled the ice. He is fiercely private and deeply loyal, and the force of Orr's singular presence has not waned

BY S. L. PRICE 2/3/2009

OF COURSE THE PARENTS TRY TO STAY COOL.
But when the phone rings and that voice says, "This is Bobby
Orr . . ." some can't help themselves. "No!" they'll say, or giggle and talk too loud: Just the idea of telling the cousins, the
folks at work, *You won't believe who called last night*, is enough
to get the nerves jangling.

Still, this is their boy's future at stake, so they usually recover
and manage a few hard questions, and then the conversation
will start sailing along and, *Why, he's just so easy to talk to, so
down-to-earth, like everyone said,* and soon it's just two people
gabbing, no starry-eyed stuff until the voice says something
about coming by to talk a bit more. Then it sinks in: *Come by?
Him?* And, still listening, now there's this quick scan of that family room in Thunder Bay or Hull or whatever Canadian town
happens to have produced the next raw piece of hockey talent, a
desperate glance at the stains on the coffee table, the drapes that
long ago needed replacing. . . . *Here?*

"It's unbelievable," says Barbara Tavares, mother of top Canadian
junior John Tavares. "Your legs are like jelly."

Bobby Orr – for many the greatest hockey player ever, the
defenseman who altered the essence of the game – has been
making his living as an agent for thirteen years now, and he's
become, as celluloid agent Jerry Maguire put it, good in the living room. He and partners Paul Krepelka and Rick Curran
incorporated his Orr Hockey Group in 2002 and have built a
clientele of thirty-three active NHL players (fourth most of any
agency) that includes Ottawa center Jason Spezza, Carolina's

PREVIOUS PAGE: **Bobby Orr back in his playing days. The
mismanagement of his career by agent Alan Eagleson would inspire
his own career as an agent.** *(Photograph by John D. Hanlon)*

Eric Staal and Cam Ward, and Philadelphia forward Jeff Carter, who last June signed a three-year, $15-million extension. Neither lawyer nor marketing expert, Orr leaves negotiations to his partners, serving as all-around adviser, player counselor, exemplar, and conversation stopper. "We were talking to different agents, but once I met him, my decision was pretty much made," Spezza says.

Who, after all, could better understand the pressure of becoming a national darling at fourteen, the psychic toll exacted by injuries, the threat of business "advisers" ever ready to sink their teeth into an athlete's balance sheet? Who better to remind overpaid kids of their responsibilities to their talent, teammates, and public?

Indeed, "Bobby Orr: Agent" might make perfect sense, except there's simply no precedent for a generational icon to enter this long-derided trade and even less reason to think the fiercely reticent Orr would be the first. Even now, it's no secret that he regards player representation as a generally dirty business; in 1996, when Orr began working as an agent, the irony was lost on neither friend nor foe.

"I found it hard to believe," Alan Eagleson says.

Yet here Orr is, despite – or perhaps, because of – the fact that Eagleson, the fallen power broker whose hockey empire grew out of his role as Orr's agent, left him all but broke as part of one of sport's most spectacular financial scandals. Here Orr is, knees and fortune rebuilt, sixty years old and rounding a corner in 2009. He has now been an agent for longer than his run as an NHL star and with his clientele growing and his firm embroiled in a big-time fee dispute with Islanders goalie Rick DiPietro, Orr is playing hardball. And on his terms: All agents alternate between vocal advocate and secret-keeping consigliere, but Orr has taken the public-private shuffle to new extremes, keeping his face before the Canadian public in TV ads that highlight his self-deprecating humor and that eternally boyish Bobby-ness, while keeping any thoughts on the league, his business and his life under tight wraps.

Orr hasn't given a substantial interview in nearly two decades and doesn't need to. Thirty years after the Boston Bruins retired his number four, the hockey world is still dazzled by the magic of his name: Parents will always take his call, team execs and coaches who played against or idolized him will always agree to meet. And once inside Orr works to defuse any hero worship. He'll giggle and tell jokes at his own expense, recall how it was for him to be young and homesick and crying, how it felt rising so fast. He'll steer the conversation to what he can do for your boy. Sometimes, though, the family will want a little more. And when, in the case of a prospect like Spezza, whose Canadian junior career nearly matched Orr's for bated-breath mania, a cocky little brother pipes up at the dinner table, "I bet you can't score on *me*!" well, sure, Orr will take that bet: ten shots, score fewer than five and the kid wins.

So it was that, in the fall of 1998, eleven-year-old Matt Spezza found himself scrambling down to the basement in his Mississauga, Ontario, home to strap on goalie pads, gloves and mask. Finally Orr pushed away from the table, hobbled downstairs in his golf shirt and slacks, and picked up one of Jason's sticks. He flipped the first two shots up, easy to block, but Matt was cocky and started taunting the man who scored 296 goals, the player known in practice to gather a puck off the ice as if with a spoon and with back to the goal swat it on a line into the top corner of the net. "Is that it?" Matt said. "Come on, let 'em go."

It happened fast: *Boom, boom, boom.* One low, right under the glove, then another, and another; everybody laughing, but the room getting warm. "You could see it," Matt says. "He could put it wherever he wanted." Then as quick as it came, the moment passed. Orr eased up, let the kid knock away the last pucks and win by one, done with remembering what Bobby Orr could do.

"HE RAN A TIGHT ROOM," FORMER BRUINS CENTER Derek Sanderson likes saying about the man who helped save his life, but that doesn't do the matter near enough justice – not with Orr's first Boston coach, Harry Sinden, calling him the Godfather and his last, Don Cherry, relating how teammates shortened it over the decade that Orr played a kind of hockey no one had ever seen. "God here yet?" the other Bruins would say, or "Where was God last night?" But not to Orr's face. Not once.

God came to Boston in 1966, eighteen years old, and within two seasons the once-pathetic Bruins had been transformed into a spectacular, mean, winning bunch. Some of that was due to the 1967 trade that brought in scoring machine Phil Esposito and forwards Ken Hodge and Fred Stanfield, but it was Orr, the working-class product of Parry Sound, Ontario, who set the tone. His on-ice artistry – coupled with a willingness to hurl that six-foot frame in front of any slap shot, into any opponent – endowed him with ultimate authority. He barely had to say a word.

Game days, Orr would arrive at 2:30 for a 7:30 start, play cards, bang around the emptiness, sort through the 144 sticks sent him every few weeks – weighing them, selecting two, maybe three, discarding the rest – getting himself ready. His teammates would file in at five or six o'clock. He'd wander about then with one stick weighted with lead or with pucks taped to the blade, shifting it from hand to hand. Locker room music rarely played. "I have never run into any player who brings the intensity that he brought," says Sinden, who spent forty-five years as a coach or front office executive. "His silence, his looks, were enough to tell you if he didn't like what was happening. And he made the rest of us the same way. You could not be around him without feeling that and getting in line."

If you had a bad period? Or dogged it? Sanderson's locker was by a pillar, and he'd set his chair so the pillar would block Orr's view from across the room. "Is he looking?" Esposito would whisper. Always, Orr would be staring lasers. Sanderson only felt worse when Orr would wait until he was alone, come over and mutter, "You got to pick it up. We need you."

Then Orr would hit the ice again, and it was wondrous to see – for the fans, yes, but even opponents found themselves entranced. When Bobby Clarke was a rookie center for the Philadelphia Flyers – the team that later raised the ante on Boston's bruising ways – he found himself all but cheering Orr's speed and control; he couldn't help himself. It wasn't just the end-to-end rushes, Orr's thick legs pushing him to a gear few could match, to scoring levels unheard of for a defenseman. It was his style. There was just one strip of black tape on Orr's stick and the puck seemed glued to it, that fine detail so compelling that Boston strippers took to sporting the equivalent of today's French bikini wax – a thin strip of pubic homage dubbed "a Bobby Orr."

During one penalty kill against the old Seals in Oakland, Orr swooped behind goal in possession, tussled with an opponent and lost a glove. "He went around by the blue-line, came back, picked up his glove – still had the puck," Esposito says. "[Goalie] Gerry Cheevers was on the bench, and I'm standing there and I hear Cheesy say to me, 'Espo, you want *The Racing Form*?' I said, 'Might as well; I'm not touching the puck!' Bobby killed about a minute and ten, twenty seconds of that penalty – and then . . . ," with even the Oakland players cheering now, " . . . he scored. Greatest thing I ever saw."

In 1969–70 Orr became the only player to sweep the league's top awards – MVP, best defenseman, playoff MVP, and scoring title – and capped it off by scoring the Stanley Cup–winning goal over St. Louis in overtime. The following season, the Bruins scored 124 more even-strength or shorthanded goals than they gave up when Orr was on the ice, and that remains his most lasting monument; the man most mentioned as Orr's rival for the title of greatest ever, Wayne Gretzky, never cracked plus-100.

Yet Orr bristled at the attentions of superstardom, would tell coaches to find reasons to bawl him out like the rest. His last good season, 1974–75, he scored forty-six goals but probably gave away a half dozen more by insisting that teammates had deflected the puck in. It's no accident that his signature play – and the one that won the first of his two Stanley Cups, against the Blues – was a give-and-go. Orr's best rushes were never look-at-me affairs but a storm he brewed on one end of the ice, gathering in his fellow Bruins for the inexorable sweep forward. When he began to move, says former Montreal goalie Ken Dryden, the sensation was unique: All the Canadiens began backpedaling in a small panic, like beachgoers sighting a coming monster wave.

"He brought others with him; he *wanted* them involved," says Dryden. "That's what made him so different: It felt like a five-player stampede moving toward you – and at his pace. He pushed his teammates, [because] you're playing with the best player in the league and he's giving you the puck and you just can't mess it up. You had to be better than you'd ever been."

LORD, DO THEY REMEMBER. FOR HARD MEN OF A certain age, and for Canadians, especially, the mere mention of Orr can undam a rush of feeling. "Guys make fun of me because I'm always talking about him," says Cherry, whose second life as a hockey broadcaster gives him plenty of opportunity. "My son made [an Orr highlight] tape to Carly Simon – *Nobody Does It Better* – and I cry every time I see it. I don't know why."

It's no mystery. Orr did it all: blocked shots, dealt out punishing blows, endured the swooping hits of players desperate to stop him, somehow. When it came time to defend a teammate or himself, he fought. Gladly. "Too much," Esposito says. "He didn't have to, but he had a temper."

The fact is, despite his schoolboy haircut and shy grin, Orr was a killer on the ice. He laid out the Blackhawks' Stan Mikita with a perfect forearm cheap shot, hammered the hell out of Mikita's teammate Keith Magnuson at every opportunity, waited a year to get his revenge on Toronto's Pat Quinn – Orr jumped him in a brawl – after Quinn knocked him unconscious with a riot-sparking hit in the 1969 playoffs.

"Pound for pound, he might've been the toughest guy in the game," Quinn says. "He wasn't a hold-and-throw like a lot of guys. He could go with both his hands, like a prizefighter."

A game-changing talent, a taste for blood: Those were enough to make Orr a hockey hero for life. But vulnerability is what makes him resonate still. A recent TV ad shows Orr sitting silently while a lengthening scar on his famous left knee serves as a time line of victory, and loss; he played, really, only eight full seasons, and operations on both knees left him a near cripple at thirty. Ever since, commentators have made him the equivalent of Jim Brown, Sandy Koufax, even John F. Kennedy, shooting stars who left the world wondering what might have been. His last hurrah, the 1976 Canada Cup series, provided the perfect, bittersweet coda: Orr in so much pain that he couldn't practice, beating the Russians on one leg, outplaying the Czechs single-handedly, "the most courageous that I've ever seen a hockey player," says Clarke, the captain. Hockey nation didn't disagree.

"He *is* Canada," says Barb Tavares, whose son nevertheless ended up signing with another agent. But if Orr is how a certain segment of Canadians want to see themselves – self-effacing, self-sacrificing, quietly great – there's a glint of recognition too, in what lies beneath the forced politeness, the goofy charm. In any conversation there's a tension that never leaves Orr, the feeling that his spring-loaded temper might snap and turn the warmest banter to ice. When first contacted by SPORTS ILLUSTRATED, Orr couldn't have been more welcoming, shuffling through his calendar for interview dates; in a second phone conversation he declared that he didn't want, as he has told many journalists, "a story about the agent business." He never returned another call.

Cherry has felt more than one freeze-out as Orr's coach in the 1970s and even after the two battled as celebrity coaches in the annual Top Prospects Game a few years ago. That time Orr didn't speak to him for six months. "Great heart, but he hates pretty good," Cherry says, and when asked how Orr was to coach, he pauses.

"I got to be careful here," he says finally. "You had to handle him right. You had to know when to talk to him; he was not an easy guy. He could spot a phony a mile away. There were so many people after him all the time that he became suspicious; he was never really friendly with a lot of people. When I first went there, I made the mistake: He was eating alone, and I made conversation. How was the fishing this year? And he picked up right away that I was just making conversation, and he didn't like that. He didn't like any bull——, and you know what? He's exactly like that today. He's pretty unforgiving. If you cross him, you will never get the chance to cross him again."

Eagleson crossed him the worst, of course, exposing a weakness as damaging as any knee injury. Once the cocky and high-flying master of the hockey universe, an irresistible force who rode Orr's celebrity into a multihatted – and conflict-ridden – position as executive director of the NHL Players' Association, hockey's most powerful agent and chairman of Hockey Canada's international committee, Eagleson would be accused of pilfering money from player pension funds and disability payments, and in 1998 he pleaded guilty to multiple counts of fraud, including those involving the theft of hundreds of thousands of dollars in Canada Cup proceeds. He served six months in a Toronto jail, was disbarred, got kicked out of the Canadian Sports Hall of Fame.

Eagleson's bargaining tactics had made Orr the NHL's highest-paid player as a rookie, and Orr expected to be a millionaire when he retired in 1978: Eagleson had promised him, after all. But in 1990 Orr told a Canadian newspaper in detail how, in blindly following Eagleson's tangled financial advice, he had ended up with just $450,000 in assets – and tax bills that wiped him out. He had his homes in Boston, Cape Cod, and Florida and a name to sell, but a wife, Peggy, and two sons, Darren and Brent, to support. And the money was gone.

For press and public, Eagleson's crime against Orr was best summed up by the pair's final contract negotiation with the Bruins in 1976. Boston offered a multiyear deal that included an 18.5 percent ownership stake in the team, worth an estimated $49 million today. Though Eagleson made that offer public, Orr insisted that he didn't know about it until years later and, more to the point, believed Eagleson when he said there was a better deal to be gotten with the Chicago Blackhawks – owned, it just so happened, by Eagleson's close friend Bill Wirtz. Such obliviousness seems incredible, but then Orr had known Eagleson for fifteen years. "He had total control," Orr said in 1990. "He said we were brothers. And I trusted him like a brother."

For his part, Eagleson won't talk about specifics and says, "I wouldn't do anything differently. That's how I was and that's how it is, and in the long haul of life the truth will eventually out."

What's not in dispute is the depth of Orr's trust. Esposito didn't like Eagleson, but Orr wouldn't hear a harsh word against him, and the tension between the teammates became palpable anytime his name came up. One day in the spring of 1976, with negotiations at an impasse – Orr would eventually sign a five-year contract with the Blackhawks, but injuries limited him to just twenty-six games in two seasons – Cherry was alone at one end of the Boston Garden dressing room, fixing a stick for his son, when he noticed Bruins president Paul Mooney walk in and approach Orr as he sat pedaling on an exercise bike.

"Bobby, can I speak to you a minute?" Mooney said, puffing on a pipe.

"F—— off, Paul," Orr replied. "You're trying to drive a wedge between Al and I."

"Just let me talk to you for thirty seconds."

"F—— off. Don't talk to me."

Mooney shook his head and walked out.

"They were going to offer Bobby all that money, 18 percent," Cherry says. "Nope: 'F—— off.' That's how loyal he was to Eagleson. You couldn't convince him. Once he made up his mind? Forget it."

RICK CURRAN FIRST HEARD THE QUESTION SIX years ago, after he became Bobby Orr's business partner. Does Bobby participate? He's got the name, and you guys do all the work, right? Come on, Rick: Is he *involved*?

"You don't understand. This guy gets up 5:30, 6:00 every morning," Curran says. "By the time I talk to him – and we talk every day between 7:00 and 7:30 – I can tell by the sound of his voice whether our clients had a good or bad night the night before. He knows how everybody did; if someone's minutes are down, we know he's either injured or hasn't done what he should've been doing. And by the end of the conversation we have a list of seven or eight items for that day that we're going to address. Involved? He still lives and breathes it."

Endorsement contracts and public relations work had lifted Orr out of the financial ashes left by Eagleson, and in 1996 Orr bought into the Boston agency created by Bob Woolf. Now agenting gave him a chance to attack business as relentlessly as he did the game. "Dozens of calls every day – to players, to scouts, to skill coaches: How's our guy doing?"

says Jay Fee, who worked at the agency before going out on his own in 2002.

Orr also drew a clear line: His agency would not handle – as Eagleson had – player finances. "Being victimized by a bad agent, I think Bobby wanted to run a business that would never do that to anybody," Fee says.

Still, Orr leaves much of the on-the-ground detail to his partners. The Flyers' Jeff Carter – handled primarily by the Philadelphia-based Curran – emerged as a breakout star for the firm this season, and he has scarcely any relationship with Orr. Meanwhile, Orr's Boston-based partner, Paul Krepelka, is the agent of record in DiPietro's case; he represented the Islanders goalie up to and including the moment DiPietro signed a record fifteen-year, $67.5-million contract in 2006. The relationship frayed soon after and DiPietro fired the firm, refusing to pay its percentage because he had never signed a standard player-agent contract. Last summer, Orr filed a grievance with the NHL Players' Association, but DiPietro – who declined to speak to SPORTS ILLUSTRATED – says he owes nothing. Krepelka agrees that DiPietro didn't sign a contract with the Orr Group, but says he negotiated the pact and should be paid. The grievance is expected to be heard this spring and "could segue into a lawsuit," Krepelka says.

Orr's role, though, was never about pen and paper. Then and now, he has traveled widely to take in college and pro games, bundled golf rounds with contacts in coaching and broadcasting, used his stature to gain an entrée denied rival agents. He often showed up unannounced at the Maple Leafs' offices when Pat Quinn, his old sparring partner, was coach and general manager from 1998 to 2006. Quinn usually didn't deal with player reps, but he always welcomed Orr. Eventually talk would turn to a client like defenseman Tomas Kaberle, and Quinn says, Orr would "get to where he wanted to go. And it was always about the kid, about his best interest." When, during Kaberle's 2001 holdout, hockey analyst Gord Miller of The Sports Network in Canada took an on-air shot at Kaberle's defense, Orr got in Miller's face, stats at the ready, snapping, "You'd better rethink that!"

Orr's loyalty to the faithful is just as fierce. If he has refused to donate signed pictures or gear to a desperate fan, or refused a charity golf tournament or hospital visit, no one has heard of it. In 2006 a story ran in *The Boston Globe* about a high school hockey player, Bill Langan, who played in a regional title game on the day of his mother's wake; the kid mentioned that his mother used to watch Orr play. Orr called, asked if he could help. Langan asked him to come to a team dinner. Orr made no promises. But he showed up without warning and stayed an hour.

As for the big, bad – and now old – Bruins, Orr is, Sinden says, "still the Godfather." When the flamboyant and reckless Sanderson showed up in Chicago in the winter of 1978 stoned and unable even to hold a cup of coffee steady, Orr personally checked him into a hospital and was there when Sanderson woke up with three doctors staring at him. "Who's going to tell him?" one said.

"I'll tell him," Orr said and then leveled with Sanderson: "You're a full-blown alcoholic and a drug addict. It's over. You've got to go to rehab." Orr paid for that first stint. When Sanderson relapsed, he says, Orr paid to send him back. And then again. "He never left me," Sanderson says.

When Sanderson finally cleaned up, and began a new life as a financial adviser for athletes in the 1990s, Orr invested with him, gave Sanderson the chance to work with Orr's clients too.

Orr also paid for rehab stints for former Bruins trainer John (Frosty) Forristall, his roommate during his first years with the Bruins and an irreverent bon vivant whose alcohol problems led Esposito, then the general manager of the Tampa Bay Lightning, to let him go in 1994. Forristall returned to Boston jobless, and soon after he was told he had brain cancer. Bobby and Peggy took Forristall into their home for a year until he died in 1995 at fifty-one.

"I'm glad somebody was there for him," says Frosty's older brother, Bill, from Florida. "He wouldn't come down here. I was a little too hard-nosed; I wouldn't put up with his drinking." Orr stood by Frosty to the end, hovering over him in the hospital, serving as a pallbearer at his funeral. But he wouldn't speak to Bill.

"Bobby wasn't too happy with me," Bill says. "John apparently said something that put me in a bad light. I've never been able to figure it out."

MAYBE IT WAS THE FACT THAT HE'D JUST TURNED sixty, or that two knee-replacement surgeries had freed him of cane and pain. Maybe he figured he could finally take the onslaught of memories without breaking. But on November 27, Orr relented at last, stood on the ice at the General Motors Centre in Oshawa, Ontario, and allowed the junior team he left in 1966 to retire his number.

Still, he could barely sleep for two nights before. Oshawa, after all, had known him all the way back in 1962 when Orr was raw, wide-open, fourteen years old and missing his parents, Doug and Arva, up in Parry Sound. Oshawa was where Wren Blair, a G.M. in the Bruins system, planted him and where the Eagle got his hooks in.

But Arva died in 2000 and Doug in 2007, both in winter, and when Orr took the microphone that night, his voice quavered and his eyes filled. "I know my, uh, mom and dad are watching tonight," he said. "I know they're very, very happy . . . very proud. My mom and dad were the perfect minor hockey parents. Their whole philosophy was, Look, go out and play, have fun, and let's see what happens. And I wish there were more parents that thought like that when it came to their kids playing hockey. . . ." And the standing crowd cheered the dig at hockey parents gone wild, cheered how things used to be.

Yet as much as he doesn't like being called an agent – "He'd rather it be, 'family representative,'" Sinden says – that's what Orr is. He famously never put either of his sons on skates, but he has his oldest, Darren, thirty-four, working for The Orr Group in Boston. Bobby Orr is now part of the machinery of parents, media, teams, and agents dedicated to finding the next Bobby Orr.

In January, Orr returned to Oshawa to coach against Cherry in the 2009 Top Prospects Game, the annual showcase for top junior talent. It was Orr's tenth appearance; he took part in the inaugural event in 1996 as a celebrity, but once he became a player rep, competing agents cried conflict of interest – he would, after all, be coaching a game designed to help determine draft order, salaries and the size of an agent's commission. Orr offered to withdraw. Organizers wouldn't hear of it.

On the morning of this year's game Orr and his team of prospects posed for the traditional team photo. Afterward, the coaches and players scattered to the locker room, leaving their chairs and platforms and mess behind. Orr didn't say a word. He grabbed two chairs and skated them off the ice. Then he went back for a riser, bent over, and shoved it slowly to one end of the empty rink: wrong door. He wheeled and shoved it the length of the ice again, leaving it at the right one so the arena crew would have a bit less work.

The players returned after a few minutes and began circling the ice counterclockwise. Orr joined in, dipping into the flow and skating hard again, reversing time if only for a few laps. Cherry hadn't seen Orr on the ice pain-free in thirty-five years. "Before, it was push and glide, really sad to see," he said. "Now? You would never know."

Orr gathered up a puck and wristed it low into the empty goal, making the net shiver. He stopped, began feeding all the young men as they swooped past, clockwise now: Foligno, Holland, de Haan, Tavares, O'Reilly. He tapped gloves with one, cracked a joke with another. Now Eakin, McNabb, Roussel flashed past, and now Schenn, and Orr motioned with his stick, and Schenn passed back the puck, maybe three inches wide. "Hey!" Orr snapped, and banged his stick on the ice to say, right *here*, and Schenn got closer with the next one. Orr gave him a grin.

He came off the ice later, and the press gathered and someone asked if he remembered what it felt like to be that young. He spoke about playing as a kid, outdoors mostly, shooting through the fierce cold on the Seguin River, on Georgian Bay, scrapping on icy parking lots. "No coaches, no parents," he said. "Get the puck and just go.

"It was never a job for me. Even during my pro days, it was never, ever a job. That's what these kids have to understand: Just enjoy it, keep that love and passion for the game. I think what sometimes we do – we, the pressures, the coaches and parents – we just suck that love and passion from our kids. And I think that's wrong."

He and Cherry had a bet on the game, $100. That night Orr's side won 6–1, and Cherry gave it up at the handshake. "Money goes to money, you see that?" he said.

And then Orr, icon and agent and coach all in one, raised the bill over his head and waved it in triumph. Thousands roared. Thousands laughed. Their Bobby was back, no limp, and eyes shining. It felt perfect, the way any church does when the ceremony goes off without a hitch and the light streams just so.

3. TORN ASUNDER

The inner conflicts that drive St. Louis Blues coach Mike Keenan
to succeed also make him the most reviled man in hockey

BY GARY SMITH 8/5/1995

HIS HOME WAS A THREE-BEDROOM UNIT ON THE sixteenth floor, filled with the furniture of forgetting. All whites and blacks and glass and metal; each morning, in such a place, was surely the dawn of a clean, fresh start.

The one old thing was his leather briefcase, worn and cracked as an old fisherman's face. "It's the only thing in my life," he remarked, "that I haven't thrown out."

But, it turned out, that wasn't quite true. Late one night, as he tried to explain himself over Amarettos, he fell silent and knelt in front of a small bookcase in his living room. Finally he stood.

"No one who has ever written about me," Mike Keenan said, "has a f——ing clue who I am." Then he handed *The Great Gatsby* to me, as if that were proof.

THE PAPERBACK BOOK WAS A QUARTER-CENTURY old, yellowing and marked in a variety of inks: sentences he had underlined, words and exclamation points he had scribbled in the margins at different junctures since he was a teen. His eyes glittered as he watched me leaf through it. "It's much more complicated," he pointed out, "than anyone really thinks."

He was not much of a reader, he admitted; too many winds whistled through him for him to sit and hear the quiet rustlings of a book. And so even he found it extraordinary that he had read *The Great Gatsby* five times and that every now and then he skimmed it again in order to . . . well, he couldn't quite say

PREVIOUS PAGE: Mike Keenan is one of the most successful NHL coaches of all time, with nearly 700 wins and one Stanley Cup. (*Photograph by Bob Rosato*)

why; it was all feeling, not thought. The first underscored passage I opened to: *Everyone suspects himself of at least one of the cardinal virtues, and this is mine: I am one of the few honest people that I have ever known.*

The main character in F. Scott Fitzgerald's book is Jay Gatsby, a man who, out of nowhere – *poof!* – appears in an opulent estate on the shores of Long Island in the 1920s, throwing lavish parties for guests who whisper speculations about his past and the source of his fabulous wealth. No one realizes that the mansion, the boats, the cars and the weekend revelry are just props, details painstakingly wrought by a poor boy who has poured everything into a pure dream: the pursuit of a beautiful married woman with a low, thrilling voice.

But no, that's not exactly true. The main character in Fitzgerald's book is actually the United States, a land where such a man could invent himself. A land where an eighteen-year-old Canadian named Mike Keenan arrived one autumn day in 1968 and knew in the beat of a heart that he belonged.

Passport official: The purpose of your visit to Canada?
Traveler: Business.
Passport official: What's your business?
Traveler: I'm a writer.
Passport official: What are you writing about?
Traveler: Mike Keenan.
Passport official: Go ahead. He's a bastard.

Odd – or was it fitting? – that a keeper of Canada's gates would issue such a warning, as if some national interest were at stake. But perhaps people everywhere, always, will dispute who Mike

Keenan really is. In Philadelphia, as he coached the Flyers to two Stanley Cup finals between 1984 and 1988, players gave him *Heil Hitler* salutes when he turned his back. In Chicago, where he coached the Blackhawks from 1988 to 1992, Mike willed another average team into the finals but soon lost his job and his marriage. RAT and SCOUNDREL screamed the New York headlines when he fled the Rangers a few weeks after leading them to the Stanley Cup last year. His mailbox was blown up.

The St. Louis Blues hired him immediately, of course, as coach and general manager, and their executive vice president called him the messiah. He drove the Blues to a strong second-place finish in the NHL's Central Division, but he and his new bosses had already gone to war. "The management there," he seethed, sounding oddly distant from his own team, "has promoted superstar status without the team concept. They filled the building without developing a winning culture. They produced a very selfish culture."

Each new place, Mike spoke of how he had learned from the traumas in the previous city, how he had grown and changed. "The ability to grow, change, and adapt," he wrote in his resume for his first NHL job, "are the foundation of the method." So it was strange indeed for Mike to find himself crying recently over things that had happened long ago to the person he used to be.

HIS FRIENDS WERE SICKENED BY THE EVER-SPREADING image of Keenan as rodent and cur. "His marketability today is zero," Gary Webb, a close friend and business partner, says in disbelief. "He's perceived as unethical and morally corrupt." To them Mike's truest self was the man they drank beer with and laughed with till tears came to their eyes. The one who would appear at a party dressed as a fat man or a baseball catcher for the sheer hell of it, who would bolt to the CD player and re-cue *All I Wanna Do*, by Sheryl Crow, eighteen straight times. Or sit at his gleaming white piano, fingers flying over the keys, eyes shut, head jerking back and forth as if in the throes of creative rapture, crooning in a voice so antimelodic that it was almost beyond belief . . .

Sing us a song, you're the Piano Man/Sing us a song tonight/ Well, we're all in the mood for a melody/And you've got us feelin' all right . . . waiting for his flabbergasted listener to realize that the performance was all just bravado and bunkum, a player piano activated by a programmed disc. This Mike, with the blue musical note tattooed on his back and the green shamrock high on his thigh, this free spirit ripping through the countryside on his Harley-Davidson Fat Boy – how had things gotten so twisted that almost no one knew he existed? All those terrible things he had been whispered to have done to players – didn't people understand that they were simply tactics he used to excel in a world where the only measure of a man's worth was *performance*, and that they had little to do with *him*? That the four trips to the Stanley Cup finals he had made, the Calder Cup he won in the American Hockey League, the two Canada Cups, and the Canadian national collegiate championship justified every ugly bit of business along the way? "You have to understand," says Gary Green, a friend of Mike's and a former NHL coach, "this man is two totally different people."

As for Mike himself, he seemed to sense that another self lay one layer closer to bedrock, one level beneath either of the contrasting faces he showed to his friends and to the hockey world. He was still standing over me, watching me thumb through *The Great Gatsby*, as I came to another underscored sentence: *He had been full of the idea so long, dreamed it right through to the end, waited with his teeth set, so to speak, at an inconceivable pitch of intensity.*

Yes, Mike said, his jaws ached in the morning, he ground his teeth so hard at night. He continually cricked his neck, trying to undo the tension. He didn't need much sleep. "Humans overrate sleep," he said. "I've trained myself to sleep from two to six."

He was a dreamer, wide awake. That was the thing one might never suspect of a person so tautly controlled. He would stand for hours on the deck of his lake cottage or on his high-rise balcony, staring at water or sky, dreaming. "I was a visionary even as a kid," he said. "I just wasn't as preoccupied until I got older. One of the problems with being a visionary is I could see things in people that they just couldn't bring themselves to do. I'd picture the whole and then break it into all the little parts. People have this image of me as a knee-jerk decision-maker. But there's almost nothing I do that I haven't thought about for months, down to the smallest detail. You can't compromise on details, because details are what lead to the whole." He smiled. "You may think I'm f——ing nuts. But that's O.K., because I am."

It was ritual now, with each team he took over, each fresh start. He would sweep through the locker room, a fleet of assistant coaches, trainers, therapists, physiologists, equipment managers, public relations personnel, video experts, and carpenters trailing him as he pointed left and right, barking, "Change this. Move that. This shouldn't be here. We need more space here. More light there." Who understood better than he the power of atmosphere and image, the dynamic of the fresh start? What land yearned for it more than his new country, forever turning on televisions and opening magazines for yet another dose? When Mike was done, there would be a crisp new coat of paint in the team's colors. A new carpet with the design of a hockey rink would cover the floor. A state-of-the-art video system would fill one side room, a squadron of exercise bicycles would fill another, and a killer stereo system would pump adrenaline-jacking music into every nook and crevice.

The garbage can in his locker room would know its place, and those little balls of discarded tape had better, too. If the players were wearing red socks in practice, they *had* to wear red tape; white tape with white socks, black with black; off the ice with you if you didn't match. That stick rack, that Gatorade table – clearly they conveyed more order, more success, when arranged in the far corners than the near ones. Soon, as he traveled around the league, there would be grown men, gentlemen of integrity, entering every visiting locker room minutes before he did, stomachs in knots, asking themselves, *Is the room right for Mike?*

The centerpiece in the home locker room, of course, would be the framed color photograph of the Stanley Cup, ceiling track lights focused on it in the way that crucifixes are illuminated behind altars. After all, as he would promise fans in a new city: "We're going to do everything we can to bring the chalice here. The Holy Grail. You have to go through hell to get it."

Most dreamers were vague – floaters in the fuzzy glow of the scenes they imagined. A rare and dangerous thing was the dreamer who squinted, who insisted ruthlessly upon the particulars of his vision. A rare and dangerous thing was a man who would subordinate his popularity, his family, his past to his dream. "I gave up sanity to chase the dream," Mike says. "That's why I win, I guess.

I'm willing to pay the ultimate price. Whether it's worth it or not, it's *my* choice. You preserve your integrity when you do that. You have to have that purity to be a champion." A glint enters his eyes. "It's a good life," he says, "if you don't weaken . . ."

So he invented just the sort of Jay Gatsby that a seventeen-year-old boy would be likely to invent, and to this conception he was faithful to the end.

IN THE AUTUMN OF 1973, AT THE TRAINING CAMP of the World Hockey Association's Vancouver Blazers, fate brought Mike Keenan and Jimmy Adair together. Mike approached him, shook his hand and thanked him for saving Mike's life. Jimmy, who had never met Mike before, just blinked.

Jimmy Adair was the chance event, the distant random molecular movement that led to the invention of the man we see today behind the Blues' bench – shoulders extraordinarily square, arms folded, eyes squinting, head tilted back as if he were sniffing the air for something akin to his own excellence but never expecting to find it. Jimmy was the kid who accepted and then backed out of St. Lawrence University's sixth hockey scholarship in 1968, propelling a man to walk up to Mike and ask the five-foot-seven teenager with the C-plus average if he would care to attend a small, prestigious, private American university for next to nothing.

Mike could have screamed *Yes!* He could have seized the man by the lapels and dragged him to the General Motors plant in Oshawa, Ontario, where Mike's father would work for 31 years, his uncle Bob for 35, his uncle Bill for 38 and his grandfather, the poor bastard, for 51 – that vast, squat corrugated-metal factory with its forest of smokestacks, one of them just waiting, waiting to suck Mike inside it, too. Mike could have dragged the man inside the brick box house in Whitby, one of Oshawa's little satellite towns, where for years Mike had flinched while his parents were at each other's throats. He could have jerked the man's head up to the stars that Mike had been staring at as long as he could remember, full of a hunger so ferocious that it frightened him because he had no clue what could fill it.

Instead he just swallowed and nodded.

His parents drove him across the Canadian border and dropped him off at St. Lawrence University in Canton, New York. *Yes,* Mike could have screamed. Around him were beautiful brick buildings, facilities the likes of which he had never seen before. There were eighteen-year-old girls unloading horses they had brought to school in trailers, young men carrying skis to use at St. Lawrence's lodge in the Adirondacks. Kids from all across America – what kind of land was this, where a teenager might travel several thousand miles to attend college? Kids noticing his hockey jacket and welcoming him – didn't he know that hockey was St. Lawrence's only big-time sport, that anyone who would lace on skates to lead the team against Michigan and Harvard and Cornell was automatically someone special? *Yes, yes!* Mike could have screamed, but instead he just closed the car door and waved to his parents as they headed back north. He wouldn't call them Mom and Dad anymore. He would call them Thelma and Theodore. Nothing personal, but they could have kept driving all the way to the Polar icecap, the way he felt that day. That life, that Mike, was done.

"The second our feet hit the ground," recalls Gary Webb, another Canadian hockey player at St. Lawrence, "we absolutely loved it! Mike and I would just look at each other and say, 'Double A!' It was our signal word. It meant *all-American*. Every time we got excited – it could be over a blonde walking across the quad, or a great party – we'd say, 'Double A!' It meant, *This country's great! Let's go for it!* A place where you either made it on your own or you didn't, where you could go as far as your creativity and convictions could take you. No more socialist crap, no government to bail you out or unions to protect your ass, no laid-back approach to life like we'd both grown up with in Canada. For people like him and me, St. Lawrence and America were paradise. Double A!"

How many noticed what was digging inside of Mike, the burr from his past that would go with him each step of his journey: *Am I worthy?* "Here I was, this poor Canadian country kid," Mike says. "Did I belong there? I felt I owed it to that school to fit in, to survive. They had given me my chance."

He flunked out after his freshman year. He cried. "Ejection from paradise," his pal Webb called it. Mike looped a tie around his throat, prayed feverishly to the god he had once served as an altar boy, and walked into the dean's office, begging for one more chance. The gate to paradise creaked open a crack. Mike would have to sit out one semester, somehow earn enough to pay St. Lawrence's considerable tuition the following semester, and pass all his courses to regain his scholarship. There was only one place for him to turn – back to the brick box house, to the GM plant waiting to bend one more Keenan over an assembly line.

The jungle line, workers called the section Mike was assigned to that summer and fall. Every ten seconds another car rolled before him to be spot-welded – another spray of sparks hitting his goggles, blackening his teeth and spit, scorching his eyebrows and hair, another man's features vanishing in the thickening blue smoke. He worked twelve-hour shifts to earn most of the money, his father made up the difference by cashing in a life insurance policy, and Mike raced for the exit his last day on the job, shouting as he hit fresh air, "You'll never see me here again!"

And they didn't. Back at St. Lawrence he awoke before dawn to study. He made the honor roll. He ran five miles a day. He captained the hockey team. He even took a job laying railroad tracks back in Canada during the summer, sleeping in a boxcar with his money under his ear while grizzled French-Canadian coworkers sometimes rolled with the local squaws a sleeping bag away – anything rather than return to GM and the brick box, the anonymous life to which he was born.

He remembers the terrific energy and vigilance he needed each day, the observation of every American nuance, the caution required not to make a mistake. "It was a lifestyle I wanted," he says. "I knew simplicity would be lost. But I didn't care what adaptations it would take. I was going to do it."

He coughed up the puck – and an easy goal – in his own zone during a game in his junior year. His coach, George Menard, summoned Mike to his office. "I'm not going to tolerate it," Menard fumed. "You did that on purpose. You threw the game. You won't suit up for any more games."

Mike walked out, thunderstruck. This new country, this fickle Double A blonde – was she about to pull the rug out from under him again? "He was in a total fog," recalls Webb. "Looking in the mirror, thinking, I couldn't have thrown a game, but . . . but maybe I have to be stronger so I don't ever even give off the *appearance* of weakness again. The mind games Mike plays on his players today . . . some of that had to come from Menard."

The result? Mike sat for two games but played harder than ever in practice, crushing everything that moved. His teammates unified behind him, one even threatening to quit, and then Menard relented. *Hmmmmm. . . .*

Mike and a half-dozen teammates moved into an old warehouse – black lights, purple posters, garbage-dump furniture, motorcycles in the living room. At Mike's suggestion they formed their own band, Nik and the Nice Guys. "Mike didn't play any instrument," recalls Webb, a member of the band, "and he sang in this incredibly flat voice, but he wanted so badly to be center stage. He would sing that Sly and the Family Stone song *I Want to Take You Higher*. He'd get everybody in the room down on their knees, then wiggling their rear ends, then flopping like fish on the floor of some beer-soaked frat-house basement. It was hilarious! He'd compensate for his lack of ability by bullying the crowd into doing what he wanted."

All the prevailing breezes in his life now were southerly, American, except one. For love he turned and tacked north, hitchhiking home on weekends to see the girl he had met just months before entering St. Lawrence. Rita Haas was a farmer's daughter – cautious, understanding, smart, *rooted*, the granddaughter of a Hungarian Jew killed at Auschwitz. In her home Mike felt warmth and closeness, the absolute absence of tension. It was pure, another antithesis to the life he had known. Not seeing the trap, he wanted that too.

But his heart was in a constant, turbulent riot. The most grotesque and fantastic conceits haunted him in his bed at night.

IF RITA ASSUMED THAT THEY WOULD BOTH BE teachers and raise a large, close-knit family somewhere in the Canadian countryside, couldn't she be forgiven? Her bridegroom couldn't put his dream into words exactly, any more than he could explain why such sentences in *The Great Gatsby* hit him like the back of a shovel to the gut. It had to do with excellence and passion, with refusing the safer, wider road when life, with her unreadable smile, beckoned a man toward a narrow, mysterious path. After a year of minor league hockey in Roanoke, Vermont, Mike knew that his boyhood dream would have to be replaced by an adult one, but he couldn't quite see it yet. In 1975 he took a job as a coach and phys-ed teacher at Forest Hill Collegiate Institute in Toronto – a wolf about to learn that his appetite was larger than his forest.

He would awaken at 5:30 A.M., drive nearly an hour from Oshawa to the school and coach the girls' swim team at 7:00. Teach all morning, jog a few miles at lunch, teach and coach the boys' hockey team all afternoon. Then drive 45 minutes and, at 6:00 P.M., begin coaching the Junior B Oshawa Legionaires, whom he would lead to back-to-back championships. He would be home by 9:00 P.M. if it was only a practice, by midnight if it was a game, and start all over again in darkness the next morning.

It was during a teachers' strike in 1975 that he realized this life could never fulfill his dream. It happened as he walked the picket line beside unionist typing and trigonometry teachers already earning more than he was, demanding raises based on seniority rather than on how much of their hearts and souls they poured into their work. At age twenty-eight, when the Major Junior A Peterborough Petes offered him a full-time job as coach and general manager, he seized it. No more wide, safe roads. He was in the jungle now, and it felt just right.

Well . . . almost. "I'm too sensitive," he would fret to Rita. "I have to get harder to survive in this world." He had developed a few tricks. The one he learned back in Oshawa – he would secretly hack a hockey stick until it was nearly in two, then disguise the break so that he could dramatically shatter the stick during a between-periods rant in front of his team – worked splendidly. But he would need more, much more.

A model, that's what he needed. If he couldn't find sufficient hardness in himself, he would find it in someone else and imitate it. Another minor adaptation, one might call it. Every day, in the halls of the Memorial Centre in Peterborough, Mike walked by a framed photograph. *Perfect*. Scotty Bowman had coached Peterborough to the league title in his first season, just as Mike was doing. Scotty Bowman had just won four consecutive Stanley Cups with the Montreal Canadiens. Scotty Bowman had done it the hard way, as an outsider who had never played in the NHL – just as Mike planned to do it, too. It seemed as if the gods themselves were hitching Mike's star to Scotty's when Bowman, having jumped from Montreal to Buffalo in 1979, hired Mike in 1980 to coach the Sabres' minor league team in Rochester, New York. "When Scotty introduced him at that first press conference in Rochester," says Webb, "Mike was like a puppy dog following his master. He siphoned every ounce of Scotty he could."

There were no more off-nights. If Mike's team wasn't playing, he would drive five hours and scout an opponent, returning at sunup . . . or drive to Buffalo and study Bowman's every twitch behind the Sabres bench. For hours Mike would pepper Yvon Lambert – one of Bowman's former Canadiens who had been sent down by the Sabres to play for him – with questions about Scotty. Just like Scotty, Mike would hold his shoulders and head more and more erect, as if a winch were being tightened in the small of his back. He would chew on slivers of ice the whole game, the way Scotty did. In his late thirties, Mike would even appear one morning with his hair slicked back. Just like Scotty. It was perfect.

Well . . . almost. "Sure, there were a lot of similarities," says Lambert. "They both didn't give a f—— about anyone. They'd both do anything to win. Mike wanted to be as tough as Scotty, but there was one problem. Away from the game, Mike was friendlier. He cared what you thought about him."

Those who would come to know Mike away from the game couldn't fail to notice the paradox. So swiftly did he walk that everyone accompanying him was forcibly swept into step. But once he reached his destination – a restaurant, a bar, a scenic overlook – he would become the child seeking confirmation again and again, asking, "Isn't this a great place? Isn't this beer excellent? Isn't this an incredible view?" He would sneer at schmoozers and fame hounds but shoot looks at all strangers who passed his restaurant table, searching their eyes for that spark of recognition. He was the first to say, "How are you, sir? Nice to see you, ma'am." He was the one in a photograph who put his arm around the fan, not vice versa. This was no merging of the uncertain boy and the authoritative adult. It was screeching lane changes.

Bowman played those uncertainties like piano keys, grilling Mike to explain every decision he made. An uncanny similarity in their coaching styles soon became clear, an emphasis on instinct over system. Mike wanted control over every detail in a player's preparation – his diet, his fluid intake, his conditioning, his state of mind – but on the ice he wanted no blueprint, no patterns. Months might pass without his teams practicing the power play or penalty-killing. He didn't want to restrict his players' creativity, and besides, if he told them what to do, that gave them an excuse if it failed. Whetting will and hunger became Mike's specialty: Let them eat the damn meal with any utensil they wanted. But let them nowhere near the table if they weren't starving.

Systematic hockey filled his nose with the old scent, the GM blue haze; it suffocated his soul. Spur of the moment, seat of the pants, play the hot hand, plank the superstar, yo-yo the goalie, juggle the lines, defy the percentages, anticipate the sea changes – when it was cooking, it was difficult to explain, and it felt like jazz. Bowman played jazz too, so why in hell was he asking for explanations?

Mike's sport still crawled with stegosauruses, old-school coaches, ex-NHL players who had never been to college, Canadians uneasy with change. Never having made it to the top level, Mike felt like the outsider, the unknown, the one who had to one-up the system. He turned his uneasiness to his advantage: He would be cutting edge. Mike would herd his Rochester team into a downtown fitness center for aerobics classes. Mike would put calipers to the players' bellies and masks to their mouths, measuring body-fat percentages and aerobic thresholds four times a year. Mike would pioneer in the AHL the use of video, interval training, circuit weight training. Later Mike would award short-term segment bonuses and quarterly incentives, just like a sales manager. Mike would use computer programs to analyze the comparative efficiency of every line combination in the league. Mike would be Double A.

He read all the motivational and management books, picked the brains of all the men he met in corporate America. In a few years he would begin to dress as they dressed – in dark blue suits and crisp white $100 monogrammed shirts – and to talk in CEO-speak too. His old buddies from St. Lawrence knew it was all just an artist's conception; one of them, Tim Pelyk, approached Mike at a party and gave one of those $100 shirts a button-bursting neck-to-navel rip, just to be sure that Mike knew that, too. Perhaps that's why Mike wore the tattoos and that white shirt with the hole near the armpit under his suit now and then: hidden memos to himself that he wasn't a clone, that he was still the most devout Double A individualist in the land.

No, others speculated, the hole near the armpit was a bullet hole. Mike grabbed players by their jerseys, right at the throat, and screamed in their faces. He instituted curfews on team buses: lights out, total silence. Against Nova Scotia his entire team rose in horror at a blunder that let in the game-tying goal, and Mike knocked over the bench in a rage. "Sit down!" he screamed, and so traumatized were the players that fourteen fannies hit the deck.

"Yvon Lambert told him to back off, or he wouldn't be alive today," recalls Rochester's leading scorer that year, Geordie Robertson. "It was clash after clash after clash. Each team Mike coaches needs a player who has won four or five Stanley Cups, like a Mark Messier or a Lambert, to tell him to slow down. He'd panic sometimes. He'd go into the coaching office between periods and pull into himself, go into a shell, and you'd be on pins and needles because you could feel he was ready to explode. But he was the greatest practice coach ever, ran the shortest and most productive practices you've ever seen."

The Death Skate occurred during a losing streak in 1983, Mike's third year at Rochester. Two hours of nonstop skating, no water, players crumpling on the ice, players vomiting. "I was panicking," recalls trainer Jim Pizzatelli. The team won twenty of its next twenty-four games and the Calder Cup. Mike and the Cup slept together that night in Portland, Maine.

But no reward came from Bowman, no promotion to the Sabres. Mike was thirty-three, for god's sake, stuck under his mentor's thumb, and life was evaporating. A man who would order his team's traveling secretary to enter the cockpit when their plane was stuck in a holding pattern and instruct the pilot to land the plane now . . . did you expect him to wait?

"The whole point of life to me," says Mike, "is to risk." He stunned Bowman by taking a job as coach at the University of Toronto, knowing the only way it wouldn't be seen as a backward career step was if he won the Canadian national championship in 1984. Which he promptly did.

He consented to a one-week vacation in Fort Lauderdale that spring with Rita and their five-year-old daughter, Gayla. Mike holed up in their motel room with a typewriter and wrote a position paper, informing the Philadelphia Flyers how he would win them a Stanley Cup. The essay was filled with sentences such as: "In this paper I hope to be able to integrate the general and the particular, the theoretical and the practical, the idealistic and the realistic, into a final presentation which projects an accurate image of me as both a person and a manager-coach."

Gayla learned to swim that week in Fort Lauderdale. Rita told Mike all about it.

He had intended, probably, to take what he could and go – but now he found that he had committed himself to the following of a grail.

TO ALLUDE ONLY TO GATSBY, HOWEVER, WOULD BE
to slight Bugsy. Bugsy was Benjamin Siegel, the real-life 1940s
gangster depicted in *Bugsy*, the Warren Beatty movie that struck
Mike with nearly the same visceral wallop as *The Great Gatsby*
had. "The similarities between Mike and Bugsy are uncanny,"
notes a friend. Bugsy, like Gatsby, was an extravagant criminal
who staked his life on a long-shot dream: the construction of a
posh casino-hotel in the Nevada desert that would eventually
blossom into Las Vegas. To steel himself, to suffocate any remorse
after killing someone, Bugsy repeated over and over a phrase:
Twenty dwarves took turns doing handstands on the carpet.

Mike memorized the phrase and recited it to friends. Now
that he was an NHL coach, hired by the Flyers in 1984, the stakes
were even higher, and surely he recognized the utility of such a
mantra. Twenty just happened to be the number of men who
suit up for an NHL game.

"He'd get Peter Zezel in the stick room between periods and
motivate the hell out of him," hints Flyer fitness specialist Pat
Croce. *Twenty dwarves took turns . . .* "It wasn't just me," says
Zezel. "He'd throw sticks at other players" . . . *doing handstands
on the carpet. . . .*

"My temper is only a tool," says Mike. "I lose my temper for
the right reason, to make players better."

He skated straight at players who made mistakes in practice,
as if he were going to knock them heels over head, then came
to a halt inches away. In his office he stood over a seated player,
brandishing a hockey stick and seething as the player cowered,
thinking he was about to be hit.

"Most people think I enjoy conflict," Mike says. "*I hate it.* Rita
and I never argued or shouted, even at the end. I saw so much

conflict when I was young, I'm *sick* of it. I'd walk away from doing those things to players, and I'd feel awful inside."

Twenty dwarves took turns . . . "Who haven't I benched this year yet?" he would ask an assistant coach. He would get a name and then bench that player, just to make him wonder if he could play a little harder. "He pitted you against your team-mates," says ex-Blackhawk Steve Thomas. "He always made you feel you were letting them down." In Philadelphia he gave Ron Sutter an ultimatum: Play better, or else your brother Rich won't dress for games.

"The owners gave me s——, so I gave it to the players," Mike says. "I felt I *owed* it to the owners to be that way. I came into the NHL as a complete unknown. They'd given me an opportunity."

Twenty dwarves took turns . . . He shut off the locker room lights between periods and left his team in darkness. He called for prac-tices at 11:59 A.M. just so that players would scratch their heads and wonder why.

"I carried this fear every game," Mike says. "The fear that this would be the last game I'd ever coach. The media read me all wrong. They thought I was arrogant. I was really just scared. It's a great way to hide fear."

"Eventually," says Thomas, "he just drove us physically and mentally insane." *Twenty dwarves, twenty dwarves, twenty dwarves* . . .

And it worked. God, did it ever work. He was Coach of the Year in his first season, driving a Flyer team laden with rookies and second-year players to the league's best record and the 1985 Stanley Cup finals, in which they fell to the Edmonton Oilers. Two more division titles followed, another march to the finals in 1987, with the Flyers denied the Cup again by a supe-rior Edmonton team. He took over the sorry Blackhawks in

1988, whipped them to two division titles and an unexpected trip to the 1992 Cup finals, at which they lost to the Pittsburgh Penguins. In fact, if he stays in the game long enough, nearly every NHL career coaching record will likely come down to a dogfight between him and – of course – Scotty Bowman.

"Mike wouldn't tolerate one bad practice or one bad shift," says Thomas. "That's what made him different. Not *one*. Not even from a superstar." Poor play he took as a personal insult, one so overwhelming that sometimes, in the middle of a game, he simply stopped coaching. After a loss Mike wanted to trade half the roster. Players, trainers, secretaries, janitors – under Mike they either fell by the wayside or they had their most productive years.

His objective was to make losing so dark and confusing that his team's only choice, its one way out of the tunnel, was to win *everything*. Anything short of the Stanley Cup was failure. If the anxiety this produced was too much for a half-dozen players each year, well, then, the sooner he learned this, the better, for how could he possibly rely on such men in Game 7 of the finals? And so he was forever testing them, rolling little sticks of dynamite beneath their feet – *Does your father work, Tony? Does he work hard? Why don't you work that hard, Tony?* – forever demanding more, until their heads spun so fast, they could no longer be sure what the correct answer was. Did he want them to bend over backward to show him how committed they were? Or did he want them to stand up and challenge him, prove their integrity, their spine? There was no correct answer, the smart ones finally realized; anxiety was the goal. Riddle me this: If his own pain and confusion had created such a vast hunger to win, didn't he owe each of his players a personal heaping of pain and confusion?

In his words: "Teams get too cozy. I don't like cozy. You can't win with flat-liners, not even with self-motivated flat-liners. You go first-class in everything, you give them clarity, cleanliness and comfort . . . and then you introduce confusion if need be. If you feel a sigh of relief on your team, even for a moment – *bang!* – you've got to shake them up. There must be a dynamic. If I'm completely unpredictable, the players have to stay focused. They have to always be thinking, *When is the sonofabitch gonna call on me?* I learn instantly who can be rocked."

His teams had camaraderie; his vision was so white hot, it fused them. There were delights as well as horrors around each hairpin curve. On a day's notice, during a break in the schedule, his players were suddenly flying to a lovely mountain resort for a three-day retreat. He took them to fashion shows, musicals, and movies. He could spend hours driving around, talking with a player who had lost his father; could spend thousands of dollars buying everyone, even the locker room broom man, beautiful Christmas gifts. So deeply did he install himself inside the psyches of his men that when they suddenly found that they were no longer part of the crusade, they were unsure whether to feel relief, sadness, or rage.

Thomas: "I know what it takes to win because of Mike."

Zezel: "He taught me things that have added five goals a year."

Robertson: "Every player he has will be critical of him, but every player wants to play for him and win the Cup."

Even Bobby Clarke, the general manager who fired Mike in Philadelphia, says, "In hindsight I probably should've changed some of the players instead of Mike." Perhaps all the conflicting feelings he left behind were inevitable, radiating from the contradiction at Mike's core. The same man who could blame the world for his actions, who at times felt like such a victim, was the one whose whole life was based on the Double A premise that a man with guts and heart could become whatever he wished. The contradictions became so glaring that one night, when the man the Flyers called Adolf rented a hotel ballroom for a party and grabbed the microphone to sing with the band, his players flopped on the floor like fish at his urging and hoisted him so high that he banged his head on the shimmering disco ball.

BUT YOU'RE STILL WONDERING WHAT HAPPENED TO Rita, and with just cause. After all, what was left for Mike to give when he came home? He would return from a road trip or another long day, wrap the stereo headphones around his ears and check out of the universe. On a Saturday off-night, he would stand in front of the TV for two hours – after all, he was scheduled to play in Vancouver in just two weeks, and he couldn't scout the Canucks sitting down. Summers, you ask? He spent two of them coaching in the Canada Cup, two more felling trees from dawn to dusk and then building a cottage on the shores of Lake Huron's Georgian Bay, the body of water he would stare at for hours to heal his disillusion, to dream anew. It was just a few miles from where he had summered as a child, from where his mother had grown up. "There was nothing constant in my life," says Mike. "I needed that cottage. It was my roots, my solace, and sanity."

When he slowed down for a few hours, the softness that he had walled off poured out upon his daughter. He would gaze at Gayla with adoring eyes, stroke her hair, lavish her with praise.

Rita maneuvered around the wide space he needed, moved with him from city to city, losing friends almost as soon as she made them, unable, as a foreigner in the U.S., to work. "She came with me to the NHL out of loyalty, but she never came psychologically," Mike says. "It was never the life she bargained for. God, I was selfish. You look back and wonder what you were doing."

Rita was his liaison with his past, the one who called family members and old friends whom he almost never saw. "Mike," his father would plead, "give Marie and Cathy a call once in a while. They're your *sisters*." Relatives who drove for hours to see him would turn around and drive for hours back home if his team lost, never exchanging a word with Mike rather than risk his wrath. Tim Pelyk, his close friend from St. Lawrence, wrote him a letter after one futile trip to visit him in Chicago. "You'd think two old friends could have more than five minutes together in four days," he wrote.

Mike grabbed a telephone. "You don't understand, Tim," he protested. "I have a blowtorch on my neck."

"Mike," said Tim, "we all have blowtorches on our necks."

IT FELL APART IN PHILADELPHIA, AFTER FOUR YEARS, when the players mutinied. What earlier had stimulated them, in the end only wore them down. It disintegrated in Chicago after another four years, when the owner decided that Mike lusted for too much power. "You give 120 percent of your soul, you give up your family life, and then they kick you in the balls," Mike says. "In all three places I've been in the league, someone was either jealous of me or felt their position was threatened and began undermining. There are snakes everywhere in this jungle."

One day not long after he lost his job in Chicago, he jogged a few miles across the sand in Myrtle Beach, South Carolina, then slowed and looked at his old college pal, Webb. There it was again: "That same look of utter rejection that he had when he flunked out of St. Lawrence," says Webb. "He asked me, 'Do you think I'll ever get a job again?' I said, 'Mike, with *your* record?' But it's like a theme running through his life, this feeling that maybe he doesn't belong here. Like he's still the foreigner, the teenager from the small-town, blue-collar Canadian family, and he's conned his way into this great party, and nobody's found him out yet. So he has this drive to justify that he does belong."

There would always be another NHL job, of course. Another general manager who, like Neil Smith of the Rangers, would say, "I can deal with the devil as long as he wins." Another owner in another city eager to buy Mike's hunger, or at least rent it for a few years, willing to pay the price. But Rita? She looked at her teenage daughter. In a few years Gayla would graduate from high school and be gone, and Rita would be alone again in a new city. Rita looked at Mike. She couldn't say the words. So he did. "You're not going to move with me, are you?" he said.

She asked if he would give up pro hockey.

"You don't even know me," he said.

She played the piano the day he packed – just some cardboard boxes of books and clothes. He saw her waving from the doorstep as he drove away from their twenty-five years together and headed to his new job in New York.

A sudden emptiness seemed to flow now from the windows and the great doors, endowing with complete isolation the figure of the host. . . .

HIS FOOTSTEPS ECHOED INSIDE THE TEN-ROOM
house he had bought for $1.3 million in Greenwich, Connecticut.
He walked outside. Yes . . . *exactly*. "Exactly like *The Great Gatsby*,"
he says. "All those big houses, and you'd never see the people
who lived in them." The teenager who had raced away from the
GM plant in Canada had finally made it. Double A.

Months passed. Most of the rooms remained empty, the refrig-
erator virtually bare. Some nights, rather than go home, he slept
on the sofa at the Rangers' practice facility in Rye, New York.
Some nights he never slept at all. He pretended that Gayla had
gone away to boarding school. "Pain," he says, "beyond what
you can imagine."

It was not just the pain of a failed marriage. It was pain from
all across the map of his life; the past that had seemed to evap-
orate behind him was now dripping down his cheeks. The six
miscarriages Rita had suffered as he was hurtling up the ladder, one of them occurring as late as seven months into her
pregnancy . . . God, he had never stopped to mourn them until
now. The knock on the door when he was four, the policeman
standing there telling his parents that Mike's baby brother had
just died of pneumonia in the hospital . . . somehow it had never
really hit him until now. Suddenly, driving down a street, he
would find himself sobbing for the little altar boy with the big
black glasses. "Just a likable, easygoing kid," recalls his sister
Marie. "Never controversial. Everyone wanted to be his friend."
The little boy who couldn't understand why his parents were
the only ones who screamed at each other, why his father was
the only one in the world who came home smelling of alcohol,
why his mother was so compulsive that when her three children stumbled out of bed early on a Saturday morning just to

go to the bathroom, they might find their beds stripped by the time they stumbled back.

Moments before Ranger practices began, it could happen to Mike; it was scary. Tears for the adult who still couldn't bring himself to go back to 225 Lee Avenue and look at the home of his childhood. Tears for the impatient young man who fled at eighteen, in too much of a hurry to appreciate the gifts that came from that home: the self-discipline from his mother, the love of song and laughter from his dad, the scrimping that a man and woman without high school educations had done to make sure that Mike always had skates and sticks and lessons.

But it had all been just too extreme, too contrary – control and chaos at the same dinner table. Ted coming home after a twelve-hour shift and a few "brown pops" at the Legion hall, wanting to keep the good times rolling; Thelma returning from six hours selling men's clothes feeling as if she had to be the one who asked why every B wasn't an A and every jacket wasn't in a closet. Ted hissing at Thelma to leave the kids alone, and Thelma. . . .

"You know, sometimes I wish I could've done what Ted did, just drink a couple of beers, let go, relax, party time," she says. "But I had to be the ogre. I'd say to Mike, 'You could've done better,' no matter what he did. Our family doctor said he'd never seen a son turn out to be more like his mother.

"I know what he's feeling because I'm the same way. I just wish I could let my emotions out and hug somebody, and I know he feels that way too."

Yes, it was true: Inside, he felt just like his father, who could cry at the crooning of *Danny Boy*. "That was my shortcoming from the beginning," says Mike. "I was oversensitive. I'd keep it all in – I was the stiff-upper-lip oldest son – but inside I kept thinking, 'I'm way too soft.' I knew I'd get chewed up if I didn't change."

So he set out on the longest journey that any boy can make – to become his father's antithesis – and he got there. Why, then, in his mid-forties did he find himself, just like Dad, crying at the crooning of a song? Every room he entered, every car and bus, he switched the station on the FM stereo to country and western, to the brotherhood of American longing and pain. His Rangers would groan. The man whose life was all about winning suddenly *had* to hear people singing about losing.

But his anguish was also his hope; it meant that he had failed to pave himself over completely. He shocked his father, on Ted's sixty-fifth birthday, by sending him an airline ticket and spending six weeks with him in the *middle* of the season. Mike began calling his mother nearly every week – once to ask her how to bake potatoes. "I began wondering," he says, "if the pain I was feeling was the price for the pain I'd inflicted on others. You bury that old Irish-Catholic guilt, but sooner or later it bites you in the ass. I wondered, Did I need people more than I thought? And if I did and I needed to change. . . . Could I change just a little? God, that's scary. Everything had been so all-or-nothing. If I changed it just a little, would my career fall apart?"

He tried to read the meaning of his pain. Was it a signal that he had chosen the wrong path, given too much of himself to the quest? Or did it mean that now, having sacrificed even his family, he had made the quest even more sacred and himself more worthy of its highest reward? Life seemed to answer his question: Even as he feuded with Neil Smith, the Rangers won more games than any other team in the league, and Mike won his first

Stanley Cup. Obliterating the past – maybe that's what it took to dispel the Rangers' curse of fifty-four straight years without a championship. Maybe that's how it works in America.

"It was my most fun year of coaching," Mike says. "There were only a half-dozen times I had to be a sonofabitch versus forty the year before."

He took the Stanley Cup to his empty home and stared at it. "The goddamn thing is unbelievable, I tell you," he says. "It has its own personality. Like it's talking to you – talking of all the broken hearts, the broken legs, the broken families that went into it. For a small period of time, all the heartache goes away. I just looked at it and cried."

SO HOW DID IT ALL FALL APART AGAIN? HE HAD planned to take the Cup to his cottage on Lake Huron, invite all the family and old friends over so they could stare at it and listen to it, too. He wouldn't have to explain anything to them after that. The Cup would justify it all. But he never got the chance.

A few weeks after the season, he infuriated the city that had just toasted him: He quit. He claimed that his contract, which had four years remaining, had been breached when the Rangers sent out his playoff bonus check a day late, and two days later he signed a fatter five-year deal that gave him almost complete control of the Blues. NHL commissioner Gary Bettman called it an "unseemly spectacle," punishing Keenan with a sixty-day suspension and a $100,000 fine.

"Of course, it wasn't the one-day-late payment of the playoff bonus," says Webb. "Mike couldn't stand Neil Smith. To him Smith was the ultimate spineless corporate wimp, and Mike was floored when the Rangers wouldn't let him run the operation after he'd delivered them their first Cup in fifty-four years. What else did he have to do?"

Keenan and the Rangers, of course, have wildly contrasting versions of the events, but a league gag order on the case prevented either from publicly going into details. So it depends on whom you want to believe: the people, like one member of the Rangers, who say, "Winning with Mike Keenan made you feel like a whore," who point out that Mike, even during the playoffs, vowed that he was committed to staying, even though a member of the Detroit Red Wings' front office later claimed that Mike's agent had already made contact about the Red Wings' then vacant coaching job. Or do you believe Mike, who swears that he was going to be kicked out the door by Smith as soon as the Rangers slumped? Mike, who even after he had finally clasped the chalice and attained his dream, still seemed to smell the smokestacks of the GM plant waiting to suck him in? Mike, whose past somehow hadn't gone away after all?

But the deed was done. Mike was running the Blues, he had the fresh start. . . . So why was it that it didn't feel fresh? All the old anecdotes and vitriol followed him, the horror stories dredged up again until he was ready to explode. He thought he had an understanding with his new country, one more inviolable than his pact with the Rangers. You succeed, and the past is forgotten. You move, you leave people behind, but that's permitted too if you win. Wasn't that the promise he had smelled in the air when he crossed the border a quarter of a century ago?

"You can have all the stories and all the s——, and all the reporters and players can call you a sonofabitch, but at the end of the day you've either won or lost, and that's all that matters," Mike snaps. The more he thought about it, the more bewildered he became, the more cheated he felt. "Ask all those players now: Did they mind going to the Stanley Cup finals? They say I burnt them out – *screw* that. It's s——, all these complaints, and it pisses me off, and I'm sick of hearing them. Most of it's from a lot of s—— lazy writers. They regurgitate these stories over and over and never give my side. No one writes about all the good things I've done for players. I'm not going to go around telling people that. I'm not a f——ing P.R. guy. And so 10 percent of my personality is always written about, never the 100 percent. I won't take responsibility for that. A monster's been created, and now everyone wants to come see the monster. Now I *do* need a huge P.R. machine to deal with it. I'll tell you one thing, my P.R. department better do their f——ing job."

And besides, he insists, it's all irrelevant anyway, because he finally has the authority to trade players, finally has been given the power that will allow him to be more human. "I can coach in a far more palatable way now," he says. "I can surround myself with people who are willing to go the distance. I've realized I can't change people. I can only change the teams they play on. I'm sick and tired of being sick and tired. You reach a point where you have enough security, and you say, 'I'm just not going to do it anymore.' Ask the players I coached last year who knew me from before. I'm a lot more patient, so these questions don't apply to me now."

But, Mike, what about what you said about the manhood of the four Russians on the Rangers when you cornered them last season?

"Hey, my reputation precedes me now, so I don't have to be that way anymore," he says. "Fear is a factor already. So I can be softer and be a lot more effective."

But what about . . .

"Look, I've come to realize I'm a decent human being, and I'm a goddamned good coach, and I've had enough of people running over me."

But . . .

"People are so far behind in terms of where I'm at now, they're antiquated. I've changed *that* radically. There *are* choices. I *can* make them. All that matters is that you learn from your mistakes. All that matters is that you're growing."

IT WAS LATE, AND I HANDED THE GREAT GATSBY back to him. I rose from the furniture with no past, wondering what becomes of a man like Mike. Gatsby and Bugsy ended up plugged with bullets, but there's reason to hope for much better than that.

As I went to the door, I was thinking of what Nick, the narrator in the book, said to Gatsby the last time he saw him: *"They're a rotten crowd," said Nick. "You're worth the whole damn bunch put together."*

"They" were the petty frauds who whispered about Gatsby, the backslappers who had compromised their dreams long ago, the schmoozers who hadn't the courage for the magnificent quest. They, Nick decided, were far more corrupt.

And what had I decided? Mike said he had changed, grown, and in ways he had, but in my notepad there were quotes like "I don't want to spend my life alone. Hopefully I can find someone who'll understand it when I say, 'Hey, I'm in the playoffs, I can't talk to you for thirty days.'" He said his experiences had softened him, but in my memory was the glint in his eye when he said, "I'll tell you one thing, my P.R. department better do their f——ing job."

And so I left, I guess, just like everyone else who has written about him. The more I knew, the less I had a f——ing clue.

4. LESS THAN MURDER

*When Jesse Boulerice laid out Andrew Long with a vicious high stick,
was it just hockey, or something much worse?*

BY JEFF MACGREGOR 22/3/1999

SOMETHING TERRIBLE IS ABOUT TO HAPPEN. THERE, in the upper-left-hand corner of the screen. Behind the goal and a step to the left. The videotape is probably a copy of a copy of a copy, as grainy as a Navajo sand painting. A hockey game. The camera pans too fast, too slow, chasing knots of players back and forth across the ice. Medium wide-angle coverage, very likely shot from the press box, panning blue-line to blue-line, blue-line to crease, blue-line to blue-line. It looks like team tape, overbright and jittery, something coaches use to show players how a penalty kill broke down or to mock their clay-footedness on a breakaway. The date – April 17, 1998 – appears across the bottom of the screen.

You've been told about the incident, so you know what to look for, and where. You think you know how bad it's going to be. The camera pans left and then rests, showing an area from the blue-line to the goal. A clumsy rush forms and dissolves, and a blocked shot shakes the puck loose. It squirts into the corner, left of the goal. Two men skate in on it. They look small, but they aren't. The white jersey gets to the boards first; black jersey vectors in a second later, delivering a cross-check to the back, left elbow high. The puck slides past them and is cleared up the ice. White jersey turns, gives black jersey a shove, and they both glide toward the net. They are three feet from each other, no more, the black jersey a step nearer the goal. They pause for a second or two, the time it takes to read from here to *here*. But the moment seems to stretch on and on, elongated and made dense by the number of possibilities it contains.

PREVIOUS PAGE: Andrew Long, seen here playing with the Miami Matador's of the ECHL, would recover from his injuries and continue to play hockey, though he never made the NHL. *(Photograph by Bob Rosato)*

Then it happens. White jersey lifts his stick and swings it hard at the head of the player in the black jersey. The long, flat arc of the swing drives the heel of the stick into his face, and he goes down. Goes down like an empty suit of clothes dropped to the floor. Goes down and stays down. The player in white stands over him as the camera pans away to the right. The tape abruptly cuts to a shot of the scoreboard.

Several seconds later you remember to breathe again.

This is a sports story in which no one wins. Everyone involved has already lost, and all that's left is the reckoning.

WHO YA GONNA BELIEVE?

From hockey officials, on the record: "I didn't see it."

From hockey officials, off the record: "The worst thing I've ever seen."

THE SYNOPSIS

On Friday, April 17, 1998, during an Ontario Hockey League playoff game at the Compuware Sports Arena in Plymouth, Michigan, nineteen-year-old Jesse Boulerice swung his stick into the face of nineteen-year-old Andrew Long. That fact is not in dispute. It is, after all, on videotape. Jesse was in white jersey number eighteen; Andrew wore black jersey number nineteen. It was early in the first period of the fourth game of a seven-game series. Jesse's team, the Plymouth Whalers, was down three games to none. Andrew's team, the Guelph Storm, was on the verge of advancing through the divisional elimi-nations toward Canada's lesser grail, Major Junior hockey's Memorial Cup.

When Jesse swung his stick, he produced immediate consequences for Andrew: a broken nose, multiple facial fractures, a Grade III concussion accompanied by seizure, a contusion of the brain, two black eyes, and a gash in his upper lip the size of a handlebar mustache. Had the stick landed a hand's width higher or lower, Andrew might have been killed.

The consequences for Jesse, arriving more slowly but with a grinding weight and gravity of their own, have been these: a one-year suspension from the OHL and a suspension from the American Hockey League, his next step up the professional hockey ladder, that ended last November 15. He has also been charged by the Wayne County (Michigan) Prosecutors Office with a felony: assault with intent to do great bodily harm less than murder. A conviction could carry a $5,000 fine and ten years in prison.

For every action there is an equal and opposite reaction. These are the applied physics of violence. Arc and acceleration, cause and effect. Swing a hockey stick hard enough, and you can bring the world down on yourself.

A QUESTION OF FACT

On April 30, at the Toronto Marriott Hotel, the OHL held a hearing on what it called the Jesse Boulerice/Andrew Long Matter. The video was reviewed. Reports were taken from game officials, coaches, the players, and their agents. Jesse and Andrew were interviewed separately and did not talk to each other.

The OHL's confidential thirty-five-page report is largely what you'd expect: witnesses explaining what they saw, agents and coaches speaking about the character of their players and the viciousness or the unintentional nature of the hit. A few intriguing points emerge. The first is Jesse had broken his right hand several games before the Guelph series, and he was wearing a playing cast on the night he swung that stick. The OHL report says Jesse was on painkillers that night, but no conclusions are drawn as to how that might have affected his behavior. Also interesting are these questions to Jesse regarding what he said as he was led off the ice that night.

Question: *Do you recall the statement allegedly made by yourself to Referee [Pat] Smola, "You didn't even see what happened"?*

Answer: *I knew what I did was wrong – I was upset – I was not sure what else I should be saying.*

Question: *Do you recall the statement to linesman [Steve] Miller, "but Smola did not see what I did"?*

Answer: *I knew what I did was wrong and I was not sure what I should be saying or doing.*

It could be argued that Jesse had checked to see where the referee was looking before he hit Andrew. Prosecutors expect to seize on this when the case goes to trial.

OTHER THINGS JESSE SAID ON APRIL 30
"When I went into the boards, my hand got crushed."
"I have been picturing the incident ever since."
"I never meant to hurt him like that."

SOME THINGS ANDREW SAID ON APRIL 30
"All I want to know is why."

"I don't understand why [he] would do that."

"I don't understand why."

WHAT IT ALL MEANS PART I

So far the story unspools the way these stories always do: good guy-bad guy, right-wrong, black-white. You don't have to read past the headline to know what happened and form an opinion. It is another tidy front-page morality play that teaches the kiddies a valuable lesson in sportsmanship before working its way backward through the newspaper until it evaporates completely. Seen out of the corner of your eye among the NBA box scores and the strip-joint ads and the PGA Tour money list, the story is just another messy collision between sports and the law, a not very memorable footnote to an age in which athletes seem to spend as much time in court as on it.

But to understand any part of this story, you have to understand all of it.

OH, CANADA

There is no analogue in the U.S. for the almost chromosomal role hockey plays in Canada's national life. It is omnipresent – everywhere and in everyone – at such a molecular level that even Canadians who hate the game (and there are a few) understand its nuances. In a nation with so much winter and so much ice, hockey is an inevitability; it is as inexorable as the weather. In Canada hockey is the manufacturer of good character. It is myth and science. It is a kind of national dream state. Baseball, the only fitting point of comparison in America, has always been optional, no matter what George Will says. Hockey is to Canada what capitalism is to America: a functioning ideology.

Hence Major Junior hockey.

MAJOR JUNIOR, JUMBO SHRIMP

There are as many divisions in organized Canadian hockey as there are diminutives in the language.

Before a Canadian is old enough to lace up his own skates, he has a league to play in. (Yes, the sport is still mostly about boys, although girls' and women's hockey is growing.) By the time a boy is ten or eleven, it's time for him to start taking the game seriously. His family should, too, because that's when it gets ruthless. And expensive: Equipment. Gas. Registration fees. Food and a room for those weekend tournaments. If you've got more than one child playing the game, better buy a minivan because the average hockey bag is now the size of a Lake Louise summer cabin. And bring a book, because your kids are going to be playing more than seventy games a year by the time they're twelve. And don't forget to set aside some cash for power-skating camp next summer. Little Pierre and Gump Jr. and Sue had better attend; by the time they're thirteen, if they're any good, they're already being scouted.

At the top of this food chain is Major Junior, last stop before the pros. It is made up of fifty-three teams in three leagues: the Western Hockey League, the Quebec Major Junior Hockey League, and the Ontario Hockey League. Together, they make up the Canadian Hockey League, which advertises itself as the largest hockey league in the world. If it is not, it is at least the most complicated.

CHL teams are spread over eight Canadian provinces and four U.S. states (Michigan, Washington, Pennsylvania, and Oregon). A few teams are in big markets such as Toronto, Ottawa, Seattle, and Calgary. (The Plymouth Whalers, for whom Jesse played, are a suburban Detroit franchise.) The heart of the CHL beats loudest, though, in small towns, places like Kamloops, Kitchener, and Kelowna; Lethbridge and Medicine Hat; Moose Jaw, Swift Current, and Victoriaville; Brampton, Belleville, and Guelph.

Players between the ages of 16 and 20 are eligible, but the bulk of the CHL is made up of kids 17, 18, and 19. These are most of the best young players in North America. They are drafted (yes, drafted) out of the regional or divisional minors at 15 or 16. In western Canada they can be drafted at 14. That's why scouts start tracking these kids in utero. According to CHL figures, 70 percent of the NHL's coaches and 65 percent of its players graduated from the Major Junior system, including Gretzky, Lindros, and Lemieux.

Young as they are, these kids may move thousands of miles to join their new teams. Billeted with local families, they carry a full high school schedule while playing more than sixty games a year (not counting playoffs) in front of crowds that often exceed the population of a team's home town. They practice almost every day. For this they receive room and board and a stipend of about forty-five bucks a week. If they choose to continue their schooling after the CHL, the teams provide for that, too. CHL folks are very proud of the league's record in educating players, and they resist no opportunity to define Major Junior hockey as a largely educational enterprise.

Upside, players are being scouted by almost every team in the NHL almost every night they play. Downside, it's tough to finish that book report on *Ivanhoe* during a seven-hour overnight bus ride.

Upside, every team has an educational counselor. Downside, it's likely to have a boxing coach too.

Upside, players become local celebrities. Downside, they might miss the prom because they've been traded.

Upside, players wear the best equipment money can buy. Downside, they need it.

Upside, this is their best chance to make it to the NHL. Downside, only one in hundreds ever does.

The CHL boasts season attendance of more than six million and pumps nearly $200 million into the Canadian economy every year. The league has more than 1,800 employees. It supervises more than 1,900 games annually. It has a comprehensive new four-year television package to broadcast games regionally and nationally. Again, this is amateur hockey, not to be confused with professional hockey. In pro hockey the pay's better. And there's no homework.

UH-OH, CANADA

Any character-building system this elaborate and profitable involving young people – children – is going to have critics. Major Junior hockey has plenty. Every decade or so Canada undertakes to reform its national game. Generally this involves a series of scathing editorials in newspapers and some self-loathing rhetoric in magazines. Canadians bemoan the state of the grand old game for a few months, rending their garments and tearing at their hair. Then the two-line pass rule is modified, and everyone heaves a grateful sigh and shuts up.

Whereas in the past it was the quality of the game and the players that engendered those cyclical reexaminations, now it is the nature of the system in which the game is learned and played that is coming under scrutiny. The Graham James sexual abuse scandal in 1996 arrived just in time for one of hockey's ten-year checkups, and the stakes went way up. For those who don't remember, Graham James was a Major Junior coach convicted of serial sexual assaults on Sheldon Kennedy, who later made it to the NHL. (In the space of one week last October, James was released to a halfway house on parole and Kennedy entered rehab for substance abuse.)

The most immediate fallout from the James case was a hurried investigation of the CHL *by* the CHL that was later criticized as a whitewash. But the investigation – and the events that precipitated it – stirred Canada to take a long look at every aspect of the business of Major Junior hockey. Toronto's *Globe and Mail* published a four-part series scalding the CHL for its win-at-any-price philosophy. It referred to the players as "slaves to a junior hockey monopoly that is run by a gang of buccaneers who would do Blackbeard proud." The systematized violence of junior hockey and the intractable code of silence surrounding it were also roundly denounced. Its editorial pages recommended scrapping the junior draft and remaking the entire development system. In addition to being morally unsound and Dickensian, it was, worse yet, not turning out very good hockey players. (The number of Canadian players in the NHL has been going down steadily, so Canada is losing gold medals *and* jobs to players from Europe whose names read like bad Scrabble racks.) The *Globe and Mail* also asserted that verbal, emotional and physical abuse of players occurred because "the Canadian Hockey League structure demanded that you keep your mouth shut and do as you were told. Anyone who did otherwise – and to this day, anyone who does otherwise – in Tier I junior hockey in Canada risks never playing again. Period."

Laura Robinson's 1998 book, *Crossing the Line – Violence and Sexual Assault in Canada's National Sport*, has also been brewing up rancor with its delineation of drinking, brawling, hazing, and sexual assault throughout junior hockey. "Violence is the vocabulary" of the game, Robinson says. In November, *Maclean's*, Canada's leading newsweekly, ran a piece slugged "Thugs on Ice" that looked hard at the manly traditions of goonism and the quick fist.

Off the record you'll hear plenty of horror stories about a *Lord of the Flies* hierarchy that prevails on and off the ice. The entire system seems pressurized by a get-tough-or-get-out Darwinism. And it is druidically secretive. "These kids are terrified," says one leading agent who knows Canadian junior hockey, "but they learn never to say anything to anyone about it." Jesse Boulerice may be from upstate New York, but he is entirely a product of this Canadian system.

Major Junior hockey still thrives because it is part of the golden mythology of Canada. For generations it has been a way to rise above a lifetime of bucking bales at the grain elevator in Wakopa or Assiniboia or Cut Knife. It is the rural equivalent of boxing or ghetto basketball, a ticket out. And it inspires as much false hope. But even mythology changes when it has to. Major Junior hockey is under a cloud right now, under the microscope, under the gun. Any business with that many metaphors ganging up on it is in trouble.

WHAT THOSE LAST 2,732 WORDS ADD UP TO

Andrew and Jesse still want more than anything else to play in the NHL.

WHY FIGHTING IS STILL ALLOWED IN HOCKEY

It is by definition a violent sport. Apologists for the game say that fighting acts as a safety valve, preventing other, more serious expressions of frustration with sticks or skates. "They're always saying that," says Kevin Young, a sports sociologist at the University of Calgary, "but I'd like to see the study that proves it. There isn't one."

When asked in a recent Internet poll by the OHL if fighting should be banned from hockey, more than 85 percent of respondents said no. Unscientific, but perhaps indicative.

Fighting is a leading cause of injury in the NHL. It is also a great tradition.

CLICHÉS MAKE THE MAN . . .

Andrew is referred to as a "skills" player, a "finesse" player. Jesse is regarded as a "physical" player, a player with "some skills," a player "who sticks up for his teammates" (no pun intended).

. . . AND THE NUMBERS DON'T LIE

In four seasons at Guelph, Andrew played in 189 regular-season games. He scored 48 goals and had 92 assists. He accumulated 96 penalty minutes. In three seasons at Plymouth, Jesse played

150 games. He scored 32 goals and had 42 assists. He had 529 penalty minutes.

THINGS YOU MIGHT NOT EXPECT

Jesse turned down a chance to attend Brown to play in the OHL. He played on two U.S. World Junior teams. He is a regular churchgoer. His favorite television show is *Jeopardy!*

THINGS YOU'D NEVER EXPECT

Jesse and Andrew seem like nice young men with a lot in common. Both are right-handed forwards. Both are polite in conversation. No brag or swagger in them – like sitting next to the deacon's son at a box social. Both are tall and move with the space-creating assurance that characterizes professional athletes. The two have similar features and share a smudged sort of handsomeness. Despite his injuries, Andrew's face is still the more smoothly engineered. Jesse's face is all broad angles and worried planes. Pale in the sickroom way that only fictional Victorian heroines and real-life hockey players are pale, each young man has wavy hair; Andrew's is black, Jesse's brown. Andrew has hazel eyes and a big, terrific smile. Jesse hasn't smiled much lately. His eyes are blue. Jesse and Andrew were born on the same day: August 10, 1978.

Each has a steady girlfriend. Both enjoy video games. Jesse is crazy about golf and plays whenever he can. Andrew enjoys golf too and is starting to play more often. (They are much longer off the tee than you are.) Each has one sibling and two parents at home. Both young men were selected in the fifth round of the

1996 NHL draft. Andrew went 129th, to the Florida Panthers; Jesse went four choices later, to the Philadelphia Flyers.

People speak highly of them, both as players and as young men. They seem never to have been properly introduced.

They also have in common the fact that each, directly or indirectly, may have shortened or destroyed the other's career. Both suffer troubling thoughts about the future. And there must be times, maybe before the morning skate, or after dinner, or late at night, balanced on the dark edge of sleep, when they hate each other with a purity and purpose you couldn't begin to understand.

PLYMOUTH AND GUELPH

Plymouth, where Jesse played, is about twenty-five miles west of Detroit. Downtown Plymouth is as small and neat as a hatbox, with gift shops and bookstores and a restored Art Deco movie theater. The Compuware Sports Arena is on the western edge of town. It is nearly new, and the money that went into it shows. There is a landscaped pond out front, and you can reach one of the arena's entrances by a bridge that spans across the water. Inside there are two rinks and a nice restaurant. The 4,300-seat rink where the Whalers play is bright and open and has four suites. There are a couple of brightly painted concession stands that look like the kind you'd stop at for a $4 hot dog on the Universal Studios tour.

The team draws a youngish crowd, enthusiastic, with plenty of puck bunnies: high-school-age girls wearing cocktail-party makeup. During breaks, the P.A. system plays the same deafening rock-and-roll snippets you hear at big league games. The whole thing is like a one-quarter-scale rendering of an NHL arena.

The Guelph Memorial Gardens in Ontario, where Andrew played, is a half-century-old barn of a place, like a zeppelin hangar with a rink in it. It is downtown, across from the Black Stallion Saloon and Acker's Furniture. The training area is in the oldest part of the building; one wall is whitewashed stone. (Players must feel as if they're lifting weights in a root cellar.) Up in the rafters, in the dark, is a banner from the 1951–52 Biltmore Mad Hatters of the old Ontario Hockey Association. This rink is the one where, some say, the phrase *hat trick* was born. The banner may make the trip across the street to a proposed new 5,500-seat arena.

The crowd in Guelph is older than the one in Plymouth: lots of former players, guys thick through the hams and hunkers, with graying crew cuts that look as if they were done with a belt sander. One codger spends the night roaring like Lear whenever a fight breaks out. He's as deaf as a post, but he knows what he likes. Amid the cowbells and the great farting horns, the P.A. plays the same denatured rock, but you can't hear it; the sound system isn't very good, so the canned excitement dissipates into the rafters like smoke.

NEWMARKET AND MOOERS

Newmarket, Ontario, is a northern suburb of Toronto. The Longs have lived there for ten years, in a two-story brick house with blue trim dropped onto rolling farmland. David and Brenda Long share the house with Ryan, Andrew's older brother, and Rudy, a schnauzer. Andrew's bedroom, at the top of the stairs to the right, is pretty much as it was when he left home to play Major Junior hockey. There is a bunk bed along one wall, and next to it are shelves that hold many of the plaques and trophies he has accumulated. He was on skates for the first time when he was four.

David and Brenda are in their early fifties. Brenda works part time in publishing, and David is the president of several professional associations. David is a good-looking man, gone a bit gray at the temples. Brenda is a blonde, pretty woman who gets animated when she talks about what happened to Andrew. David grew up in the same neighborhood as Ken Dryden, a Hall of Fame goalie for the Montreal Canadiens and now the president and general manager of the Maple Leafs. They used to play a little hockey together and are still friendly.

Sitting in their kitchen, you begin to understand what all of this has done to them. "Andrew was nearly killed," says Brenda, "and Boulerice gets to go right on skating? It's not fair." The kitchen table is covered with newspaper clips and Internet downloads about the incident. David and Brenda both look tired. There have been a lot of interviews and phone calls and conversations since the assault last April. It's late. "I've never seen anything like this," David says. "He took two hands and swung his stick into Andrew's face."

Do they want to see Jesse go to jail? Brenda answers. "No," she says, as though measuring the word, "but somebody should take his hockey away from him for at least a year."

On the big-screen TV in the den, David plays the video of that night. He has seen it many times. He talks until the moment Andrew gets hit; then he is silent. A few seconds later he says, "I'll never get used to that." Brenda is still in the kitchen. Brenda still hasn't seen the tape. She can't bring herself to watch it.

It's late when you leave, when you've heard all their stories about the distant tournaments and the driving and the many successes and the rare failures. About how happy and jokey a kid Andrew is, and about the grind of trying to get organized hockey to pay attention to what was done to him.

Mooers is in the northernmost corner of New York State, only forty miles south of Montreal. It is farther north than Toronto and Guelph and Plymouth. Like lots of rural towns, Mooers is just a few tattered businesses laid out at a crossroads – the A&L Cafe and Monette's Furniture and Dragoon Farm Equipment. The Boulerices have lived outside Mooers for nineteen years, in a trim white farmhouse. It's pretty country, dotted with dairy farms. You can see the Adirondacks rolling away to the southwest.

Mike and Lisette Boulerice share the house with Marie, Jesse's younger sister. Jesse's bedroom, at the top of the stairs to the right, is much as it was when he moved to Plymouth to play Major Junior hockey. There's a low bed along one wall and a dresser and a few jerseys hanging in the corner. Leaning on their stocks next to the dresser are two shotguns that Mike and Jesse use when they go bird hunting. There are no trophies or medals; those are across the hall in a little attic space. There is also a letter in there from some local school kids saying that Jesse is their favorite hockey player.

Mike and Lisette are in their forties. They celebrated their twenty-third anniversary on Valentine's Day. Lisette works for a commodities company that handles grain. Mike works for the highway department, doing roadwork and plowing snow. He takes extra work doing construction and welding when he has time. The Boulerices used to run the 148-acre farm as a dairy operation, with sixty cows, but they had to sell out a few years ago. "You can't go fifteen years just breaking even every year," Mike explains. They kept the land.

Lisette is a pretty blonde who still has Quebec French in her voice. Mike has curly brown hair. He is meaty through the chest and shoulders, like most farmers. He gets agitated when he talks about their son's impending trial but doesn't always have the words to express his feelings.

Sitting in their kitchen, you begin to understand what all this has done to them. "We think it was a terrible thing," says Mike, "but this kid has had no trouble with the law *whatever*." Mike and Lisette both look tired. There has been a lot of bad press about all this and a lot of talk around town. "You really find out who your friends are," Mike says. Lisette says she has tried to talk to Jesse about that night, "but he doesn't say much, just keeps it all inside."

What would they say to the Longs if they had the chance? Mike knits up his face and says, "We're sorry, I guess – we're just so . . . I wish we could just get in a room and talk to them . . ." Tears well.

"How sorry we are," adds Lisette.

It is nearly midnight. You've heard all the stories: Jesse driving a tractor when he was eight, putting in a full workday like a hired man. How he started hockey late, at ten, and practiced out front shooting into a goal Mike welded up himself; about what a good kid he was and is, and how nobody here can make sense of this. How hard he worked to overcome his late start. How tough he had to make himself.

You walk out into a night so dark you can't see the keys in your hand to unlock the car, and you remember what Mike said about driving back from the arraignment in Plymouth: "You cry all the way home. Nine hours. Then you get home, and you cry some more."

THE TIME LINE, PART I

Jesse's stick was most likely traveling between fifty and seventy-five miles per hour when the heel of it slammed into Andrew's face. It probably crashed into that little groove that runs from your nose to your upper lip. Doctors and dictionaries call it the philtrum. The blade of the stick bowed Andrew's face shield back into his nose, cutting him, but the shield didn't shatter. Remarkably, neither did Andrew's teeth, although he wasn't wearing a mouthpiece. The blow fractured his nose and his right cheek and a small bone tucked away inside his sinuses. It opened three cuts under his nose, the longest of which ran laterally and was the length of a tall man's little finger. The force of the blow may have slammed Andrew's brain into the front of his skull, because the contusion that the doctors found on the brain was just behind the forehead. Or the bruise may have occurred when Andrew fell and the back of his head hit the ice, his brain sloshing forward in his skull on the rebound. He was knocked unconscious.

Shane Mabey, the Guelph Storm trainer, got to Andrew first. "I knew he was in serious trouble," Mabey says. "When I got back there behind the net, he was curled up in the fetal position and in seizure." After kneeling to assess Andrew's condition, Mabey jumped up and beckoned team doctors onto the ice. The paramedics in attendance were taken under the arms by players, lifted, and literally skated out from the bench.

Getting knocked cold slows bleeding, so until Andrew regained consciousness, it was mostly a matter of making sure that he was breathing and that there was no spinal injury. When he came to, though, the bleeding from the broken nose and the facial lacerations started in earnest. "I had to have my equipment guy wipe my face off three times, because every time Andrew breathed out he was blowing a lot of blood," says Mabey. "I had blood all over me. He was sort of blowing it out like a whale. Two feet in the air."

Head trauma is often characterized by disorientation and agitation. Andrew experienced plenty of both for the next twenty minutes. "He didn't really know what we were trying to do for him," says Mabey. "We had to hold him down to work on him." Six men couldn't keep Andrew still enough to get an oxygen mask on him or start an IV. He was screaming and swearing in the sold-out, now silent arena. "He was yelling 'f——' a lot," says Mabey.

By this time the refs had skated Jesse off the ice with a match penalty for attempting to injure another player. He went to the locker room.

A fan who witnessed the incident and wrote a letter offering to testify in any case that might proceed from it said, "Parents were grabbing the many young children to remove them from the sight." Several Guelph players admit to having cried on the bench that night, no small thing in what is often described as the toughest league in hockey. "We knew it was bad when the coach went out on the ice," one player said. "Coach never goes out on the ice."

Andrew remembers only shards of this.

Andrew's parents were at home in Newmarket. In their bedroom they listened to all this being described on the radio.

THE TIME LINE, PART II

It took several minutes to get Andrew stabilized and restrained on a backboard, to put a cervical collar around his neck and wheel him off the ice. By the time Mabey saw him put in the ambulance, play had resumed. The trainer went into the Plymouth dressing room to clean up. "I looked around and saw that Jesse was sitting beside me," Mabey says. "He was in his underwear. He was crying. My clothes were all covered in blood. I remember him saying he didn't mean to hurt him."

With lights and siren it was a twelve-minute ride down to St. Joseph Mercy Hospital in Ypsilanti. Andrew arrived there Friday night around 8:30. Mabey got there around 11:30 and spent the night. When Mabey arrived, Andrew's parents had been called and told what to expect, and Andrew had been stitched and scanned and tested and was out of immediate danger.

Jesse left the arena, perhaps on the advice of the Whalers' staff, and went back to his billet. He changed clothes and met up with his teammates a few hours later for what had become a somber season-ending party. (Plymouth had lost the game and was done for the year.) Jesse was still upset. According to Robert Esche, a Whalers' goalie and Jesse's best friend, "He felt really bad about it. It's not like he planned it or anything."

Andrew's parents arrived the next morning, and Jesse was still asking his coach if he could go to the hospital to apologize to Andrew. He was told not to, that the Longs were too upset. He called Andrew instead. That didn't go well. Neither of them remembers exactly what was said, but it wasn't enough.

By Sunday the nineteenth, Andrew was ready to be released. His performance on the neurological observation flow sheets and Glasgow Coma Scale tests was nearly normal, and CAT scans revealed that the bruising to his brain had stabilized. He was told not to play any contact sports for three months and to have his own doctors monitor his condition. His parents took him home to Canada, where he spent a lot of time on the couch watching TV and eating pasta one strand at a time. The long-term prognosis was good.

Andrew visited his teammates a few times as they made their postseason run at the championship. He cracked some jokes in the locker room, led stretching exercises, and saw how his mates all touched his jersey, which hung by the door, for inspiration on their way out to the ice. While watching them play, however, Andrew got very worried. "The game was so fast, so confusing, I couldn't really follow it," he says. "It didn't seem like I'd ever played it."

There is a newspaper photo from an appearance Andrew made in Guelph about a week after he was hit. The crowd has just given him a standing ovation. He is smiling as best he can, but the face in the picture looks like a pillowcase full of doorknobs.

On May 6, 1998, the OHL, saying that Jesse Boulerice had "used his stick in a most alarming and unacceptable fashion," suspended him for one year. It meant that he could not return to the league, which he was unlikely to do in any case, since he would move up to the American Hockey League at the start of the following season. It was the most the OHL could do under the circumstances. The OHL has refused further comment on the decision.

On May 17, the Guelph Storm lost in the eightieth Annual Memorial Cup Tournament to the Portland Winter Hawks, 4–3 in overtime. According to former Storm coach George Burnett, Andrew, one of the team's leading scorers and playmakers, might have made the difference.

That same week AHL president, CEO, and treasurer David Andrews ruled that Jesse would be suspended for the first month of the AHL season. Though the AHL and OHL are not affiliated, Andrews has been severely criticized for not honoring the junior league's one-year penalty. The assault "didn't happen in our league," Andrews has said, adding that there was a potential civil liability if his league interfered with Jesse's right to earn a living. "Under the circumstances, I'm comfortable with the decision." The AHL is the primary minor league for the NHL. The NHL has never formally commented on the Boulerice-Long matter.

During the last week of May, David Long called the Plymouth Township police department for instructions on how to file a criminal complaint. On June 4 Andrew Long filed a formal assault complaint against Jesse Boulerice. On July 6 a warrant for Jesse's arrest was issued by the Wayne County Prosecutors Office. On July 14 Jesse, accompanied by his parents, surrendered himself to Plymouth Township police. He was fingerprinted, and his mug shot was taken. Later that afternoon he was arraigned in 35th District Court and released on a $10,000 personal bond.

Over the summer Jesse was allowed to attend the Flyers' training camp. In the fall he joined their AHL affiliate, the Philadelphia Phantoms. He practiced with the team but was ineligible for game play until November 15.

Andrew's rehabilitation continued over the summer. He was able to cycle and work out, but he began skating again only in July. He played some shinny games, practiced with friends in Guelph, and felt well enough to go to the Panthers' training camp in late summer. He joined their AHL affiliate, the Beast of New Haven, in the fall.

On August 17, five months to the day after he was hit in the face with that stick, Andrew took the stand in a preliminary hearing in Detroit to determine if the case would be brought to trial. Jesse and several of his Plymouth teammates were there, too, but they were not called to testify. Andrew identified Jesse as the man who hit him and testified that Jesse had called him the day after to apologize. The court's decision at the end of the hearing: "It is a question of fact that the crime was committed and probable cause exists to believe this Defendant committed the crime. He will be bound over."

A defense motion to dismiss the charges has been denied, and a trial could begin as early as this summer. Jesse has options that would avert a jury trial: alternative programs that allow for a lengthy probation but no jail time. But they would require a guilty plea, which is unacceptable to Jesse on principle and would increase his exposure in a civil lawsuit, even though the Longs express no interest in filing one. "This isn't about money" has been their assertion throughout.

Precedents in the criminal matter are hard to come by. Eleven years ago Minnesota North Stars winger Dino Ciccarelli spent a day in jail as part of a plea bargain for whacking Toronto Maple Leafs defenseman Luke Richardson in the neck with his stick. In 1969 Wayne Maki and Ted Green of the St. Louis Blues and the Boston Bruins, respectively, were both charged with assault when they went at each other with their sticks. Both were acquitted.

Sports and the law coexist uncomfortably in situations like this, the rules of one having little to do with the rules of the other. All that's required for a hung jury is one juror who watches the tape and thinks, It's just part of the game.

JESSE AND ANDREW

Trying to talk to Jesse about all this is frustrating. He is a quiet young man by nature, and his attorneys are present to make sure he stays that way. Questions about the incident are off-limits.

The programs list him at six-foot-two, 200 pounds, and he's every bit of that. He has huge hands – not much scarring on the knuckles yet – that he folds and unfolds while he talks. He freely admits to having made himself tough to get ahead in the game, but he is surprised how far all this has gone: "I never thought I'd be in trouble with the law for playing hockey." He sounds genuinely sorry that he hurt Andrew but seems determined to view it as an isolated incident, an aberration. Has the experience changed him or changed the way he plays the game? "No," he says, honest enough to give his real answer.

When Jesse skates hard, he is all ass and elbows, effort and angles. Off the puck, sizing up the play, he is as expressionless as a guy waiting for a bus. He is tough to get out of the crease, goes into corners as if he's got a lifetime gift certificate for chiropractic therapy, and skates much bigger than he is. Splitting time between the Phantoms and the New Orleans Brass of the East Coast Hockey League, Jesse has amassed 120 penalty minutes in 36 games. The Flyers consider him to be one of their top prospects.

Andrew hasn't played much for the Beast of New Haven. Because it's affiliated with both the Panthers and the Carolina Hurricanes, the Beast roster is large for an AHL team, and ice time is scarce for first-year players. He has been loaned out twice to the Miami Matadors of the ECHL to get more ice time.

Andrew remains a very upright, fluid skater. At six-foot-three and 190 pounds, he is nearly willowy compared with some of the bruisers he skates against. He seems to be aware of everything in the offensive zone and sends passes where they need to be before you even see the opening for them. Good wrist shot, good slap shot, good nose for the goal. He is a playmaker and has, as they say, all the tools.

The game he's had to play against himself has been the toughest part. "I almost talk to myself about it, just kind of convince myself that stuff like that can't happen again," he says of the Boulerice incident. "And I'm not worried about it happening again – it's just that. . . . sometimes I ask myself, What if I take a big hit tonight? I try to say to myself, You gotta do it, because I want to play in the NHL. If I'm scared out there, I'm not going to make it."

Andrew's only ongoing medical concern is his concussion, so he wears a helmet with a little extra padding. It was his third concussion, and he's only twenty years old. When New York Rangers forward Pat LaFontaine retired last season because doctors said he couldn't risk another major concussion, he'd had five. He was thirty-three years old. The Panthers have been patient with Andrew and foresee no special problems in his development as an NHL player.

Does Andrew want to see Jesse go to jail? "I don't care to see him go to jail," he says. "What I really, really want – and I talked to the prosecutor about this – is for there to be a precedent, some sort of serious probation, and for him never to be able to lift his stick, or do something even *remotely* close to that on the ice. Anything even close to that, like an 'attempt to injure' penalty, and he's gone. Never play again. Playing in this game and not being able to bring his stick up when guys are coming at him would be punishment enough."

WHAT IT ALL MEANS, PART II

This is a sports story in which nobody wins. The final reckoning won't fit in a box on the sports page or add up clean in the mathematics of a nightly highlight show.

Stories like this drag too many questions behind them. What was turning in the heart and mind of Jesse Boulerice on the night of April 17? Was there criminal intent? Or was it simply iron-man hockey? Does the tape show Jesse sliding his hands up the stick? Did he shift his weight to get a lumberjack's leverage on the swing? And how do you differentiate this act, other than by its terrifying result, from 1,000 other unseen moments in that same game, the many small, subtle acts of enthusiastic violence that hockey prizes? What is most surprising about the Jesse Boulerice-Andrew Long matter is not that it happened, but that it doesn't happen more often.

And when it does happen, who bears responsibility? What about the hockey factories that tirelessly promote themselves as "quality organizations" and "builders of character"? If what they manufacture short circuits, should they not be held accountable? They're always eager to talk in the euphemisms of risk, of "role players" skating close to "the edge." But when they lose a kid, when the edge crumbles and he falls, you won't hear a word. The code of silence won't allow it, and locker-room signage is sparse on the topic of regret. Players spend years in junior hockey practicing to do things right. How much time is spent learning to do the right thing? Is Jesse Boulerice, then, a criminal or simply the product of his elite education?

And what about us, you and me, fat and happy as a couple of whorehouse bedbugs up in the seats in our souvenir jerseys, spilling our beer and screaming for brain matter whenever two guys drop the gloves? How much responsibility do we bear?

Hall of Famer Ken Dryden knows better than most: "We love to turn up the temperature, in part because it means that we go off into territory we've never been as players, and it's exciting to be where you've never been. The problem is, where you've never been may be where you shouldn't be.

"Whether it's the motivation of the coach, the chanting of the crowd, the taunting of the crowd, the rhythm of the music inside the arena – all of those things are intended to pitch the emotions higher and higher and higher . . . and then, when something really dumb happens, we sort of step back and say, 'You fool, how could you allow that to happen?' Then we shake our heads and walk away."

And something terrible has happened.

5. WHY GOOD TEAMS FIGHT

*With hockey's dark art making a comeback, star players have to be protected.
Call it insurance or self-defense, but clubs are muscling up with a new
breed of tough guy*

BY MICHAEL FARBER 13/10/2008

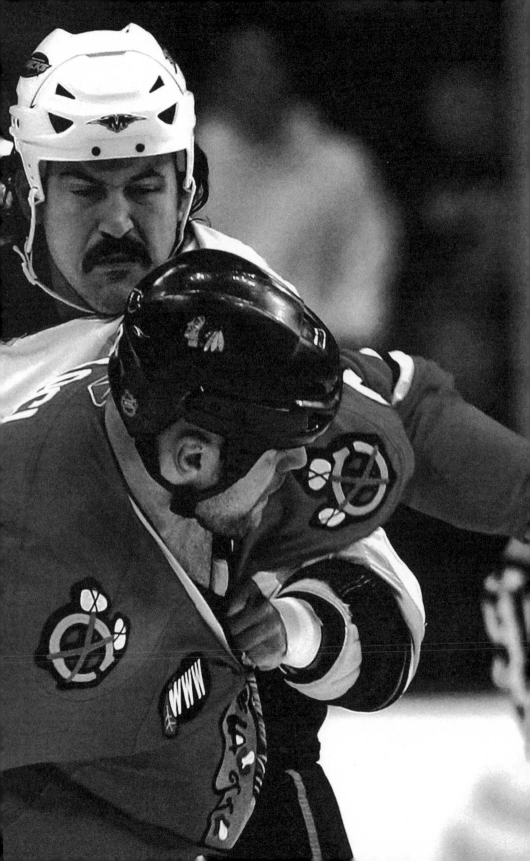

THE MONTREAL CANADIENS' NEW BODYGUARD
stands six-foot-three and weighs 255 pounds. He enjoys moon-
lighting as a radio deejay, fostering humanitarian causes and,
when professionally advantageous, punching people in the
head. This would be an eye-catcher in the personals, but Georges
Laraque never has to advertise. Now on his fourth team in two
and a half years Laraque, seventh among active players with
118 career fights, signed a three-year, $4.5 million contract at
thirty-one, an advanced age for a hockey player who earns his
living primarily with clenched fists. The surprise was not the
generous terms for a gregarious fellow who had been entrusted
to score the occasional goal and keep the flies off Sidney Crosby
for the past year-plus in Pittsburgh but that it was Montreal
ponying up for a player who averages less than eight minutes a
game and who did not even dress for the last five matches of the
Stanley Cup finals.

Considering that the Canadiens had the best regular-season
record in the Eastern Conference last season without employ-
ing an enforcer, and that Laraque turned into an outsized hood
ornament deep into the playoffs, why were they smitten with
Big Georges? Montreal coach Guy Carbonneau is still dubious
about fighting's role – "There were lots of times last year when
I came into the [dressing] room between periods and told them
I didn't want them to fight," says Carbonneau, whose team
ranks next to last in the league in fighting majors over the past
three seasons with seventy-two – but he categorizes Laraque as
a "good insurance policy." (Slogan: Grab a piece of Laraque!)

PREVIOUS PAGE: George Parros, one of the league's most feared
pugilists, is tasked with protecting the Ducks stars night after night.
(Photograph by Jonathan Daniel/Getty Images)

As general manager Bob Gainey said of his new windup toy, "He helps us check off an area where we don't want to be vulnerable. We're not a big team. We have new, formative offensive players. Many are Europeans. It's nice to have a big brother in the schoolyard."

Minnesota Wild coach Jacques Lemaire, whose team retains six-foot-seven, 258-pound brawler Derek Boogaard, understands completely. "We all say, 'No, no, it's not necessary [to have a fighting presence]' before we go out and do exactly what they did," Lemaire says. "They needed [Laraque]. Otherwise they wouldn't have gotten him. It's that simple."

As the 2008–09 NHL season begins, fighting – for the first time in the postlockout era – is back with, well, a vengeance. Although the league does nothing to market fighting (new Tampa Bay Lightning coach Barry Melrose thinks the league is embarrassed by its resurgence), and skill and speed are at an all-time premium, players pairing off and pounding away is trending upward. There were nearly 1.1 fighting majors per game last season, up about 57 percent from 0.7 in 2005–06, the first season after the lockout. (If you have never seen 0.7 of a fight, you missed the powder puff between Montreal defenseman Andrei Markov and Ottawa center Jason Spezza in April.) Fighting won't ever return to the donnybrook days of the 1970s, but after a period of restraint much of the league has remembered that a player with thunder in his fists can still change a game – or in the case of the Carolina Hurricanes, perhaps a season.

CAROLINA HADN'T HAD AN INTIMIDATOR FOR NEARLY two years when, in a game last December 26, New York Rangers ruffian Colton Orr wallpapered Hurricanes center Matt Cullen coming across the blue-line. The fallout from the hit was a broken nose and a concussion for Cullen, and a promotion from the minors for six-foot-four, 225-pound tough guy Wade Brookbank. Carolina captain Rod Brind'Amour speculates that if Brookbank had been on the roster for the New York game, Orr might not have laid out Cullen with such force. Brind'Amour credits the arrival of Brookbank and, later, Tim Conboy, another enforcer from the AHL, for a 16–6–2 record over the final two months of last season. "Teams weren't so willing to run our guys," Brind'Amour says. "If you have [an enforcer] on the bench, other teams know there's going to be some retribution."

Coach Peter Laviolette had a no-fighting policy during the Hurricanes' 2006 Stanley Cup run, but this year the question among NHL coaches and front-office thinkers is not whether to fight – moral ambivalence, incidentally, is practically impossible to find – but simply how often to do it and who to entrust with the responsibility. In the traditional model a team carries a full-time head-bopper like the Philadelphia Flyers' Riley Cote. "Cote doesn't even realize there's a puck on the ice," an Atlantic Division center says of the up-by-his-bootstraps player who averaged a little more than four minutes of ice time per game last season. But with the salary cap inhibiting investment in such one-dimensional players, more clubs are entrusting fisticuffs to players who can also help in other ways. Consider the NHL's reigning fight leader, Columbus forward Jared Boll, a six-foot-two, 206-pound stripling who also chipped in five goals last year. "Boll is part of a new generation of fighter because he can play [a good amount of] minutes and fight, too," star Rick

Nash says of his twenty-two-year-old Blue Jackets teammate, who averaged eight minutes and engaged twenty-seven times last year. "He's a good player."

The Chicago Blackhawks, who dispensed with pugilist David Koci (now with the rock 'em–sock 'em Lightning), will try fighting by committee this season, relying on tough guys with some skill such as Adam Burish, Ben Eager, and James Wisniewski. The Boston Bruins, second in the East to the Flyers in fighting majors last season, don't have an old-style tough because of players such as rampaging sophomore Milan Lucic, an impressive winger who battles as well as he plays. ("Lucic played his role to perfection in the playoffs, trying to get into [rough-and-tumble defenseman Mike] Komisarek's head and abusing him a little," Carbonneau says. "I'm sure with a guy like Georges around, Lucic will stay a little quieter.") The dukes-up Vancouver Canucks, third in the league in fighting majors last season, are trying it both ways: Just as having Laraque in Montreal means Komisarek can sidestep some fights, signing one-dimensional Darcy Hordichuk to a three-year, $2.3 million deal relieves the fighting burden on core defensemen such as Willie Mitchell and Kevin Bieksa, who'll still get their swings in.

Anyway, enough with the prelims. On to the main event. Since the lockout two teams have appeared in a league-best eight play-off series. Each has won a Stanley Cup. In the black-and-blue corner, the Anaheim Ducks, who have lapped the rest of the league in fights with 178 since the lockout. And in the Greenpeace corner, the Detroit Red Wings, a one-off who are tougher than shoe leather but who also have been last in fighting majors in each of the past three seasons, totaling an astounding 141 fewer than Anaheim has.

To borrow from ring announcer Michael Buffer, let's get ready to ruminate.

WHEN THE RED WINGS BROKE TRAINING CAMP IN 2005, new coach Mike Babcock was concerned about the team's level of grit. Babcock, who had most recently coached Anaheim, believed intimidation was one of hockey's cornerstones. One of his favorite teams had been in Spokane, where his junior players would "make you so scared, you couldn't play. Even when they were ahead, they would fight so you couldn't get back into the game." He was uncertain this Detroit team had sufficient gumption. On the eve of a season in which Babcock's Red Wings would finish the regular season with a Gandhi-like six fighting majors, then get shocked by Edmonton in the first round of the playoffs, the coach asked G.M. Ken Holland, "Where's the toughness?"

"I told Babs that toughness is five guys clicking on the power play," Holland recalls. "That it's about four lines not backing off, about players going to the hard areas on the ice and winning battles."

But Detroit, as Lemaire says, "is different, special." The Red Wings are the exception to the fighting rule because, following a philosophy championed by Scotty Bowman when he coached there in the 1990s, they have drafted and developed a team that is a unique blend of high-end skill and two-way grit. There's no other NHL roster like theirs.

Yet even Detroit has wavered. Holland brought journeyman fighting specialist Aaron Downey to training camp in September 2007 following a discussion with star forward Henrik Zetterberg, who convinced the general manager that the team was low on muscle. Downey had been a cipher at his previous stop in Montreal – he dressed for a total of forty-six games in two seasons – but Babcock played him a career-high fifty-six games. When Colorado's Ian Laperrire injured Norris Trophy defenseman Nicklas Lidstrom with a questionable hit last February, Downey fought the Avalanche pot-stirrer twice in the game. Says Babcock, "I thought Downey looked after that situation very well."

Downey, who had ten of Detroit's twenty-one fights while averaging four and a half minutes a game, never dressed in the playoffs, but he'll likely be a fixture again this regular season. The Red Wings also have Darren McCarty, a grinder and occasional fighter whom they repatriated late last season after he'd been out of hockey for a year. The Wings will remain the NHL's most reluctant pugilists this season, but they have to some degree joined the party. On the way to the Cup in 2007–08 Detroit fought five more times than it had in the previous two seasons combined.

Anaheim, Team Truculent, might have exacted a far heavier toll than Downey did on the Avalanche had some brazen opponent mussed one of their stars. Although Anaheim wins with fundamental hockey elements – excellent goaltending, franchise defensemen such as Scott Niedermayer and Chris Pronger, superb young forwards such as Ryan Getzlaf and Corey Perry – its identity is almost cartoonish, like its former name and logo. General manager Brian Burke can live with the stereotype. "You bring a toolbox into the arena for every game," Burke said. "There's lots of things in that toolbox: speed, goaltending, scorers, intimidation. If you make a team pay a physical price, many nights that's going to influence the outcome of a game."

With fourth-liners George Parros and Brad May eager to scrap (the NHL's favored euphemism for fighting), the Ducks' 2007 Cup campaign sometimes was perceived as a regression to the 1970s Era of Bad Feelings. Actually the Ducks merely returned fighting to historical levels. In 1989–90, for example, ten of twenty-one NHL teams had more than the league-high seventy-one fighting majors that Anaheim accumulated in its fractious championship season.

"We didn't do anything revolutionary," Burke says. "We were merely honoring the past, the way the game used to be played, at the highest skill level and intensity level. But I do think you're seeing teams getting bigger and meaner in part through our influence…. Look, we're charged with entertaining you. From the time the puck is dropped, that's what our team will do. That's done with goals, big saves, scoring chances, a big hit, a fight. I guarantee you – without the requisite level of hitting and fighting, we'd have empty buildings."

This is the NHL's dirty secret. Many editorialists may hate fighting, but fans of a league that relies heavily on its gate revenue seem quite content to extract a brawl for their ticket price. Consider that in a sophisticated, standing-room-only hockey market such as Minnesota, four-minute-per-game Derek Boogaard's jersey outsells every other Wild player's except franchise star Marian Gaborik's. Says Penguins general manager Ray Shero, whose father Fred coached Philadelphia's Broad Street Bullies in the 1970s, "The two things that get people to their feet are the anticipation of a fight and the anticipation of a shootout. For many of our fans, these might be the two most exciting things in the game, too."

WITH THE SHARKS LEADING 3–0 LESS THAN THIRTEEN minutes into Game 3 of a first-round playoff series against Calgary last April, Patrick Marleau was lugging the puck head-down along the boards in his own zone when Flames defenseman Cory Sarich vaporized the San Jose captain. There was much milling after the seismic hit, but other than Matt Carle's shove of Sarich, the Sharks had no significant response. Carle was assessed a roughing minor, and Calgary scored on the ensuing power play, starting a comeback that would end in a 4–3 Flames home ice win. As Barry Melrose, then an ESPN analyst, watched in the studio, he concluded that the absence of a fight had been a momentum changer. "If San Jose had jumped in and fought," Melrose says, "I think the message would have gotten through to Calgary. The Flames wouldn't have won that game."

Not surprisingly the gloves are off this season in Tampa Bay, where Melrose has Koci, Ryan Malone (nine fights in 2007–08), and Shane O'Brien (twenty over the past two seasons) to ward off anyone who even looks cross-eyed at prized rookie Steven Stamkos. Melrose, who hails from an area of Saskatchewan that produced fabled punchers Joey Kocur, Kelly Chase, and other tough guys, adores enforcers for their willingness to protect teammates and the team logo. For Melrose, a fight can be a wake-up call for a sluggish club, a warning of dire consequences to an opposing player who is running amok, simple retaliation, or sheer intimidation.

Coaches don't need to explicitly tell enforcers when or upon whom to whale; most fighters have an intuitive grasp of the right time to step into their roles. In some ways they serve a similar role to that of the chorus in Greek drama, offering a pause in, and a commentary on, the narrative that drives the play. In this sense, fighting is scripted. "The biggest misconception is that fighters are mad at each other," Melrose says. "In fact, fighters are very much in control ... like [players] taking a slap shot. They do it for a reason."

Viscerally appealing if intellectually indefensible, part of the show or sometimes merely a sideshow, fighting is a cultural artifact in the NHL, and it is very much back in vogue.

6. ON THE WILD SIDE

From a tiny Canadian town 200 miles south of the Arctic Circle, Jordin Tootoo
will soon be in Nashville, trying to become the first Inuit to play in the NHL

BY E.M. SWIFT 18/8/2003

THE STORM HAS PASSED, LEAVING HUDSON BAY –
at least that portion surrounding the little town of Rankin Inlet
– as flat and gray as milled slate. Into the dreamy calm slides a
broad-beamed, twenty-two-foot Moosehead canoe that easily
holds its five passengers and a spare fifty-five-gallon gas drum.
Stolid and sleek, with a fifty-five-horsepower engine, it is a
canoe on steroids. The engine sputters to life, and as the craft
weaves past dozens of rock islands, it leaves a perfect white
wake through the leaden bay, startling flocks of eider ducks
into skittering takeoffs. The lingering clouds hover low over
the water like smoke.

The canoe's occupants are standing and watchful. In the
bow, wearing yellow slicker pants smeared with bloodstains, is
twenty-year-old Jordin Tootoo. Rifle in hand, he looks every bit
the predator – or is it Predator? A fourth-round choice by the
Nashville Predators in the 2001 NHL entry draft, the five-foot-
nine, 190-pound Tootoo, whose hard-nosed, fearless play at forward for Team Canada in last year's World Junior tournament
elevated his standing in the hockey world, signed this summer
with Nashville. If he sticks with the big club after training camp,
Tootoo, already the most famous citizen in Rankin Inlet (population 2,300), will become the first Inuk and first resident of
Nunavut to play in the NHL.

On this day, however, Tootoo has other things on his mind,
like hunting seals, beluga whales, caribou, and geese. "Anything
that swims or moves is fair game," he says from his perch in the
bow. "I'm a predator looking for prey."

PREVIOUS PAGE: Jordin Tootoo of Rankin Inlet, Nunavut, would
become the first player of Inuit descent to play in the NHL. *(Photograph by
Todd Bigelow)*

"Eleven o'clock," Jordin's father, Barney, calls from the stern. Seventy yards ahead, above the glassy surface of the bay, the black head of a bearded seal is bobbing. It looks the size and shape of a football helmet. Barney cuts back on the throttle, and as the canoe glides smoothly ahead, Jordin shoulders his .22 Magnum rifle and fires twice. The first shot skips a few yards short of the target. The second splashes beyond the seal's head. With a gurgling rush, the seal sounds.

Barney eases the canoe to where the seal went under, and they wait. A full-blooded Inuk, Barney's skin is the color of saddle leather, darker than Jordin's. (Barney's wife, Rose, is of Ukrainian descent.) Father and son are broad-chested and short, with bright, dark eyes, and high cheekbones. There is no tension in the boat. It is more in the nature of the Inuit to laugh at a missed opportunity to kill than curse it, and the Tootoos are here to have fun. No one will starve if the seal escapes. Of greater concern is the retrieval of the carcass if Jordin shoots one, because seals have little blubber in the summer and sink. "You have to get to them quickly and stick them with a harpoon," Jordin says. "Seals are one of the hardest animals to shoot because everything's moving – the waves, the boat, and the seal."

It is several minutes before the seal comes up for air. "There," Barney starts to point, but Jordin, who's been hunting with his father since he was six, has already seen it surface, some sixty yards away. Quickly, he shoots twice, and misses. The seal resubmerges. The men wait, patiently scanning the flat gray surface, as Barney makes slow circles with the canoe. After some minutes they decide to move on. The seal has escaped.

IT IS DIFFICULT TO GRASP THE ISOLATION OF Rankin Inlet. It is 1,000 miles north of Winnipeg and 200 miles south of the Arctic Circle. Beyond those numbers, it is an inland island, cut off from the rest of Canada by seemingly endless tundra. No roads lead into town. The only way to get there is by plane or boat.

Nunavut is one of the least populated expanses of North America, a 770,000-square-mile expanse that was carved out of the central and eastern parts of the Northwest Territories in 1999. Just 28,000 people live in an area three times the size of Texas, or about one person per twenty-eight square miles. Eighty-five percent of those residents are Inuit – Eskimos to Barney's generation – people who have traditionally lived off the land by fishing for cod and arctic char, and hunting caribou, seals, whales, geese, ducks, and even polar bears. No trees grow on the tundra, so until gas and electricity arrived in the 1950s and 1960s, the Inuit rarely were able to cook their food. They dried fish in the breeze after dipping it in salt water, or ate it raw, as they did with their meat. "To us, fast food is when you shoot an animal and eat it right there," Tootoo jokes.

The traditional ways are still practiced to some degree in Rankin Inlet. Caribou is dried into jerky, seal is eaten raw, and the skin of the beluga whale – muktuk – is chewed as a delicacy. "The meat of the beluga is too rich for us, so we cut it up and give it to the dogs," Tootoo says. "We only eat the skin, dipped in soy sauce."

Until recently muktuk was the primary source of vitamin C in an Eskimo diet. But now Rankin Inlet has a stocked grocery store offering everything from iceberg lettuce ($3.43 per head) to fresh corn ($1.35 an ear) to orange juice ($7.59 per half gallon).

Most of the residents live in ranch-style single-family homes with electricity, telephones, and gas or electric ovens. Many, like the Tootoos, have satellite TVs and Internet access. There's a pizza shop, a store that rents DVDs, and a sixty-five-room hotel. All the comforts of a rural Canadian town.

But Rankin Inlet is different in other ways. Upon entering someone else's home, "no one knocks," Barney says. "Only the RCMP [Royal Canadian Mounted Police] knocks." Everyone from ten-year-old kids to eighty-year-old grannies gets around on all-terrain vehicles (ATVs). And in the summer, when there's sunlight for as many as twenty-two hours a day, time is suspended. It is nothing to see ten- or eleven-year-old children riding bikes through the streets or bouncing on trampolines at 2:00 A.M. "What I love most about Rankin is there's no schedule to follow," Tootoo says. "You just go with the flow. Everyone knows you, and you know everyone. Being around simple, straightforward Inuks."

In the winter snowmobiles take over the streets from the ATVs, and the windchill can drop to -60 degrees. The sun rises at 10:00 A.M. and sets five hours later. Since the mid-1980s Rankin Inlet has had a covered outdoor hockey arena that seats 1,500, but there is no refrigeration system to keep the ice frozen. The surface usually doesn't freeze until mid-November, and by April it's melted.

Still, Rankin usually puts together some loosely organized hockey teams. Barney Tootoo managed the rink and was a coach when Jordin and his older brother, Terence, were growing up. (There is also an older sister, Corinne Pilakapsi, twenty-seven, who has two children.) It was too expensive to fly the teams to other communities for games, so the Rankin Inlet kids skated in a house league three times a week, scrimmaging mostly, and when weather permitted, they had pickup games on Williamson Lake. "We only had one team per age group [in the town], and we just played each other," Jordin recalls. "It was shinny, and we made the rules as we went along."

Barney had learned the game in Churchill, 300 miles south, where he was raised. A right wing, he played semipro hockey for the Thompson Hawks of the now defunct Canadian Central League, but he made his living as a miner and, later, as a plumber. Barney liked the game to be played rough. He taught his team to bodycheck. Terence, three years older than Jordin, was the fiercest hitter in Rankin. "My brother and his friends were always hard on me," Jordin says. "That's where I got my toughness. They'd tell me to bodycheck the boards at full speed, and I'd do it. They just wanted to laugh at me, but when you're nine and they're twelve, it's intimidating. My dad always told me, 'If you want to play with the older kids, you'll have to stick up for yourself.' He'd just laugh when I got beat up by my brother and his friends."

If Terence and Jordin were going to go anywhere in hockey, as those who watched them at summer hockey camps in Winnipeg believed they could, Barney knew they'd have to leave home and play better competition. So in 1997, when Terence was seventeen and Jordin was fourteen, the boys moved on. Terence played Junior A for the Opaskwayak Cree Nation (OCN) Blizzard in The Pas, Manitoba, a team he helped lead to three championships, and captained twice, over the next three years. Jordin played AAA Bantam in Spruce Grove, Alberta. Everything about playing and living away from home was tough. Stoplights? Jordin had never seen one before. The traffic and speed of the cars? "A lot of times I just stayed inside," he says.

The hardest adjustment was living in a town where people didn't know who you were. "I was the only Inuk in the area, and for the first time I experienced racism, at school," he says. "I was living with a friend, Justin Pesony, who was aboriginal, and gangs of kids would come to the house yelling that we weren't going to take over their school. I had my battles off the ice. Little did they know I'm a crazy Inuk who eats raw meat and could butcher them up, no sweat. Eating that raw meat makes me a little wacko sometimes."

He must have had a big meal before his first home game in Spruce Grove, because Jordin beat up another player so badly that he was suspended for seven games. Says Jordin, "I thought, What's the big deal? I figured you could do anything you wanted on the ice."

It was his first time playing against kids his age on a regular basis, and his coaches kept telling him to back off – he was too rough. The next season he joined Terence in Junior A at OCN, where, at fifteen, he was the youngest player. At the end of the year he was voted the team's most popular player by the fans. "My brother and I always looked after each other," he says. "If he fought, I fought. We were wild. He was five-foot-eight, but he played like he was six-foot-three."

They looked alike and played alike, small and feisty and fearless. But Jordin's skills were developing faster than his brother's. The next year Jordin went to play for the Brandon (Manitoba) Wheat Kings in the Western Hockey League, where his style of play made him the team's most popular player in each of the next four years. As a seventeen-year-old he was voted the best bodychecker in the Kings' conference. He captained Canada's gold-medal-winning entry in the Four Nations tournament in

Slovakia for players eighteen and under. At the Top Prospects Skills Evaluation in Calgary that winter, he had the hardest shot (96.1 mph) in the competition. He may have started as a rough-neck, but Tootoo was showing people he also had skill and lead-ership. For such a physical player he has soft hands and projects to be a twenty-goal player in the NHL. He can score on rebounds in the tough areas around and outside the crease.

"It was his skating ability that caught my eye," says Craig Channell, the Predators' chief amateur scout, "and he's the best hitter I've seen in my life."

"He's a human bowling ball," says Parry Shockey, a scout for the Los Angeles Kings. "In one game I've seen him throw five strikes, a couple of spares, and a gutter ball when he missed a guy. He hurts people."

"He's like Stan Jonathan with wheels," says Detroit Red Wings scout Bruce Haralson, comparing Tootoo to the Boston Bruins fireplug of the late 1970s and early 1980s, who at five-foot-eight was one of the most feared instigators in the league. "He's a little ball of hate. Some people think he'll struggle in the NHL. Nah. I think he'll just keep pissing people off like he did in junior."

It was the dream of Barney to see Terence and Jordin play in the NHL. Terence wasn't drafted, but he played professionally in the East Coast Hockey League for the Roanoke Express in 2001–02, scoring twenty-five points while proving his worth as a fighter. Off the ice everyone loved him – fans, teammates, management. He was always smiling, talking about hockey and Jordin and Rankin Inlet. He and Jordin called each other after every game they played, and each listened to the other's matches on the Internet.

They were Team Tootoo. The brothers had their own website, TeamTootoo.com, which sold caribou jerky and hockey souvenirs such as T-shirts (with inscriptions that read MOVE, AND YOU'RE FAIR GAME) and pucks. Both wore number twenty-two. They were the talk, and the pride, of Rankin Inlet.

Then last August everything changed. Terence was visiting Jordin in Brandon, working out with him to get ready for the hockey season. On August 28, they went out for dinner and drinks, and afterward Jordin stayed with a friend for the night. Driving home alone, Terence was stopped by police and charged with driving while impaired. After impounding his vehicle, two policemen dropped him off at the house where he was staying. When Terence didn't show up for their training session the next morning, Jordin reported him missing. The RCMP went to the house and found Terence's body in the bushes behind the house, a twelve-gauge shotgun by his side. He had committed suicide. The only note he left was for his brother: *Jor, Go all the way. Take care of the family. You're the man. Ter.*

No one saw it coming. "He was one guy you'd never thought would do something like that," says Ron Roach, the municipality manager of Rankin Inlet and a family friend. "We'll never know what was going on in his head."

If anything, the tragedy made Jordin more determined to succeed, and he buried his grief in hockey. "It's almost like there's two of us playing in one body now," he says. Last season he had a breakout year with Brandon, tying for the team lead in scoring with 32 goals and 39 assists in 64 games while getting his customary 200-plus penalty minutes. He was also a key contributor to Canada's silver-medal-winning performance at the World Junior tournament in Halifax, Nova Scotia, running over guys, drawing penalties and dogging the opponent's top line. He was named Canada's player of the game in its 4–0 win over the Czech Republic.

"When you looked outside during the tournament, the [Rankin Inlet] streets were empty," says the town's mayor, Quasa Kusugak. "Everyone was watching him on TV. That's all anyone talked about. Jordin's impact isn't just on our community, but all Nunavut. His success shows kids of his generation that they can go out and make something of themselves. When he came home after the tournament, 500 to 600 people met him at the airport – more people than went to see the queen a few years ago. And none of it has gone to his head. If anything's gone to his head, it's that he wants to help the kids in this community more."

He already has. Spurred by Tootoo's success, the government has come up with $400,000 to help pay for the installation of a refrigeration system in Rankin Inlet's arena. "Now we'll have ice by mid-September," says Roach. "Enrollment in the program will be up."

BARNEY, WHO HAS A YOUNG MAN'S EYES, SPOTS six caribou grazing in the sedge meadow beyond the rocky shore, less than 1,500 yards away. A discussion of freezer space ensues. Two days earlier the Tootoos came upon 20,000 caribou near the Diana River, so many that the trick was not just to shoot one, but to shoot one without the herd stampeding. As a result of their success, the family's caribou larders are full, and these three bulls and three cows are left to graze the tundra in peace.

Most of the seals are twenty-five miles offshore, probably near Miracle Island. The beluga whales, which usually migrate past

Rankin Inlet at the beginning of August, came three weeks early this year, and the Tootoos haven't seen one since Jordin returned in the second week of July. Rather than go home empty-handed, Barney stops the canoe at a favorite fishing spot, and in twenty minutes they catch a half-dozen cod on jigs. He fillets them on shore in the endless twilight of a northern summer evening as Jordin loads the canoe on the trailer. It is 12:30 A.M. when the hunting party returns.

Rose, the family matriarch, is still up. Blunt and salty-tongued, she would tell a queen or a prime minister where to take a hike. And she is protective of her men. "She roars like a lion," says Barney, "but is a kitty inside."

Rose takes the fillets from Barney and starts preparing the fry pan, melting butter and Crisco. She dredges the fillets in flour, salt, and pepper. After cooking them, she sets the steaming-hot fillets on a paper towel. Picked up by fingers, they are Arctic candy. Then Rose announces she's heading out to play cards with the ladies. It's 1:15 A.M.

"You know what our family motto is?" she asks, turning from the door that has never known the rap of knuckles. "We're not the best, but we're hard to beat."

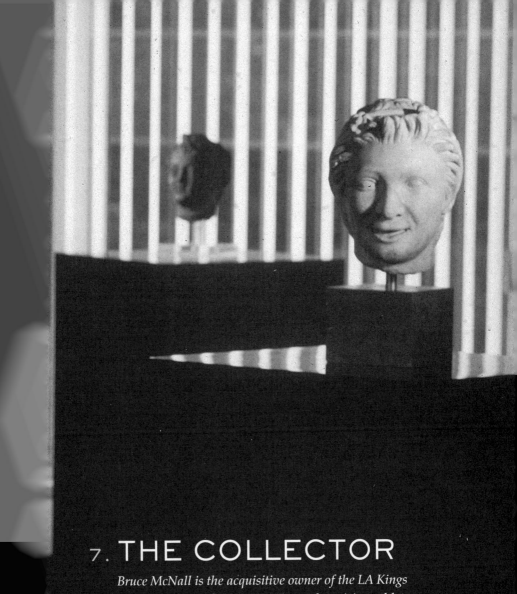

7. THE COLLECTOR

Bruce McNall is the acquisitive owner of the LA Kings
whose tastes run from antiquities to the priciest athletes

BY RICHARD HOFFER 13/5/1991

BRUCE MCNALL HAS ALWAYS BEEN INTRIGUED by the idea of undiscovered value. When he was in the third grade, shortly after he had been introduced to the world of coins by one of those little starter kits, he wandered into a numismatic shop in Arcadia, California, and happened upon a pair of 2,000-year-old Roman coins.

Get this: The coins were on sale for a dollar apiece. "Can you imagine?" he says. "Something 2,000 years old, with all that history behind it, selling for one dollar?"

The notion boggled his eight-year-old mind. It was as if he had just been introduced to a world populated entirely by schmoes. Remarkable value was to be had just for the poking around, just for the asking. Just for a dollar!

This was powerful knowledge, and here is how he used it. At fifteen, with inventory he had built through his own mail-order business in ancient coins, McNall opened a numismatic shop. At sixteen, having sold out to enroll at UCLA and study ancient history, he had $60,000, a Jaguar XK-E, one apartment near campus and a grander one a little farther away. At twenty, cajoled back into business by some of his professors and their wealthy friends, he opened a new coin shop, this time on Rodeo Drive. He appraised a coin collection belonging to J. Paul Getty and told Getty it was "junk," after which he became Getty's adviser on numismatics.

At twenty-four, in 1974, McNall bagged the Athena Decadrachm, known to collectors as the *Mona Lisa* of Greek coins. Valery Giscard d'Estaing, who would become president of France, had wanted it. So had Aristotle Onassis. Until McNall bought the Athena Decadrachm, the record price for a coin sold at auction had been $100,000, but, to his way of thinking, that coin had nothing resembling this one's value. He was surrounded by schmoes. He put in a winning bid of $420,000, left everyone reeling in disbelief, and within a week resold the Athena Decadrachm for $470,000. Here was another important thing to know: Whoever has the best property dictates the economy of its market.

We move on. At thirty-eight, having become the country's dominant dealer in antique coins, started a film company, established a string of thoroughbreds that would number 300, and bought the Los Angeles Kings of the NHL, McNall paid the Edmonton Oilers $15 million for Wayne Gretzky, the Athena Decadrachm of hockey. A foolhardy bid, don't you think, when you consider that the entire Kings franchise, which was losing money at the rate of $4 million a year, had set McNall back $20 million? Schmoes!

Average attendance at Kings home games went from 11,667 in 1987–88, the season before McNall took over the team, to nearly 16,000 – 98 percent of capacity at the Forum – this season. Over that same span, the average ticket price more than doubled. Sellouts have become routine in a city about which former Kings owner Jack Kent Cooke once said, "There are 800,000 Canadians living in Los Angeles, and I've just discovered why they left Canada: They hate hockey." This season 34 of the 40 games at the Forum were sold out. The value of the Kings franchise may be as high as $100 million.

We move on, a little faster now. At forty, having just paid $5 million for the Toronto Argonauts, once the jewel of the Canadian Football League but lately gone to seed with the rest of the CFL, McNall decided to re-Gretzkyize Canada (it's only fair). In unlikely partnership with Gretzky and actor-comedian John Candy, McNall plucked Raghib (Rocket) Ismail, the NFL's likely top pick in the April draft, out of reach of the richer and more established league south of the border.

Ismail cost the partners $14 million, minimum, almost three times what they paid for the team, and schmoes are still second-guessing McNall on this one. How can he possibly recoup that investment in a failing league, especially with a player who may not turn out to be the Athena Decadrachm of pro football, who may in fact be nothing more than a buffalo nickel? It's easy, explains McNall: Attendance at Argo home games goes from the current average of 31,676 to 40,000, with corresponding increases in TV and other revenues – and it all happens next year. After that, the wealth that falls on McNall and his partners will be embarrassing.

Who can doubt this man, who parlayed a childhood coin collection into a personal fortune that he estimates at a couple of hundred million? Who underestimates his sporting sense, which with one bold stroke turned hockey into Los Angeles's glamour sport? Everything McNall touches turns to gold. Take Gretzky.

After arguing over proper compensation – McNall, a terrible negotiator, wanted to pay the Great One about $3 million a season; Gretzky, equally inept, wanted to play for less – the boss agreed to pay his new employee just $2.25 million a year for the next eight years *if* he were allowed to make Gretzky some money on the side. Gretzky recently earned $2 million off Saumarez, a horse McNall had put him on to, when Saumarez was syndicated. In March, McNall and Gretzky went halvsies on the world's most expensive baseball card, which collectors have since decided is undervalued at the $410,000 the two men paid for it.

Take those Roman coins. (We go back.) What do you think they're worth today, 2,000 years old, all that history? We schmoes want to know, we're resigned to our schmo-dom, we're leaning forward in our chairs. "Apiece?" asks McNall. "About a buck."

TWO WEEKS AGO THE KINGS, WHO HAVE NEVER advanced beyond the second round of the Stanley Cup playoffs, failed to do so once again, losing in six games to the hated Oilers. The defeat was especially hurtful because the Kings, who had won their division with the league's third-best overall record, believed that this was their year. Gretzky had turned thirty and, after twelve seasons in the NHL, was possibly in decline. (He's still the best in the league, even in decline.) Publicly the Kings said things like, "Sometimes you have to lose to learn how to win," but privately they expressed a sense of blown opportunity, of time having run out.

After the last game, the L.A. players wandered about the locker room in Edmonton as if they had been lobotomized. Kings coach Tom Webster, who is wrapped so tight that he ought to have TITLEIST stamped on his forehead, emerged from his dressing room and told general manager Rogie Vachon that he wasn't going to hit anything. Vachon, startled, agreed that this was sensible. Gretzky, who seems impaired by guilt when he plays his former teammates, appeared ready to weep.

Meanwhile, McNall and his wife, Jane, had already taken a limo to the airport. The most important talk of the ride concerned baby-sitting arrangements for the McNalls' two children,

Katie, eight, and Bruce, six. Later, McNall, looking very much unlike a just-defeated owner, was relaxing on the team plane, a 727 outfitted entirely with first-class seats, when the pilot hollered, "The bus is here."

Someone whispered, "Uh-oh." McNall thought for a minute and said, "Quick, close the doors and start taxiing." But the plane remained at rest until the distraught players had boarded, leaving McNall to complain, "Nobody has a sense of humor."

As it turned out, everybody had a sense of humor, sort of. However morbid the bus ride might have been – "The driver stopped on some tracks with a train coming," said a Kings official, and it was clear that he had mixed feelings about the team's subsequent escape – the flight became a minor hoot under McNall's influence. Vachon characterized one of the Edmonton players as a "bowling ball with ears stapled to his back." Even Webster was seen laughing. Plans for next season were made. Gretzky ambled forward and took some ribbing at the expense of his own ears, one of which had twenty-five stitches in it. The Kings' torment was suspended.

"I feel sorry for the players and the coaches," said McNall during the flight. "Some of those kids, when I went in the locker room after the game, were crying. This will be a long off-season for them. I went over to congratulate [Oilers' owner Peter] Pocklington, and he was shaking, just shaking. Win or lose, this is all they [members of both organizations] have." It's amazing to McNall. All they have!

The next day, in his sculpture-filled office in Century City, McNall spread out computer printouts of the results of every major horse race held in the world over the weekend. He might buy one or two of the winners. David Begelman, the former

Columbia Pictures executive who is McNall's film partner, phoned about their new movie, a teen comedy called *Mannequin on the Move*. There was also the prospect of brokering a cache of gold salvaged from the wreck of the SS *Central America* off the coast of South Carolina. And there were those Argos.

Candy, just back from shooting a movie in Rome, had plans for the halftime show at the home opener in July. He reported that Dan Aykroyd had agreed to perform with his Elwood Blues Brothers Revue. Still, you could not say the Kings were no longer on McNall's mind. "It hurts him more than you know," said Jane. But the hockey team had receded to a seasonal corner of that jumbled brain. What was it McNall had said in the limo as it pulled away from Edmonton's Northlands Coliseum? "Rocket, go deep."

This, lately, is how the world of schmoes thinks of McNall: He's the man who committed $14 million to a college junior who returned some punts and kickoffs and caught the odd pass at Notre Dame, and he is hoping to recoup this investment in a floundering league that has no national TV contract, in a country that has fewer people than California. Only three of the eight CFL teams turned a profit last season, and several are rumored to be about to fold. Among NFL players, only Joe Montana of the San Francisco 49ers has a salary comparable to Ismail's, and Montana is a proven star in a much larger market, not to mention a player who, unlike Ismail, handles the ball on almost every offensive play.

There is, in fact, no way to justify McNall's outlay, not in terms of football's traditional economics. The Dallas Cowboys, who traded up for the number-one draft pick, bowed out of the bidding for the Rocket when they learned they would have to pay close to $3 million a year to keep him out of McNall's grasp. One agent said Dallas should thank its lucky Lone Star that it didn't offer Ismail that kind of money, because for all the Cowboys' profitability, they couldn't possibly have earned a return – kick or otherwise – on the investment.

"That would have been bad business," says McNall. Bad business to pay $3 million when you are America's Team, but not bad business to pay $4.5 million when you are not even Toronto's team? (The Blue Jays are.) "The problem is they [the Cowboys] think of him as a football player," says McNall. "As a football player, he's worth a fraction of that, say $200,000. But it's not, Can he catch passes? It's, Can he fill seats?"

That is of marginal concern to NFL teams. If Ismail, all 175 pounds of him, did happen to survive in the brutish bigger league, if he did exude star power, it would make no difference to Dallas's bottom line. Ismail might help an NFL team win the Super Bowl, but he could not appreciably improve the franchise's income. Most of that comes from the league's huge television revenues, which the twenty-eight teams share equally. "But what if 10,000 more people come to see him at every home game?" says McNall. "That's 10 games at $22 a ticket times 10,000 – $2.2 million. That'd be a start, wouldn't it?"

McNall speaks from experience. The season he brought Gretzky to Los Angeles, attendance at Kings games jumped 27 percent, and the team finally went into the black. Besides becoming winners on ice, the Kings have become a marketing phenomenon. The NHL reports that Kings gear accounts for 40 percent of league-licensed products sold. North America's Team. The Kings have made so much money that Gretzky says he's now at peace with McNall; the boss didn't squander his money on him after all. "For the first time since I've come here, I haven't been thinking of that $15 million," says the Great One. "It's been repaid."

It is not lost on McNall that, unlike Gretzky when he came south, Ismail is hardly proven. He could turn out to be another Doug Flutie – a college star who has been less than sensational as a pro – although nobody thinks that likely. And if Ismail is as electrifying as McNall hopes, the Rocket might be tempted to try to leave the Argos to play for the Los Angeles Raiders, the team that selected him in the NFL draft. Yes, there are things that could thwart McNall's plans. "But I'm a player," McNall says. "Think of what we can accomplish in the CFL, in Toronto. Think of the potential."

The schmoes look at the world and see price tags and feel nervously for their wallets, but McNall looks at it, sees revenue and phones his bankers. He sees potential all around, in wonderfully diverse areas. These days, McNall scouts the world in his 727 or his JetStar or his jet helicopter. He also relies on a vast network of well-placed employees to turn up overlooked value. Those Roman coins never appreciated the way McNall thought they would, but enough other investments did to allow him to afford homes in Holmby Hills, Malibu, and Palm Springs, California; New York City; Deer Valley, Utah; and Hawaii. You just have to consider the potential.

That's what McNall always did, according to his mother, Shirley. Her husband, Earl, a retired college biochemistry professor, liked to keep their two children occupied in activities other than watching television, so he filled the house with games and books. Young Bruce, who could read at age four, methodically went through series of adventure books. But what he really attacked was Monopoly. "Boy, did we want to ditch that game," says Shirley. "He was impossible to play with. He always went for the high-priced properties, and he seemed to know right when to build."

But he wasn't headed for a career in real estate – that business bores him. Rather, he always had a penchant for collecting, a drive to complete things that could be called obsessive. To his mother, well, this trait was at least puzzling. "He'd ask to go to the bank to look through its pennies," says Shirley. "It was weird."

But, going back to those Roman coins: The idea that something from a distant time and place could be handled between your fingers fascinated him, and he was inspired to read about the emperors stamped on those coins. By the time he was twelve, he realized he had become a prodigy of sorts, an expert in a narrow field of history, not to mention a budding dealer in a thinly traded hobby. Shirley remembers the family's visit to the Louvre during a 1963 European vacation. "We spent it in the classics wing, looking at antiquities," she says. "Can you believe we never saw the *Mona Lisa*?"

"Nobody in Los Angeles knew much about that history or the coins," says McNall. Even as a teenager, he discovered that he could take advantage of local coin dealers, buying one shop's ancient coins for almost nothing and then selling them to another dealer for a profit. "It was cherry picking," he says. Eventually the shops caught on and refused to deal with him, but they did pay him to make up price lists for their ancient coins.

It occurred to McNall that he could do the same for himself. So he typed up a price list of his little inventory, mimeographed copies of it at his high school and began advertising. That led to his having his own corner at Coins of the World, Etc., a shop in Arcadia where he was supposed to sell U.S. coins for the owners. What happened, though, was that McNall steered customers away from U.S. coins to his own collection of ancients. "I didn't mean to," he says. "It was just my enthusiasm for my coins."

What money came in he committed to rarer coins. "My parents would get concerned when I bought some coin for $2,000," he says. "Then I'd have to hustle my collection to somehow pay for it."

By the time he enrolled at UCLA, in 1966, he assumed he had grown out of his hobby. The $60,000 he realized by liquidating his collection was nice, but he planned to become a professor of Roman history, and during his freshman year he devoted himself entirely to his studies. But in a way he kept plundering his old collection. He found that in many of his courses he could steer the paper toward his expertise and write on some arcane topic in ancient history. The history and the classics professors cultivated him as a kind of social pet. "I was paraded around like a freak," says McNall.

His teachers introduced him to Sy Weintraub, owner of Panavision, and other entertainment moguls like Begelman, David Geffen, and Leonard Goldberg. They began to buy coins on McNall's advice, and they began to make money. And when they made money, McNall made money, which was a problem for a nineteen-year-old in those radical times. "These weren't the eighties, remember," he says. So, for appearances' sake, he bought an old Corvair to drive around campus. The Jaguar was reserved for calling on moguls.

The dual life didn't last long. In 1971, after McNall was awarded a Regents Fellowship, a very big deal in the California university system, something snapped. With the fellowship, says

McNall, "I was working on my doctorate and making $8,000 – every graduate student's dream. Then it occurred to me I was doing $3 million in gross sales on the side. This was crazy. I quit the [UCLA] doctoral program, but not because of the money. It was the action."

He formed Numismatic Fine Arts, the shop on Rodeo Drive, and acquired an increasingly glitzy clientele and a worldwide reputation. Soon he was selling to the Louvre as well as to Nelson Bunker Hunt. McNall was making money, but he was also making important contacts. Hunt led him into sports ownership by arranging for McNall to buy stock in the NBA Dallas Mavericks. That friendship also led to horses, with McNall arranging the syndication of 400 of Hunt's thoroughbreds, two of which were the stakes winners Dahar and Estrapade. Later McNall formed his own string, Summa Stables, which has included Trempolino, winner of the $1 million Arc de Triomphe in 1987, and Golden Pheasant, winner of the 1990 Arlington Million.

Grateful clients in the movie business steered McNall toward profits in their field as well, until McNall finally said, "Let's do this right." In 1979, he formed Sherwood Productions, which gave us *WarGames* and *Mr. Mom*. Four years later he merged Sherwood into Gladden Entertainment Corp., which has produced *Weekend at Bernie's* and *The Fabulous Baker Boys*. The movie business seems to excite McNall least of all, though he promises to get more involved in it now that Candy – ol' Uncle Buck himself – has become more involved with him through Candy's interest in the Argos.

You will not be surprised to learn, after all this, that it was collecting that led McNall to ownership of a hockey team. Jerry Buss, then the owner of the Kings and still owner of the Los

Angeles Lakers, collected U.S. coins, but he and McNall had run into each other through another of their shared enthusiasms, stamp collecting. Eventually they became friends. Buss, intrigued by McNall's interest in hockey – he was a longtime Kings fan – sold him 25 percent of the team in 1986 and another 24 percent the next year. In March 1988 McNall bought the rest.

McNall tinkered with the Kings, changing the team colors and increasing the staff, but he knew he couldn't galvanize Los Angeles, a star-driven town if ever there was one, without *the* hockey star. Buying Gretzky from Edmonton was the only move that made sense to him, even at the princely sum of $15 million. This would be the most valuable piece McNall had ever collected.

The strangest part of the negotiation, though, was not McNall's dealings with Pocklington but his arrangement with Gretzky. After all, that $15 million bought nothing more than two years of Gretzky's services under his existing contract with the Oilers. "It's hard to amortize $15 million over two years," says McNall.

Thus the famous reverse negotiation, in which McNall tried to pay more than Gretzky would take. The following is not reprinted from Donald Trump's *Art of the Deal*. "[Gretzky] wrote down a figure," says McNall, "and I said, 'Don't you think that's a little light, considering I paid $15 million for you? I mean, that looks silly.'"

But Gretzky believed the franchise was too fragile for him just to take the money and skate. McNall, broke, would be forced to surround him with junior hockey players. "The Kings were drawing seven or eight thousand people," says Gretzky, under-estimating attendance by a few thousand. "How could I take $4 million a year? I wouldn't feel good. If we were to eat dinner together, I'd want to be able to look him in the face."

McNall figured that when you purchase a player for almost what you've paid for the entire team, then pay him $2 million-plus per year and expect him to quadruple your assets, you are not just hiring somebody. You are enlisting a partner. However, there was no way McNall could formalize such an arrangement. According to NHL rules, he could not give Gretzky equity in the team. Instead, he pledged to include Gretzky in his deals involving horses and collectibles.

"What did I know about horses and baseball cards?" says Gretzky. "Well, as far as horses, I watched the Kentucky Derby every year. As far as baseball cards, I used to put them in the spokes of my bicycle." But he was smart enough to see that McNall knew more than a little about these subjects and was quite a bit richer for it.

Here's how the payback began. McNall invited Gretzky to the Derby in 1989, after their first season together in L.A. Gretzky, then as now, often accompanies McNall to important events; it's only P.R., but Gretzky feels it's another way he can chip away at that $15-million obligation. At Churchill Downs, the two sat in the stands watching the duel between Sunday Silence and Easy Goer. Just as McNall had turned collectors of U.S. coins toward his ancients, he infected Gretzky with his enthusiasm for horses. As Sunday Silence pulled ahead down the stretch, Gretzky was bouncing up and down. "I gotta have a horse!" he shouted to McNall. "This is unreal! I gotta have a horse!"

What follows may say something about Gretzky, a charmed man, or something more about McNall, a shrewd one. A couple of weeks later, the Great One accompanied McNall to the Cannes Film Festival on the French Riviera. For the fun of it, he also accompanied McNall to Paris, where McNall inspected Golden

Pheasant. He was not sure about the horse, but Gretzky, suddenly smitten, pushed McNall to pay $800,000 for the thoroughbred, and he put himself in for half.

That done, Gretzky grew antsy for results. McNall explained that it would be some time before Golden Pheasant could be transported to the U.S. to run in American races. "Let me put you in with some horses I have, and you can have some action in the meantime," he said.

He sold Gretzky a part of Frankly Perfect. He won the $300,000 feature at Golden Gate Park in his next race, in June 1989; a year later, Golden Pheasant was on hand to win the Arlington Million. A month after that, Saumarez, 25 percent of whom Gretzky had bought from McNall for $250,000, won the Arc de Triomphe, another million-dollar purse, and was promptly syndicated for $8 million. "I tried to tell [Gretzky] it's not this easy," says McNall. "But he just kept winning. I've never seen a run like that." Gretzky currently has fifteen horses, calls McNall's horse people once a week and knows the *Daily Racing Form* as well as he knows *Hockey Digest*.

McNall has also put Gretzky into coins. He even persuaded Gretzky to buy a letter autographed by Alexander Graham Bell, who once lived in Gretzky's hometown of Brantford, Ontario. The letter cost Gretzky $14,000, but he has since been offered $90,000 for it.

As for the Honus Wagner baseball card, that was Gretzky's baby all the way. One off-day in Chicago earlier this year, Gretzky was killing time with an autograph hound who haunted the Kings' hotel lobby. Gretzky idly wondered if it wouldn't be fun to invest in the rarest baseball card (do you hear McNall talking here?), which he assumed would be a Babe Ruth card. That's a

$7,000 card, the hound told him. What you want is the 1910 Honus Wagner card.

Gretzky mentioned that to McNall. As it happened, the card was soon put up for auction at Sotheby's in New York City, and McNall asked if Gretzky was just talking or if he really wanted it. The Wagner was part of a full set of 1910 cards. Gretzky and McNall inquired and figured that the Wagner would go for about $300,000 and the other cards for $200,000. They agreed to go halves on the entire collection and to spend a maximum of $500,000. The 1910 cards without Wagner fetched $90,000, and where do you think bidding stopped on the Wagner? At $410,000, of course. "How did you work that out?" Gretzky asked McNall.

McNall moved Gretzky into the big time with the purchase of the Argos. Or was it the other way around? McNall was a member of the Hollywood Park board of directors along with Harry Ornest, then owner of the Toronto club. Ornest ran a tidy outfit, always making money but doing little to add to the value of the team or the league. Says Hugh Campbell, general manager of the Edmonton Eskimos, "I wouldn't say [Toronto] was failing, but it wasn't flourishing."

McNall thought that if he bought the team, he could bring some attention to it with a pair of prominent Canadians. Candy, a big hockey fan, had been bugging McNall to make the deal since he had heard his hometown Argos were for sale. Gretzky told McNall that this was a bigger opportunity than McNall knew. "This would be like owning the Dallas Cowboys," said Gretzky, getting carried away. "It's Canada's team."

Gretzky's and Candy's enthusiasm finally pushed McNall over the edge. He anted up $3 million to buy the Argos, and put his two co-conspirators on the hook for $1 million apiece. McNall wasn't sure what he would do with the team. He figured the marquee value of Candy and Gretzky would pull in some fans, and improvement in the team's performance on the field would pull in others. "I wasn't looking for a home run," says McNall. "I just thought there was a lot of tradition there, a terrific stadium, a lot of upside."

It had not occurred to him that he could find another Gretzky. Nobody in the NFL, he figured, could do for a CFL team what Gretzky had done for the Kings. The idea of drafting Ismail was actually a whim, and it wasn't even McNall's. Argo general manager Mike McCarthy claimed CFL negotiating rights to the Rocket almost for the fun of it. McNall became interested, had some figures drawn up and decided to offer Ismail $6 million over two years.

The negotiations were complicated, and the contract that the Rocket finally signed is probably not comprehensible to anyone without a Ph.D. in finance. Contrary to reports in the press, Ismail didn't receive any condos or equity in the team. The key features of the deal are $14 million guaranteed over four years, with bonuses linked to personal and team performance, stadium attendance and other team revenues. That's how speculation began that Ismail could reap upward of $25 million from the contract. "That's possible," says Suzan Waks, a McNall aide who negotiated the deal, "but then, they could have picked any number."

McNall thinks it would be stupid not to recognize that Ismail, even without equity, is a partner in this enterprise. It's he who will or will not fill the seats, attract a TV network to the CFL and generate league-wide interest. Says McNall, "People say, 'How can you pay a guy $25 million?' It's simple. If he makes you $75 million, then $25 million is not so bad."

When you talk to Ismail, he hardly mentions money. Instead, he says he was bowled over by McNall's intellect, personality and trailblazing attitude. Early in the negotiations, McNall dispatched his JetStar to South Bend to whisk the Rocket up to Toronto to look around and then out to Los Angeles so they could meet. The L.A. visit was memorable for both parties. "Have you seen his coins!" says Ismail. "It's ridiculous! Ridiculous!"

McNall was surprised to find that Ismail knew the history behind some of the coins. "I was stunned when he jumped in on some obscure topic," McNall says. For example, Ismail was conversant with the lives of some of the minor emperors.

While Ismail was in McNall's office, Gretzky happened to call. When he learned that Ismail was there, the Great One asked to talk to him. Gretzky suggested that McNall take Ismail on a shopping spree on Rodeo Drive. "I wasn't thinking," says Gretzky. "Then I remembered, I'm in for 20 percent."

McNall said, "Good idea, *partner*." And off they went.

"I promise you, dude, I saw *Pretty Woman*, but I thought it was a hoax," says Ismail. "Man, it was like a documentary. Ridiculous! And this guy [McNall] is walking down the street doing impressions of Rodney Dangerfield, cracking me up. And he's so darn smart – making money from coins – it's just ridiculous."

The shopping spree, in fact, never came off. Ismail just wanted to get some perfume for his mother, and when he finally settled on Fred Hayman No. 237, the store gave it to him for free. It *is* ridiculous. McNall was pleased to see that Ismail, in addition to attracting free perfume, was attracting attention from passersby. Maybe this was another athlete who transcended his sport. Maybe McNall really was in business.

This is increasingly risky business, however. When the deal

was done, Candy called Ismail and affected a terrible regret. "Now I'll have to do four movies a year," Candy told him. Otherwise, Candy didn't seem too pained. McNall certainly is not sweating, nor is Gretzky. The Great One has come to assume that everything he and McNall do together will work out. When McNall told Gretzky that horse racing wasn't always like this, Gretzky assumed he meant it was actually better. Nobody on this team – Three Amigos North of the Border – has had anything but success, and none of them fears failure. "We're players," says Gretzky. (Who does that sound like?)

What's interesting at this point is not whether the three partners will fail or succeed with the Argos and Ismail, but what McNall will go after next. This odd kind of trophy hunting, with the hunter and the trophy sharing in the rewards, is not likely to stop here, is it? "Probably not," says McNall's mother. "I've been calling Bruce acquisitive for thirty years, and he does get worrisome at times."

She pauses, as mothers are wont to do. Truth is, she doesn't understand her son any more than the rest of us schmoes do. "You know, I'd always hoped he'd go into medicine," she says.

8. FIRE ON THE ICE

Burning intensity, a champion's spirit, the glory and loneliness of supremacy? These qualities make Maurice Richard one of the great athletes of our time

BY HERBERT WARREN WIND 6/12/1954

FOR ALL THAT HAS BEEN SAID AND WRITTEN ABOUT
the heights of fanatic devotion achieved by the fans of the
Brooklyn Dodgers, the Notre Dame football teams, and the
Australian Davis Cup defenders, it is doubtful if there is any
group of sports addicts anywhere which year in and year out
supports its team with quite the supercharged emotion and lavish pride expended so prodigally by the citizens of bilingual
Montreal on their hockey team, Les Canadiens – the Canadians.
In June each year, four months before the next season begins,
every seat in the Montreal Forum, save 800 or so that the management holds for sale on the day of the game, has been sold out
for the entire seventy-game schedule. On playoff nights it is not
uncommon for crowds seeking standing room to run into several thousands and to swarm over Ste. Catherine Street and
beyond onto Atwater Park.

Hockey is deep in the Montrealer's blood. After a fine play
by a member of the home team or, for that matter, of the visiting
team, the Forum reverberates from the rinkside to the rafters
with sharp enthusiastic applause. But many volts above this in
feeling and many decibels above in volume is the singular and
sudden pandemonium that shatters the Forum, like thunder and
lightning, whenever the incomparable star of Les Canadiens,
Maurice (The Rocket) Richard, fights his way through the enemy
defense and blasts the puck past the goalie. There is no sound
quite like it in the whole world of sport.

A powerfully built athlete of thirty-three who stands five-ten
and now weighs 180, having put on about a pound a year since

PREVIOUS PAGE: Maurice "Rocket" Richard was the NHL's most
prolific scorer through the post-war years, setting records that would
stand for decades to come. *(Photograph by Hy Peskin)*

breaking in with Les Canadiens in 1942, Joseph Henri Maurice (pronounced Mohr-riz, with the accent about equally divided) Richard (Ree-shar'), Gallicly handsome and eternally intense, is generally regarded by most *aficionados*, be they Montrealers or *étrangers*, as the greatest player in the history of hockey. Whether he is or not, of course, is one of those sports arguments that boil down in the final analysis to a matter of personal opinion. However, as Richard's supporters invariably point out, hockey is in essence a game of scoring, and here there can be no argument: the Rocket stands in a class by himself, the outstanding scorer of all time. Flip through the pages of the record book: Most Goals – 384, set by Maurice Richard in 12 seasons (with the next man, Nels Stewart, a full 60 goals away); Most Goals in One Season – 50, set by Maurice Richard in a 50-game schedule in 1944–45; Most Goals in a Playoff Series – 12, Maurice Richard; Most Goals in a Playoff Game – 5, Maurice Richard; Longest Consecutive Scoring Streak – at least one goal in nine consecutive games, Maurice Richard; and so on and on. The record book supplies no entry for Most Winning Goals, but several Montreal fans who lovingly compile all Richardiana can document that, by the beginning of the season, their man had scored the goal that won no less than fifty-nine regular season games and eight playoff games.

It is not simply the multiplicity of Richard's goals nor their timeliness but, rather, the chronically spectacular manner in which he scores them that has made the fiery right-winger the acknowledged Babe Ruth of hockey. "There are goals and there are Richard goals," Dick Irvin, the old "Silver Fox" who has coached the Canadiens the length of Richard's career remarked not long ago. "He doesn't get lucky goals. Let's see, he's scored over 390 now. Of these, 370 have had a flair. He can get to a puck and do things to it quicker than any man I've ever seen – even if he has to lug two defensemen with him, and he frequently has to. And his shots! They go in with such velocity that the net and all bulges."

THE SEIBERT GOAL

One of the popular indoor pastimes year-round in Montreal is talking over old Richard goals – which one you thought was the most neatly set up, which one stirred you the most, etc., much in the way Americans used to hot-stove about Ruth's home runs and do today about Willie Mays's various catches. In Irvin's opinion – and Hector (Toe) Blake and Elmer Lach, Richard's teammates on the famous Punch Line, also feel this way – the Rocket's most sensational goal was "the Seibert goal," in the 1945–46 season. Earl Seibert, a strapping 225-pound defenseman who was playing for Detroit that season, hurled himself at Richard as he swept on a solo into the Detroit zone. Richard occasionally will bend his head and neck very low when he is trying to outmaneuver a defenseman. He did on this play. The two collided with a thud, and as they straightened up, there was Richard, still on his feet, still controlling the puck, and, sitting on top of his shoulders, the burly Seibert. Richard not only carried Seibert with him on the way to the net, a *tour de force* in itself, but with that tremendous extra effort of which he is capable, faked the goalie out of position and with his one free hand somehow managed to hoist the puck into the far corner of the cage.

There are two interesting epilogues to this story. The first concerns Seibert and serves well to illustrate the enormous respect in which Richard is held by opposing players. When Seibert clambered into the dressing room after the game, Jack Adams, the voluble Detroit coach, eyed him scornfully. "Why, you dumb Dutchman," he began, "you go let that Richard – " "Listen, Mr. Adams," Seibert cut in, interrupting Adams for the first time in his career, "any guy who can carry me sixty feet and then put the puck into the net – well, more power to him!" And that ended that. The second rider to the story is that Richard is perhaps the only hockey player who, to increase his ability to operate with a burden, has frequently spent an extra half hour after the regular practice sessions careening full steam around the rink with his young son, Maurice Jr., "The Petit Rocket," perched on his shoulders.

There is no question that Richard's most heroic winning goal was "the Boston goal" – the one he scored against the Bruins three years ago to lift Montreal into the finals of the Stanley Cup playoffs. It came late in the third period of a 1–1 game in which the Canadiens were playing badly, Richard in particular. Early in that period Maurice received a deep gash over his left eye. He was taken to the clinic inside the Forum, and the cut was hastily patched up. Blood was still trickling down from the dressing over his cheek when he returned to the bench and took his next turn on the ice. "I can see that goal now," Frank Selke Jr., the son of the Canadiens' managing director, reminisced recently. "Hundreds of us can. Richard sets off a chain reaction whenever he gets the puck, even if it is just a routine pass. It's strange and wonderful, the way he communicates with the crowd. Now, this time he got the puck at our own blue-line and you *knew – everybody knew –* that the game was over right then. Here's what he did. He slipped around Woody Dumart, who was the check, and set sail down the right-hand boards. Quackenbush and Armstrong, the Boston defensemen, were ready for him. He swung around Armstrong with a burst of speed, using his right hand to carry the puck and fending off Armstrong with his left, but Quackenbush pinned him into the boards in the corner. And then, somehow, he broke away from Quackenbush, skated across in front of the net, pulled Jim Henry out of the goal, and drove it home."

For ten years now because of his courage, his skill, and that magical uncultivatable quality, true magnetism, Maurice Richard has reigned in Montreal and throughout the province of Quebec as a hero whose hold on the public has no parallel in sport today unless it be the countrywide adoration that the people of Spain have from time to time heaped on their rare master matadors. The fact that 75 percent of the citizens of Montreal and a similar percentage of the Forum regulars are warm-blooded, excitable French-Canadians – and what is more, a hero-hungry people who think of themselves not as the majority group in their province but as the minority group in Canada – goes quite a distance in explaining their idolatry of Richard. "If Maurice were an English-Canadian or a Scottish-Canadian or a kid from the West he would be lionized, but not as much as he is now," an English–Canadian Richard follower declared last month. "I go to all the games with a French-Canadian friend of mine, a fellow named Roger Oulette. I know exactly what Roger thinks. He accepts the English as as good as anyone. But he would hate to see the French population lose their language and their heritage gener-ally. He doesn't like the fact that the government's pension checks are printed only in English. He feels that they should be printed in both English and French since the constitution of the Dominion provides for a two-language country. For Roger,

Maurice Richard personifies French Canada and all that is great about it. Maybe you have to have French blood, really, to worship Richard, but you know, you only have to be a lover of hockey to admire him."

NO CHEAP CONNECTIONS

As befits the Babe Ruth of hockey, Richard is the highest-paid player in the history of the game. While Les Canadiens' front office prefers not to divulge his exact salary, it amounts to a very healthy chunk of his estimated annual income of $50,000, which is filled out by his commissions for endorsing such products as a hair tonic and the Maurice Richard–model windbreaker, his cut from the sale of *Le Rocket du Hockey* and other publications about him, and his occasional appearances during the off-season as a wrestling referee. "Maurice could earn much more than he does but he has been careful not to connect himself with anything cheap," Camil DesRoches, the Canadiens' publicity director, says. "If he wanted to, he could referee a wrestling bout every night of next summer. His appearance is enough to insure the success of any affair in the province, from wrestling to a church outing." A few years ago, Richard and his teammate Kenny Reardon dropped in for lunch at the Canadian Club, a restaurant in Montreal. "When the other diners spotted Rocket," Reardon relates, "they began to pass the hat for him. It was a spontaneous gesture of appreciation. They collected $50, just like that. People can't do enough for him." Richard, in consequence, is the perfect companion to travel with should you journey anywhere in the province of Quebec. No one will let him pay for a meal, for lodgings, for transportation, for anything.

And what about Le Rocket? How does he react to this fantastic adulation? Perhaps the surest key is the way he conducts himself after he scores one of his roof-raising goals. Down on the ice, below the tumult of tribute, Richard, while the referee is waiting for the clamor to subside before dropping the puck for the next face-off, cruises solemnly in slow circles, somewhat embarrassed by the strength of the ovation, his normally expressive dark eyes fixed expressionless on the ice. In his actions there is never the suspicion of the idol recognizing the plaudits of his fans. The slow circles which Richard transcribes after he has scored serve a distinct purpose for him. They add up to a brief moment of uncoiling, one of the few he is able to allow himself during the six-months-long season. "Maurice," Toe Blake once remarked, "lives to score goals." It is not that Richard puts himself above his team or the game. Quite the contrary, in fact. But here – and he has never been any other way – is a terribly intense man who, like so many of the champions who have endured as champions, is forever driving himself to come up to the almost impossible high standard of performance he sets, whose pride in himself will not let him relax until he has delivered decisively and who, additionally, regard the veneration that has come his way as nothing less than a public trust that he must never let down. The immortal Morenz, though you would never have guessed it since he hid his emotions so well, also poured himself into hockey heart and soul. After a game in which he had played poorly and contributed to a Canadiens defeat, Morenz would warn all his friends to stay away from him and pace the street of Montreal, sometimes until four of five in the morning, until he had acquitted himself down and felt fit to live with people again. When Richard or Les Canadiens lose or when he is in the throes of a prolonged scoring slump, the Rocket does not pace the street but will brood silently, sometimes for days at a time, limiting his conversations with his wife to "pass the butter" or "more water." Success affects Richard no less deeply. After his monumental playoff goal against the Bruins he broke down in tears in the dressing room. His father came in and they talked together for a while, and then Maurice was all right. Even today, when victory and frustration are old stories for him, he remains so highly charged that he has a great deal of trouble sleeping the night before a game when the team is on the road. "Maurice can relax," Elmer Lach has said, "but not during the hockey season. After the last game, Maurice is a different fellow."

Richard's teammates remember the tail end of the 1952–53 season as the time of his most alarming mood. This was the year that Gordie Howe (playing in a seventy-game schedule) was on the verge of breaking Richard's record for goals in one season, the fifty he had scored in 1944–45 when the league was playing a fifty-game schedule. With one game to go, Howe stood at forty-nine. The remaining game was in Detroit against the Canadiens. "The night of that game, that was the only time I ever was afraid to put a hockey player on the ice," Coach Irvin said not long ago. "I remember watching Rocket's eyes as we were going across the city in the cab. 'I can't play him tonight,' I said to myself. 'He'll kill somebody.' I played him but I made sure he wasn't going to be on the ice any time Howe was. In spite of my precautions, one time they were for a few seconds, I think the Rocket was coming out of the penalty box. He skated straight across the ice and charged straight at Howe. Then he turned around and skated back to the penalty box. Rocket was proud of this record, but it was more than that. He would have felt humiliated if Howe had beaten or tied it playing against him or his team. Anyway, Howe didn't score. After the game Richard was in the dressing room breathing hard and little Gerry McNeil, our goalie, went over to him. 'Well Rocket,' Gerry told him with a big smile, "'Howe will have to start all over again with number one.'"

STOPPING THE ROCKET

Because of his own scoring proclivities, Richard has for a dozen years been subjected to far more physical punishment than any other player since the National Hockey League was organized back in 1917. To beat Montreal, you must stop the Rocket, and to stop him opposing teams assign one man and sometimes two to do nothing but stay with Richard "right into the dressing room" if necessary. Some of the men assigned to Richard play him cleanly but, more often than not, opposing "defensive specialists" resort to holding him, grabbing his jersey, hooking him, and whenever they get any kind of shot at him, belting him with their Sunday body check. One of the best ways to stop Richard, or course, is to get him off the ice. With this in mind, some of the rival teams have made it a practice to use a left wing against him with instruction to ignite deliberately the Rocket's red glare. Then, if Richard retaliates and the referee calls a double penalty, Montreal loses Richard and the other team a far less valuable man. Considering the abuse both physical and verbal he has taken from lesser men, Richard in all, has done a very good job of keeping his trigger temper under control in recent years particularly. However, if he always ranks near the top in goals, he also does in penalty time, and not all of his penalties, by any manner of means, are the result of self-protection. The Rocket probably holds the league record for misconduct penalties, ten-minute "rests" which are awarded for telling referees off in overly pungent language. And the Rocket is always up among the leaders, for that matter, in major penalties, five-minute cool-off sessions for fighting. He has lost some fights, but only when he has been ganged up on. In man-to-man combat, he acquits himself extremely well. When Bill Juzda of the Leafs challenged him one night, Maurice stripped off his gloves and flattened Juzda with one blow. In 1945 he knocked down Bob (Killer) Dill of the Rangers twice on the ice, and when Dill decided to start things again in the penalty box Richard knocked him out.

The ambition of most Canadian boys is to be hockey players when they grow up, good enough to make the National Hockey League with their favorite team — Les Canadiens, if the boy is of French descent. Maurice Richard was never confused by any other ambition. He was born on August 4, 1921 in Bordeaux, a typical parish on the reaches of Montreal, the oldest child of Onésime and Alice Laramee Richard. After Maurice came Georgette, Rene, Rollande, Jacques, Margaret, Henri, and Claude. Henri, now eighteen, plays for the Montreal Royals, the Canadiens' farm team in the Quebec Hockey League. Not too hefty, Henri has a great deal of his older brother's dash and scoring flair, and has been dubbed "The Pocket Rocket." Claude is just seventeen and also has the makings, in Maurice's opinion, of a pretty fair hockey player.

With a family soon on his hands, Richard *père* was forced to give up any ideas he had about making a career in baseball. An accomplished center fielder although he stood not much over five feet tall, he continued to play semi-pro baseball until he was forty-five, but he earned his living, as he still does, as a workman in the machine shops of the Canadian-Pacific Railroad. Maurice began to skate when he was about four. In those days Canadian winters were much more severe than they are today. From October through April snow covered the outlying parishes like Bordeaux, and deliveries of milk and bread were made by sleigh. When the snow in the street had been packed down into a hard crust, the children would skate to school on top of it. After school was out at 4:00, Richard remembers he would play hockey till 5:30 when it was time to go home for supper. "Many days I kept my skates on while I ate," he says. "Then I would go out and play some more hockey until 10:00." When rink ice was hard to find, Maurice used to skate on the treacherous Rivière des Prairies, or the Back River as it was called, since it is the branch of the Ottawa River that flows to the north or the back of the island of Montreal. Skating on the Back River was forbidden by law, but young Richard discovered that the ice within fifteen feet of the banks could be counted on to be reliable.

A STRONG RUGGED FORWARD

After finishing the ninth grade of elementary school, Maurice spent two years in the École Technique in downtown Montreal studying the machinist's trade. He played for the school team and for about four others simultaneously, a strong, rugged forward but not a player for whom you would have been instantly able to predict a glowing future. (One of the teams which Richard played represented the Garage Paquette and had been organized by a pal of his, George Norchet. The only significant upshot of this liaison was that Maurice met Georges' sister, Lucille, whom he later married. A sturdy, hockey-loving woman, Mme. Richard attends every Montreal home game. So does Richard's father. His mother misses a few now and then, but not many.)

Late in 1940, Richard was given an opportunity to join the Verdun Maple Leafs, the bottom club of Les Canadiens' farm system. He played with the Senior Canadiens in the Quebec Senior Amateur League the following two seasons, but it was impossible to get much of a line on him for he was laid up with injuries the better part of both seasons, first with a fractured left ankle, then with a fractured left wrist. He was invited to the Canadiens' training camp in September the next year but only because the team had been floundering at the bottom of the League and was grasping for any straw. He was kept on the squad only because Dick Irvin had never in his life seen a young-ster so imbued with the desire to make good. The unknown quantity started off well with Les Canadiens. He piled up five goals and six assists in the first fifteen games. In the next game he fractured his right ankle in a collision with Jack Crawford. He was out for almost the entire season again, returning only for the final game.

A recurrent mystery in sports is how a player who has never shown any signs of greatness will suddenly and inexplicably "arrive" as a full-fledged star. When Richard reported to the Canadiens training camp in Verdun prior to the 1943–44 cam-paign, everyone recognized that he was an altogether different and better hockey player. On the strength of his showing in these practice sessions, Coach Irvin, looking for someone to take Joe Benoit's place, gave Richard a crack at right wing on the first line with Elmer Lach, the superb center, and the veteran Toe Blake, "The Old Lamp Lighter," at left wing. Due to the scoring punch the new line supplied, Les Canadiens, who had finished a floundering fourth the year before, won the league championship and went on to capture the team's first Stanley Cup playoff victory in a full twelve years. Richard eclipsed all playoff records by scoring twelve goals in nine games and in one game against Toronto, went completely berserk and scored all five of the Canadiens' goals.

The Punch Line, as Blake, Lach, and Richard came to be called, played together through the 1946–47 season, a stretch in which they led the Canadiens to three more league championships and one other Stanley Cup victory. They were a marvelous line to watch. Fast-skating, spirited, and quick to take advantage of all opportunities offered them, they mapped out no set plays, but each of them, knowing his linemates' style perfectly and sharing an instinctive understanding of how a play should be developed (and the necessary alternative moves depending on how the defense reacted), always seemed to know, without looking, where the others should be, and together they could set up good shots on goal like few lines in the history of hockey. Blake's retirement in 1947, after he had suffered a fractured leg, broke up the Punch Line. Lach and Richard, working with a variety of left-wingers, continued to team up until this season when Lach retired.

A LEFT-HANDED RIGHT WING

If there was anything unorthodox about the Punch Line it was that Richard, a left-handed shot, played right wing. "I know he'd played some right wing as an amateur," Dick Irvin has said in explaining this move, "and there have always been a few left- wingers who do well on right wing. It doesn't work the other way so often. Most hockey players, you see, skate counterclockwise. Right wing was good for Rocket because it gave him a bit more leverage on his shot and a bit more of the net to shoot at. Besides, his backhand shot was as powerful as his forehand." Another aspect of Richard's sudden maturity was, oddly enough, the fact that he had fractured his right ankle the year before joining the Punch Line. After he had fractured his left ankle two years earlier, he had been inclined to overuse his right leg. After his right ankle was fractured he could no longer do this, and he began to skate with a far better distribution of leg drive. A long strider with amazingly quick acceleration, he rocks from side to side when he skates, a style that would be awkward in anyone else and which, if anything, has added to his deceptiveness. As for Richard himself, he considers that the great break of his entire career was that he was able to come back after three fractures in three consecutive years.

"DON'T DEPEN' ON ME"

The first time he saw Richard play, Conn Smythe, the head man of the Toronto Maple Leafs, offered Les Canadiens the (for hockey) fabulous sum of $50,000 for him. In making this offer to the Hon. Donat Raymond, the owner of Les Canadiens, Smythe declared, in a characteristic Smythian comment, that he was willing to go this high even though Richard was a "one-way man" – a player not remarkably conspicuous on defense. Raymond was not at all interested in selling his new star but suggested to Smythe that if they made Richard a two-way man, it would be only proper for him to double his figure. (Only a short time ago, Smythe was offering $135,000 for Richard.) Jack Adams, the Detroit boss, after seeing Richard set a new league scoring record for a single game of five goals and three assists on the evening of December 28, 1944, declared him to be "the greatest hockey player I've seen in twenty years." This eight-point spree astonished Richard more than anyone. Before the game he had stretched out limply on a rubbing table in the dressing room. "I'm all tired oud," he had yawned wearily to teammates who had gathered around him.

"Dis afternoon I move my 'partment 'bout tree block and can't get no truck. My brudder and me, we move everyt'ing. Tonight, don't depen' too much on me." After he had tallied his eighth point, to be sure, Richard's vitality perked up noticeably (Richard, by the way, spoke no English at the time he joined Les Canadiens. He resented the fact that opponents made his broken English a target for wisecracks and it is typical of the pride he takes in everything he does, the way he dresses, the way he handles his hobbies, that today he speaks just about perfect English).

Richard's eight-point night was the high point of his second complete season, 1944–45, in which he set the league record of fifty goals. By this time he was the toast of the famous Millionaires Club, a group of exuberant Montreal rooters who attended the games wearing bright wool toques and Les Canadiens jerseys. The Millionaires Club was disbanded after the war – it was a financial necessity for the management, since the members were paying only $1.25 or $1.50 for $2.00 seats – but Richard has not lost his standing in the affection of their heirs and all Montreal fans as the team's premier hero. New stars have come up, stalwarts like Bill Durnan (the six-time winner of the Vezina trophy for goalies), Emile (Butch) Bouchard (the four-time All-Star defenseman), Boom Boom Geoffrion, (the colorful, carefree youngster with the big shot who is married to Howie Morenz's daughter), Jean Beliveau (Le Gros Bill) – who made so much money as the star of Quebec's amateur team that it was a financial hardship for him to turn professional. There is room for them all in the Canadiens fan's heart, but *Le Rocket* – he has always been something special and apart. He is their oriflamme. They urge him on with a hundred different cries, but in a tight spot the Forum seems to rise up with one shout in particular. *"Envoye, Maurice!"* This is a Canadian slang form of the imperative of the verb envoyer, to send or to expedite. *"Envoye, Maurice!"* – "Let's expedite this game, Maurice!" *"Envoye, Maurice!"* – "Let's go, Maurice!" *"Envoye, Maurice!"*

TEMPESTUOUS AND INCIDENT-PRONE

Maurice has never let his fans down but there have been moments when he has worried them sick. Largely because of his tempestuous temperament, he is what you might describe as incident-prone. A few years back, for instance, during a Red Wings–Canadiens game in Montreal which referee Hugh McLean was officiating, the Rocket swooped in from his wing to follow up a rebound and in the resulting melee before the Detroit goal, was sent sprawling to the ice by the Detroit center who practically used a headlock. There was no whistle for a penalty. Boiling with indignation, Richard skated up to McLean and demanded to know what the referee was going to do about it. McLean did something about it. He handed Richard a misconduct penalty for abusive language. Burned up by what he considered a vast miscarriage of justice, the Rocket tossed all night in his berth as the

Canadiens traveled by train to New York for a game with the Rangers. The next day, still smoldering, he was sitting in the lobby of the Piccadilly Hotel when he spotted McLean. He rushed over and grabbed the official by his coat collar, but before he had time to continue his protest, Camil DesRoches and some teammates jumped on him and managed to pull him away. It was very fortunate they did. For his assault on McLean, Richard was fined $500 by president Clarence Campbell of the NHL, the highest fine ever levied by the league, but he had been restrained in the nick of time. A real assault and Richard would have been suspended.

Last year this almost happened. In a game in New York, Ron Murphy of the Rangers swung at Geoffrion with his stick. He missed. Geoffrion, retaliating, caught Murphy on the head. The blow fractured Murphy's skull and he was out for the season. Geoffrion was suspended for all the remaining games against the Rangers that season. As Richard saw it, Geoffrion had been punished all out of proportion for a fight he had not started. Richard was then "writing" via a ghost, a column for the *Samedi Dimanche*, a French-language weekly. "If Mr. Campbell wants to throw me out of the League for daring to criticize him," Richard stated in his column, "let him do it. Geoffrion is no longer the same since his affair with Murphy . . . he is demoralized and humiliated for having dared to defend himself against a sneaky and deliberate attack by a third-class player. We know that on numerous occasions, he [President Campbell] has rendered decisions against Canadiens players. . . . Let Mr. Campbell not try to gain publicity for himself by taking to task a good boy like Boom Boom Geoffrion simply because he is a French-Canadian. . . . If this brings me reprisals, I will step out of hockey, and I know that any other players on the Canadiens team will do the same."

Well, here is something – a direct challenge to the authority of the president of the league. Richard was clearly miles out of line. The affair could have been disastrous, not only for Richard but for organized hockey, had it not been handled with consummate intelligence by Frank Selke, the managing director of Les Canadiens who has been a part of hockey since 1906. At the heart of the crisis Les Canadiens returned to Montreal after a road trip. Selke was at the station to meet them. He collected Richard, Geoffrion, Ken Mosdell, and their wives and took them to dinner at the Windsor Hotel. He never once mentioned what was on his mind and everyone's. The dinner over, Richard and Selke found themselves seated alone together in the hotel lobby for a moment.

"I'm surprised, Mr. Selke," Richard said, "I thought you were going to be very angry with me."

"Maurice," Selke said quietly, "I've never known you to do a rotten thing in your life before. You're accusing President Campbell of things that aren't true. That isn't like Maurice Richard. I don't believe you wrote that column."

"No, I didn't, but I authorized it," Richard replied. "I take full responsibility."

"I want you to act like a big leaguer," Selke went on. "President Campbell's office is just across the street. I know he works nights. I want you to come over with me and see him."

Richard sat silently for a moment. Then the two got up and called on Campbell. Richard spoke up immediately. "Mr. Campbell, I want to apologize to you," he said, his deep voice almost an octave lower than usual. "I apologize not because anyone has told me to do so. I want to apologize because it is the decent thing to do. I have been wrong to say the things I said. It will not happen again."

During the weeks that followed Richard's apology, which ended the affair, many of the French papers accused him of selling out. He never batted an eye. "Maurice Richard never disappoints you," Mr. Selke said recently. "We have had a lot of dealings. When a mistake is pointed out to him and he sees it is a mistake, he has the character to recognize it and to make genuine rectification. He has great class as a person."

The Richards live in a modest, trim home in Cartierville, which adjoins Bordeaux. During the hockey season Maurice spends the bulk of his free hours at home playing with his kids – Huguette, eleven, a pretty girl who is a natural figure skater; Maurice Jr., nine, whom the family calls "Rocket" as matter-of-factly as if it were a prosaic nickname like Bud; Normand, four; and André, an infant of six months. Richard is not just a devoted father, he is crazy about his kids. During the summer, at least once a week, Richard and his wife bundle the family into the car and head for the country for a day together in the open air. It is his truest pleasure.

FISHING, SOFTBALL AND GOLF

Richard puts in some time in the summer as a sales representative for the Petrofina Company, a Belgian concern which operates gas stations in Canada, but a large part of every day goes to keeping himself in shape. It is his custom to take off on several three-day fishing trips when each hockey season is over. This is pure relaxation, but after that he plays his sports with an eye to preparing himself gradually for the coming hockey campaign.

In June and July he plays some softball but principally he golfs. A ten-handicap man, he responds so well to competition that for the last two seasons he and Elmer Lach have won the tournament for major league hockey players, which takes place before the big Canadian golf tournament, the Labatt Open. Halfway through July he switches to tennis and handball. "I think they are very good sports for sharpening the eye and strengthening the legs," he told a friend not long ago. "When it is time to go to training camp, I find it not too hard to get into condition."

Richard has mellowed discernibly in recent years. In a relaxed mood he can be wonderful company, intelligent in conversation and very responsive to old friends. His shyness with strangers has lessened somewhat and he meets people far more gracefully. He has even displayed the edges of a dry sense of humor. Not long ago the exchange for Richard's telephone number was changed to RIverside. "Just dial RI," he said with a straight face to a rural photographer who had forgotten the exchange, "RI . . . for Richard." An old friend who stood by couldn't believe his ears.

TOWARD THE 400TH

Most of these relaxed moments, it goes without saying, take place from April to September. Then another hockey season is on, and while Richard today may be a shade less volcanic than formerly as he moves steadily toward his 400th goal, he still burns with a fierce sense of purpose. During a team slump or a personal scoring drought, he is still a good man to avoid. Silent and seething, he builds up intensity to such a pitch that, eventually, it must explode. Sometimes the Rocket explodes all over the place, in fights, in arguments with referees, in overly aggressive if fruitless hockey. Sooner or later, though, he will explode with a splurge of dramatic goals. On these evenings, it is an experience to be in Montreal, for it is then that the Forum roars like one huge happy lion, the most jubilant hullaballoo you can hear in the sports world. It is not an extravagant tribute. After all, of all the great athletes of our time, none has played his game with more skill, more color, more competitive fire and more heart than Maurice Richard.

9. LEARNED IN ALL THE LORE OF OLD MEN

Hiawatha was Sault Ste. Marie's first legend, but nowadays the town hero is a teen-aged hockey phenom named Wayne Gretzky

BY E.M. SWIFT 20/2/1978

MORE THAN 7,000 PEOPLE – THE LARGEST HOCKEY crowd of the season in Canada's capital – came to the Ottawa Civic Centre one night last month to get to the bottom of a sixteen-year-old wunderkind who plays for the Sault Ste. Marie Greyhounds. His name is Wayne Gretzky. That's with a Zed-K-Y, please. The immigration guy fouled it up when his grandfather came over from Russia. In Peterborough the next night, the same thing happened: largest crowd of the year even though the last-place Greyhounds provided the opposition. The night after that, it was the same story in Hamilton: first sellout of the year for a Junior A game, and in a blizzard to boot, everyone out getting stuck in the snow to see some kid called The Great Gretzky, whom every paper in Ontario has hailed as the next Bobby Orr since he was eight years old, four-foot-four and seventy pounds.

Gretzky is not just another star of the future. He is Canada's answer to Steve Cauthen and Nadia Comaneci, one of those rare youths who leapfrogs the stage where they speak of potential, whose talent is already front and center, which, incidentally, is the position he plays for the Greyhounds. Gretzky is only a rookie in the Ontario Junior A Major Hockey Association (OHA), a league in which the players range in age from sixteen to twenty, but he has exploded onto the Junior scene like no one since Guy Lafleur – and before that Orr. If Wayne Gretzky were never to play another hockey game, thousands of Canadian kids would remember him into their dotage. He is the stuff of their dream – that, lacking size, lacking strength, lacking speed, they, too, can somehow make it.

Gretzky did. He now is a wiry (read "skinny") 155 pounds spread over five feet eleven inches, but he should fill out enough to keep the pros happy. Gretzky describes his speed as "brutal" – meaning slower than slow. All the speed in the family went to his fourteen-year-old sister Kim, the Ontario Dominion champion in the 100-, 200-, and 400-meter dashes and a good bet to represent Canada in the 1980 Olympics. Gretzky's shot is accurate, but far from overpowering. And if you expect to see him mucking it up in the corners, forget it. Still, without question, he is the most exciting Junior hockey player since Lafleur left Quebec City in 1971.

"They compare me to Orr and Lafleur, and that's very flattering," says Gretzky in his best "shucks, who, lil-ol-me?" tone. "But basically, my style is different from anyone else's." True. Nevertheless, despite the qualifier, Gretzky lives quite comfortably with comparisons involving himself and Orr, Lafleur or any other superstar who comes to mind, including Cauthen. "We're both little runts who get a lot of publicity," Gretzky says of the latter.

Gretzky's talent is all in his head. "He's the smartest kid I've ever seen," says Fred Litzen, Sault Ste. Marie's one-eyed head scout who has seen a passel of talent over forty years, even if he has missed half, as his friends suggest. Gretzky knows not only where everyone is on the ice, but he also knows where they're *going*. Uncanny anticipation, people call it.

While Gretzky's straight-ahead speed is something less than overwhelming, his mobility makes him nearly impossible to check, and his quickness – "Oh God, he's got terrific reflexes," says Litzen – makes him a superb forechecker in the mold of Bobby Clarke, the player after whom Gretzky models himself the most.

Right now, Gretzky has a knack with the puck equal to anyone's, at any level. "From the red-line to their net I play a solid game compared to anyone in the NHL," he says. And somehow such a statement from a sixteen-year-old does not have a cocky ring. It shouldn't, because it's true.

Defensively? Well, let's just say that one of the reasons Junior A hockey – the final step before the pros – is fun is that the games are often "Bombs-away LeMay" affairs. Gretzky does not return to his own zone to cover a man, he goes there only because without the puck he cannot start a rush. No one particularly worries about his defensive work, least of all Gretzky, who seems as aware as anyone that covering the opposing center is not apt to make headlines. As Greyhound coach Muzz MacPherson says, "With a kid his age, you don't take away his puck sense and tell him to play defense. He's got plenty of time for that."

One reason for the big commotion over Gretzky last month was his play in the World Junior Championships that were held in and around Montreal over the Christmas holidays. The youngest player in the eight-nation field, Gretzky led all scorers with seventeen points (8 goals, 9 assists) in six games. Team Canada, however, finished a disappointing third, behind the Soviet Union and Sweden. Gretzky was the host country's only representative on the all-tournament team and became, if not a national hero, something of a national curiosity in a hockey-mad nation.

Leading scorer at sixteen? Who is this Gretzky guy?

Dan Lucas, Gretzky's right wing in Sault Ste. Marie, was also paired briefly with him on Team Canada. "He would come in and boast to all those older guys how he was going to score four or five points against the Czechs or something," Lucas says. "I'd shake my head and think, 'What are you saying, kid?' Then he'd go out and get them. Unreal. I've had things go well for me before, but with him it never stops. If he ever has a comeuppance, it's going to be a dandy."

IT HAS BEEN THAT WAY PRETTY MUCH FOR GRETZKY since he was five. That year he made the Brantford, Ontario novice all-star team, a squad usually made up of ten- and eleven-year-olds. That led to an interview with the local television station at age six, a Toronto *Globe and Mail* feature at eight, a film clip on national television at nine. His career as a media darling was rolling. At eleven he scored 378 goals in 68 games, including three in 45 seconds in the third period of a game in which Brantford trailed 3–0. The legend grew, far faster than the boy.

After being the third player selected in the midget draft held by the OHA last spring, Gretzky was expected to need time to adjust to the rougher, faster pace of the mother lode of North American hockey. He didn't. He scored a hat trick in his first game with Sault Ste. Marie, and has been at the top of the OHA scoring race ever since. In his first 48 games Gretzky had 54 goals and 87 assists for 141 points. He already has shattered the rookie record of 137 points in a season (68 games) and may well break the OHA record of 170 points now held by Mike Kaszycki of the New York Islanders.

From the day Walter Gretzky strapped skates on his two-and-a-half-year-old son Wayne and shoved him onto the flooded backyard rink, a comeuppance just hasn't been in the cards.

HARRY WOLFE IS THE VOICE OF THE SOO GREYHOUNDS. He shouts at his microphone with such vengeance that his broadcasts can be comfortably listened to while, say, running a bath. "In twenty-five years in this business," says Harry in a quieter moment, "I have never seen a kid capture the imagination of the Canadian public like Wayne Gretzky."

Harry knows all about capturing imaginations. Ask him to rate Gretzky, and he's apt to tell you that the kid is the best Junior hockey player since Harvey Keck. That's K-E-C-K, and no immigration guy fouled the name up – he's part Indian. Plays for the Mekitina Purple Raiders. A professional scout once heard Harry talking about Harvey Keck and went so far as to get directions to Mekitina, which requires a dogsled and a clear night even in summer. A compass won't work that far north.

Keck's only weakness is that he's fictitious. "Hardest shot in hockey, and so fast he can play tennis with himself," says Wolfe. Harry has been threatening to show Keck to his listeners for the past quarter century. "Looks like it's time to bring up Harvey Keck," he will say on the air whenever the Soo Greyhounds are floundering, a pretty regular occurrence in the six years they've been a major Junior A franchise. When Harry gets into a town, the first question he asks the bus driver is: "Harvey Keck still playing as well as he used to?" Most of them will nod and point to the sign that reads PLEASE DON'T TALK TO THE DRIVER. One, however, recently startled Harry by informing him that Keck had broken his leg and was out for the year.

"The sad thing about all of this," Harry says, "is that night after night it becomes the Wayne Gretzky Show. The team's taken a backseat."

Although the Greyhounds were in the cellar, they trailed fifth-place Sudbury by just a point as they began their recent swing through Ottawa, Peterborough, and Hamilton. But they were beaten 9–5, 8–5, and 9–3 on consecutive nights, extending their losing streak to six and making their playoff prospects dimmer. One would never know it to see the press flock into the dressing room after the games.

"It's embarrassing to the other guys," says Angelo Bumbacco, the Soo's general manager, pointing to the crowd of reporters around his star. "We've got to put a stop to this. Let him hold a press conference in another room."

Gretzky is a natural showman. When his favorite number – 9 – was not available this season, he ended up wearing 99. "I tried 14 and 19 at first, but the 1's didn't feel quite right on my back," Gretzky says. "The 99 was Muzz's idea."

Muzz, an ex-goalie of no great renown, must have been sensitive to the burden of wearing a 1 on one's back. Born Murray MacPherson, Muzz has been called Muzz so long that he looks like a Muzz. He is a cheerful bowling ball of a man and a practiced referee baiter. Fans battle for seats behind the Greyhound bench to hear him carry on:

"Mike? Mike? Dandy call, Mike. Just tell me one time why that looked like a charge to you when the same play ten seconds ago didn't. Tell me that, Mike. Mike, I know you're not a homer. Don't look at me like I'm calling you a homer, Mike. You homer! Who said that?"

Muzz's hand, pudgy by nature, is swollen as round as a hockey puck from punching a railing during a recent loss. "Why not give him 99?" he shrugs. "He wanted it. The kid was going to be a marked man anyway. The way he plays, are you kidding?"

To be a marked man in Junior is not a terrific honor. For every player trying to make it into the pros as a goal scorer, there are five or six trying to get there because they can hit people into next week. Then there are the delightful few who don't worry much about next week, concentrating instead on, oh, the next three months in the hospital. Gretzky, so elusive on skates that he is nearly impossible to tag with a hard check, is subject to slashings across the wrists and legs that leave them a mass of welts after each game. Three times this season he has gone to the hospital for postgame X-rays.

"It scares me to think there might be some big son of a gun who is just out there on the ice to try to get me out of the game," Gretzky admits. "Guys are always telling me that the next time I touch the puck, they're going to stuff their sticks down my throat. What can you do? You've got to go ahead and tough it and hope they were kidding."

The Greyhounds have loaded their bags onto a chartered, thirty-year-old DC-3. Sault Ste. Marie is situated in Ontario approximately the way El Paso is in Texas, and the Hounds are the only OHA team to travel by plane. Next to Sudbury, which is a 186-mile stone's throw away, Sault Ste. Marie's nearest opponent in the twelve-city OHA is 423 miles yonder.

The crew is late, but has carefully remembered to prop open the plane's door in the sub-zero cold. The interior of the DC-3 is lined with the recycled aluminum of old ice chests, and the players huddle in the seats like cubes in a tray. To pass the time, Muzz relates the story of the four-hour roller-coaster flight they took in November of 1975, the day the freighter *Edmund Fitzgerald* sank in a Lake Superior gale. "Thought I was a goner," he says.

"Hey, Boy Wonder," someone yells. "Make some more head-lines. Fly us out of here. I'm freezin'!"

Gretzky is used to the flak. He enjoys it, as he enjoys all the attention showered on him. It is a system of checks and bal-ances devised by his teammates so that all the hoopla doesn't go to his head.

Earlier in the year, on a day he was scheduled for a television interview, Gretzky lost an eyebrow and some other, less visible hair to the razors of the Soo veterans. They also loaded his hair with Vaseline. The kid had been initiated. Undaunted, Gretzky had Sylvia Bodner, whose family he lives with in Sault Ste. Marie, apply her eyeliner to his brow and use steam, detergent, lemonade, and Bromo – "Kind of made my scalp sore" – to remove the Vaseline in time for the evening news. In another ploy, the team had the Soo police arrest Gretzky for streaking. "I've got to call my agent," he pleaded. He was innocently sit-ting in the back of the team bus in his shorts and sneakers when the police arrived. And in Ottawa a teammate, masquerading as a press secretary, phoned and asked Gretzky to lunch with Prime Minister Pierre Trudeau. Gretzky took a rain check, explaining that he had to eat a training meal.

"He's got this Boy Wonder thing under control," says Bumbacco, the man who selected Gretzky in the midget draft. Even after receiving a letter from Walter Gretzky, an employee of Bell Telephone in Brantford, in which he said he wouldn't let his son play that far from home. "I told Mr. Gretzky we were running a business, and if Wayne was available, we'd take him. Then I had to fly to Brantford and convince him to come."

He did so, but not without the help of Jim and Sylvia Bodner, friends of the Gretzkys from Brantford who had moved to the Soo four years before. "I called up Mr. Gretzky," says Mrs. Bodner, "and it was such a relief to him that Wayne could live with people that he knew. Wayne's father wants so much to be a part of everything that Wayne's going through, and he can't. I know it's hard for him."

For a general manager, Bumbacco is not a dollars-and-cents type. However, as he says, "In dollars and cents, I'd say without Gretzky we'd be averaging 1,100 to 1,200 people per game. With him, we're averaging 2,500."

Bumbacco has been managing one team or another in Sault Ste. Marie for more than thirty years. Seventy of the players who grew up under him have gone on to college on scholarships, and fourteen have ended up in professional hockey, among them Chico and Wayne Maki, Lou Nanne, Ivan Boldirev, and – the local legends – Tony and Phil Esposito.

"People told me the same thing about Phil that they tell me about Gretzky: 'He can't skate,'" says Bumbacco. "'Sure,' I tell them. 'You're absolutely right. He can't skate a lick. All he can do is score goals.'"

THE GITCHE GUMEE – LAKE SUPERIOR – IS AN EERIE white wasteland in winter. Freighters like the *Edmund Fitzgerald*, loaded with ore from the Algoma Steel plant, crunch through the channel cut out of the ice in Whitefish Bay. The city of 80,000 is as flat as the frozen waterways around it, and its rows of Monopoly-board houses are broken up only by the billowing smokestacks of the mill and Abitibi Pulp and Paper. It is here that the waters of Lake Superior, boiling into rapids, start their journey to the Atlantic.

Hiawatha was Sault Ste. Marie's first legend, back when the

Ojibway nation called that stretch of the river "Pauwating." He wasn't much for hockey, but some of Longfellow's descriptions make Hiawatha sound like something of a cross between Gretzky and Harvey Keck.

> *Out of childhood into manhood*
> *Now had grown my Hiawatha . . .*
> *Learned in all the lore of old men,*
> *In all youthful sports and pastimes . . .*
> *He could shoot an arrow from him,*
> *And run forward with such fleetness,*
> *That the arrow fell behind him!*

Sam Turco is at the Sault Memorial Gardens the night Gretzky's Greyhounds, as the Sault Ste. Marie team has been dubbed, try to break a seven-game winless streak in a game against Peterborough. He sits in the same seat he has occupied for thirty years, right behind the visitor's bench. Sam came over from Italy in 1912 and worked twenty-five years at Algoma Steel before he lost his leg to a hangnail that led to gangrene and forced him to start driving a cab.

Sam's got a handshake that Gordie Howe will be hardpressed to match at seventy-two. "Ain't afraid of man nor devil," he says with a quick, hollow rap on his wooden leg. Another night Sam glowers down at Hamilton coach Bert Templeton. "Cut out that cheap stuff. Bert!" Sam threatens. Rap, rap. "The one hit is fine, but that second shot's cheap stuff!"

A Hamilton forward has just trapped Gretzky against the boards and, surprised to have him pinned, rams the kid's face against the glass for good measure.

"Got to run into him once in a while, Sam," the coach answers with a smile. "Don't get a chance very often."

"That's cheap stuff, Bert, and you know it!" Rap, rap. "I like to give it to Bert. He's all right."

Sam sits back. "See all them little guys?" he says, pointing to the mobs of youngsters in their team jackets. "They only come to see the kid. There wasn't a one here when he was off playing in that Junior tournament in Montreal."

ROSS WINSLADE, HEADMASTER AT SIR JAMES DUNN School, which Gretzky and most of the other Greyhound players attend, is also at the game. He has a far better attendance record at the rink than they do at the school. "We've got to be honest with ourselves. They're here to play hockey," he says. "Their education is second. We do what we can." He pauses.

"Gretzky?" he says. "He's an unassuming kid who's doing a helluva job right now just rolling with the punches. I don't worry about his kind of pressure. In a year or so he'll be in my office talking about more money than I'll make the rest of my life.

"The other kids, the fringe players, are the ones with the pressures. They come to a town, settle in a school, then in two months are traded away. They're living out their parents' dreams of glory, maybe, hoping they'll be drafted by the pros – then when they're not, where does that leave them? They're the ones with pressure."

Every year about this time, some of the Greyhounds come into Muzz's office and ask him in what round he thinks they'll be drafted. Most of them won't be picked in any round. "Muzz'll tell them the only draft they'll get is on their butts as they walk out the door," says Tom McLeod, himself a fringe player now in his draft year. "So you try it as a free agent, and if you're not good enough for that, you try the International League."

"And if you're not good enough for that, you go back to Sudbury and be a miner," adds Rich Duguay, who, like McLeod, has been traded twice since the season's opening.

Gretzky is a lucky one. The luckiest of the lucky ones. Right now, the National Hockey League and the World Hockey Association have an agreement with the Junior leagues not to draft any players before they complete their Junior careers at the age of twenty. For Gretzky, that will be 1981. But there is very little chance – make that zero chance – he will have to wait that long. His agent, Gus Badali, specializes in procuring six-figure contracts for underage Juniors. Wayne Dillon (now with the New York Rangers), John Tonelli (Houston Aeros), and Mark Napier (Birmingham Bulls) all signed with the WHA while being represented by Badali. And the talent-hungry, publicity-starved WHA will require little arm-twisting to bid for Gretzky. Last September, for instance, Birmingham ignored the established rules of drafting and signed eighteen-year-old Ken Linseman to a lucrative contract.

The only serious questions are whether the pro leagues will wait until the kid is eighteen (Gretzky turned seventeen on January 26) and how long and how lucrative his contract will be. Birmingham owner John Bassett, notorious for signing under-age Juniors (Linseman, for one), has already waited nine years. He was an executive with CFTO-TVwhen he saw Gretzky play in a tournament among eight-year-olds.

Gretzky would like to play one more year at the Soo for his $75 a week. "After that, I think I'd be bored," he admits.

"Mentally, I'm ready for the pros right now, but physically I'm not."

THE KID IS PUTTING ON A SHOW FOR THE HOME

crowd. He scores five points as the Greyhounds beat Peterborough 6–3, avenging the previous week's road loss.

Sam Turco hollers with glee and goes into an ice dance, pumping his right elbow and his right knee. "Trouble with hockey today," yells Sam over the noise of the crowd, "is nobody has any fun out there on the ice. Too professional. All these guys want to do is make money. That darn kid has fun, now, don't he?" Rap, rap. "I been here in this seat thirty years, and he stands alone. Yessir. Stands alone. Don't he, Bert! Hee-hawhaw. Don't he!" Rap, rap. "I'm going to have the kid over for a home-cooked dinner some night, and what more can you say about a person than you'd like to have him eat under your own roof. He stands alone, that one."

All the village came and feasted,
All the guests praised Hiawatha,
Called him Strong-Heart. Soan-go-taha!
Called him Loon-Heart, Mahn-go-taysee!

10. THE PUBLIC ENEMY

There's one thing keeping the Penguins' Matt Cooke from being regarded among the NHL's handiest third-line wingers: He also might be the dirtiest player in the game

BY MICHAEL FARBER 14/3/2011

PENGUINS CO-OWNER MARIO LEMIEUX WASN'T
biting the hand that feeds him as much as gnawing off the entire
arm. In a scathing statement issued after a 9–3 loss to the
Islanders on February 11 that featured 346 minutes' worth of
penalties, a game that trafficked in the basest of instincts and
cruelest of NHL stereotypes, the Hall of Famer labeled the match
a "travesty" and darkly insinuated he might walk away from
hockey. The impact? Lemieux was almost immediately branded
a two-bit phony, a sanctimonious sham. From all of the vitriol
dumped on him, the outrage, basically, could be distilled to this:
Lemieux had no business sermonizing as long as he employs
the man widely considered the dirtiest player in the NHL.

"I guess," says Matt Cooke, who missed that game because he
was serving a suspension, "Mario is guilty by association."

Cooke's wry smile is punctuated by a missing front tooth,
which, in the demi-light of the Penguins' empty dressing room,
makes him look like a rueful jack-o'-lantern. He speaks softly,
at least off the ice. He is thirty-two, but his exuberance – and
penchant for dressing room pranks – suggest a player a decade
younger. He is a compact 205-pounder who would be just another
useful third-line left-winger if not for the trail of broken bodies
he has left in his wake and the recent fatwa issued against him.

Apparently the NHL does not have a violence problem as
much as it has a Matt Cooke problem. Ken Daneyko, a three-
time Stanley Cup winner as a Devils defenseman, and now a
between-periods analyst for New Jersey on MSG Network,
offered a solution. Warming to the subject on a radio show on

PREVIOUS PAGE: **Matt Cooke plays on the edge, but goes over it too
often for NHL disciplinarians.** *(Photograph by David E. Klutho)*

February 9, Daneyko said, "I'm as crazy as this: The NHL [should declare] open season for one week on Matt Cooke. You won't get suspended. Then we'll see if he'll continue [dishing out cheap hits] for the rest of the season or his career."

Cooke had already been having a turbulent week before Daneyko painted a bull's-eye on his sweater. With Pittsburgh trailing the Capitals by two goals in the final four minutes of a nationally televised game on February 6, Cooke dinged Washington star Alex Ovechkin with a drive-by, knee-on-knee check. After the match Washington's Bruce Boudreau, who coached Cooke for seventeen games in 2008, said, "It's Matt Cooke. Need we say more? It's not his first rodeo. He's done it to everybody. Then he goes to the ref and says, 'What did I do?' He knows damn well what he did." Cooke's penalty drew the maximum $2,500 fine and a rebuke from NHL senior executive vice president Colin Campbell, who told Cooke he did not want to be having any more such discussions with him in the immediate future. Two days later Campbell and Cooke spoke again, this time in a formal hearing. Insufficiently chastened, Cooke had rammed Blue Jackets defenseman Fedor Tyutin from behind into the end boards. Campbell suspended Cooke for four games, with $87,804.88 in lost salary, for a hit that former star Jeremy Roenick termed "chickens———" and worthy of a twenty-game suspension.

Campbell's ruling was hardly surprising. The shocking thing about Cooke's suspension was that it was just the fourth – and longest – of a play-on-the-edge career that has spanned 800 NHL games. For all the worst-person-in-the-world bile directed at him, his suspensions total just ten games. Disbelief has been suspended far more often than Cooke. Says former Penguins teammate Bill Guerin, "I told him he got one game for hitting from behind, one game for not thinking, and two games for being Matt Cooke."

"If people suggest our game is violent," says Brad May, the former enforcer who also played with Cooke in Vancouver, "Matt Cooke is one of the guys inciting this violence."

THERE IS ACTUALLY MUCH TO ADMIRE IN COOKE'S game. He has won a Cup, scored at least ten goals in nine of the past ten seasons – he scored fifteen last year with essentially no power-play time – and made himself invaluable on the penalty kill. In his first game back from suspension, he cashed in a short-handed goal in a 3–2 shootout loss to the Blackhawks in Chicago on February 20. (He is tied for the NHL lead with six short-handed points.) Cooke is an actual player, unlike the Islanders' Trevor Gillies, who is one of three skaters in the past ten years to have more than 100 penalty minutes in fewer than 100 minutes of ice time. (Gillies was suspended March 2, 2011, for the second time in less than a month for his hit to the head of the Wild's Cal Clutterbuck.) Pittsburgh general manager Ray Shero clearly values Cooke. Although Shero generally offers role players no more than two-year contracts, last June he signed Cooke to a three-year deal worth $1.8 million annually. "Cookie can create things," says Penguins captain Sidney Crosby, who is out indefinitely after suffering a concussion on January 5. "It's not that he's just bouncing off bodies out there."

Cooke might even qualify as an impact player, but his impact is most apparent at the point of contact. With good checks and bad, with hits that stretched rules and in one memorable case rewrote them, Cooke has earned a great living and a poor reputation. He has devastated the careers of star players. In March 2010 he concussed the Bruins' Marc Savard with a predatory blind-side hit, a check that moved the NHL to adopt Rule 48, which bans lateral hits that target the head. As a member of the Capitals in April 2008, he hit Vincent Lecavalier when the Lightning center did not have the puck, knocking him to the ice and dislocating his shoulder, an injury that required surgery. Savard, currently out for the season with another concussion, has played just twenty-five regular season games since being wallpapered by Cooke. Lecavalier scored 192 goals in the five seasons before his shoulder surgery, .475 per game. Postsurgery, his scoring average has dropped to .333 goals per game. (Cooke also shredded the knee of Canadiens defenseman Andrei Markov in the 2010 playoffs with a devastating, if perfectly legal, check; Markov played seven games in 2010–11 before reinjuring the knee, which required more reconstructive surgery.) Cooke, fined $2,500 for the Lecavalier hit but spared supplementary discipline for blindsiding Savard, also targeted the Rangers' Artem Anisimov and the Hurricanes' Scott Walker in 2009, earning a pair of two-game suspensions. Amid the accusations of headhunting, there is evidence Cooke has not ignored other body parts. In 2009 he clicked knees with Atlanta's Zach Bogosian and, in the playoffs, Carolina's Erik Cole. "There are times," Cole says, "when I think he just doesn't care if a guy is in a vulnerable position."

"Matt Cooke has found his niche and [plays] his role very effectively," says Mike Keane, who played sixteen NHL seasons, including one as Cooke's teammate on the Canucks in 2003–04. "He goes out and hits Ovechkin, hits guys from behind. If he hurts Ovechkin, who cares? The Washington Capitals won't win the Stanley Cup. He did his job. For Matt Cooke, that's perfect."

THE ONLY CHECK IN QUESTION ON THIS OFF DAY IS at lunch. Cooke is at an Italian restaurant in Pittsburgh's Strip District with John Lawrence and his family. Lawrence is nineteen. When he was sixteen, he suffered extensive brain and spinal injuries in a car accident and remained in a coma for ten months. When Cooke heard about Lawrence through his foundation last fall – Matt and his wife, Michelle, started the Cooke Family Foundation of Hope five years ago – he invited Lawrence's family to the opener in Pittsburgh's new Consol Energy Center in October and took him to practice the following day. While Cooke was being trashed in the wake of the Ovechkin and Tyutin hits, Lawrence's father called a reporter at the *Pittsburgh Tribune-Review* who previously had written about his son – John hunts deer with a crossbow from his wheelchair – to say the city should know the other side of Matt Cooke. "John admired Matt's bravery and strength and turned to that when his rehab was rough," said his father, who is also named John. "Everybody was teasing John that his favorite guy was a dirty player, a goon, but Matt's just a guy who fights for his position on the team. A battler."

Cooke had to battle to reach the NHL. At sixteen, he played Tier II hockey for the Wellington Dukes in eastern Ontario in a rink affectionately known as the DukeDome, essentially a broom closet with a Zamboni. The ice surface was 180 feet by eighty feet, twenty feet shorter and five feet narrower than an NHL rink, and the crowd was so close to the ice, an observant winger could tell who in the Whiskey Corner section had had a tonsil-lectomy. If you played for the Dukes in that crazy old barn, you finished your checks. Nonnegotiable.

He was only a middling junior prospect, Windsor's tenth-round choice in the Ontario Hockey League's 1995 draft. "The first thing Paul Gillis, who became my coach that first year, said to me was, 'You're playing the same way in the OHL that I played in the NHL; keep your elbows down,'" Cooke recalls. His elbows came down – shifting his focus from hitting to playing – and his stats went up. Cooke began his major junior career as a so-called energy player, but the speed and surprisingly sweet hands he showed in Windsor translated to forty-five goals in his second season and to an NHL opportunity when the Canucks selected him 144th over-all in 1997.

When Cooke arrived in Vancouver in 1998, the left flank was stocked with Markus Naslund and Mark Messier. He did not need a memo to know he wouldn't be a first-liner. "So I took the approach that every day I wanted [coach] Mike Keenan to go, 'Number 46? Oh, yeah, that's that Cooke kid. He ran around and hit everything,' " he recalls. "I didn't want him to go, 'Number 46? Who the hell's that?'"

Cooke played with abundant energy and menace in his early years in Vancouver, but he did not "take ownership" of his game. In the sometimes indecipherable NHL code, the phrase essentially means that he was reluctant to fight. (He did fight Avalanche forward Steve Moore in March 2004 before teammate Todd Bertuzzi's infamous assault on Moore in the same game.) In some ways his hesitance to drop his gloves explains the wide-spread disdain around the NHL for Cooke almost as much as his record of borderline hits. Cooke was a practitioner not of old-time hockey but of new-era hockey, a seminal figure in the age of the Super Pest, in which fighting your own battles was less of an obligation.

Cooke has had twenty NHL fights, according to hockeyfights. com, but only ten came in his 566 games with the Canucks from 1998 to 2008. He maintains that part of the reason was coach Marc Crawford's theory that his effectiveness as an agitator would erode if he gave opponents the satisfaction of fighting. (Crawford, now the Stars coach, says he does not recall giving Cooke those instructions.) "So many days I'd say, This guy [is] a factor; Cooke helped us win," says May, the ex–Canucks tough guy. "And other days I'd be icing my knuckles or my temple and thinking, I wouldn't have been in that fight at all except for that ass—."

Cooke has had ten bouts in just 217 games with Pittsburgh, which qualifies as accountability and maturity in the NHL. Shero reminded him before his recent disciplinary hearing to accept ungrudgingly Campbell's ruling on the Tyutin check.

"Is he a dirty player? Yeah, he's a dirty player. [Former defenseman] Ulf Samuelsson was a dirty player. But there's value in that. Is there value in injuring players and getting suspended? No. But there are football players in the Hall of Fame who were dirty. There are brushback pitchers in the Hall of Fame."

After a year in which he forced a rule change and endured the longest suspension of his career, Cooke considers himself duly brushed back. Penguins coach Dan Bylsma has actually met with the winger this season to ask why he had turned down the opportunity for more heavy hits, which Cooke explained as a hangover from Rule 48 – the Cooke Rule. He was certainly prepared for the run that Capitals winger Matt Bradley took at him on Febuary 21 in Pittsburgh's first meeting with Washington after his knee-on-knee hit of Ovechkin. As Bradley noted to reporters after the game, "You can't go hit our best player with a dirty hit without us retaliating."

"The biggest thing for me is that on the ice, there's a persona," Cooke says. "It's what it is because that's what's made me successful. But that has nothing to do with who I am."

So who's the dirtiest player in the NHL?

Cooke throws back his head and snorts. "No comment," he says, smiling. Pause. "But I don't think it's myself."

The vox populi begs to differ.

1. CHERRY BOMBS

Don Cherry, part Rush Limbaugh and part Dick Vitale, is loud, abrasive, volatile, and the most popular television personality in Canada

BY LEIGH MONTVILLE 29/3/1993

HE KNOWS THE END WILL COME SOMEDAY. MAYBE someday soon. Maybe tonight. He is pushing, pushing, pushing the limits too far, saying too much. One final piece of outrage will bubble from Don Cherry's high-volume mouth, and that will be that. *Ka-boom!* He will self-destruct in full public view, the carnage strewn across the living rooms of an entire country, from the Maritimes to British Columbia. *Ka-boom!*

"I can't keep saying these things," he says. "How can I keep saying these things?"

Things like what?

"Like asking someone to break [Pittsburgh Penguin defenseman] Ulf Samuelsson's arm," he says. "How can I say that on television? I asked someone to break Ulf Samuelsson's arm between the wrist and the elbow."

Ka-boom!

He cannot help himself. The lights come on, four-and-a-half minutes to fill on a Saturday night, a tidy little show called *Coach's Corner* between the first and second periods of *Hockey Night in Canada*, and he might as well be holding a lighted stick of dynamite while he gives his commentary. How can four-and-a-half minutes, once a week, be so dangerous? He will say anything, do anything. He will tweak noses, pick fights. He will ask for the arm – if not the head – of a Penguin defenseman he doesn't like.

Four-and-a-half minutes. One week he suddenly unfurled an eight-foot-long Canadian flag and talked about the "wimps and creeps" who opposed Canada's participation in the Gulf War.

PREVIOUS PAGE: **Nearly twenty years after this article was written,** *Coach's Corner* **continues to be the most watched and most talked about segment of** *Hockey Night in Canada.* *(Photograph by David E. Klutho)*

Another week he was wearing sunglasses and an earring in his left earlobe and talking with an exaggerated effeminate lisp. Wasn't the subject supposed to be the opposition of Los Angeles King star Wayne Gretzky and King owner Bruce McNall to hockey violence? Wasn't the subject supposed to be hockey? Couldn't he simply say what he thought? An earring. A lisp.

Cherry still can't believe he did that. He could not help himself. "I come off after wearing the earring, and I'm just shaking, eh?" he says. "I was just so pumped up. Scared. I was just shaking."

Everything has become so much bigger than he ever expected. He says these things – says anything that comes into his head – and the entire country seems to stop and listen. He is fifty-nine years old, moving hard on sixty, and he has become Canada's Rush Limbaugh and Canada's Howard Cosell. All in one. He is George C. Scott and Willard Scott and Randolph Scott. He is John McLaughlin and Dick Vitale and Bobby (the Brain) Heenan and Roseanne Roseannadanna and Cliff Clavin, mailman, and George Will and Henry David Thoreau and maybe a little bit of Mighty Mouse, here to save the day.

Polls have shown that he is the most recognizable figure in the country, more recognizable than any pop star, any politician, even any of the hockey players he discusses. He is so big that he cannot walk on any street in Canada without drawing a crowd. He is so big that he doesn't do banquets anymore, can't, because the demand is so great. He is so big that there have been petitions to put him on the ballot to replace the retiring Brian Mulroney as prime minister. Prime minister? How did this happen?

"Tomas Sandstrom," he said once on the air about the Kings' forward. "A lot of people think he is Little Lord Fauntleroy, but

Tomas Sandstrom is a backstabbing, cheap-shot, mask-wearing Swede." Actually, he's a Finn, not a Swede.

Is that something a prime minister would say? The words just came out.

"I was watching from the stands in the first period," he said another week. "There was a tipped shot, and I had to get out of the way, and it went over my head and hit this poor lady in the face. I'm telling you, when you come to the game, ladies, keep your eye on the puck. I've seen some awful smacks, and it's always a woman, just talking away, not paying any attention."

Is that any way to get the women's vote?

"The NHL is expanding to Anaheim and Miami," he said on yet another week. "Disney is in Anaheim, and the video guy [Wayne Huizenga, owner of Blockbuster Video and the Miami franchise] is in Miami. O.K., two heavy hitters like that come knocking, you'd better open the door. But TELL ME THIS. WHERE ARE THEY GOING TO GET THE PLAYERS? Would you mind telling me? You already got Ottawa. OTTAWA! Tampa Bay. San Jose, sinking fast. WHERE ARE THEY GOING TO GET THE PLAYERS?"

Did he have to shout?

Educators decry his misuse of English, his fractured syntax, his mangled pronunciations, worrying that he will breed a future generation that says "everythink" and "somethink" and won't have any idea how to make verbs agree with nouns. Hockey executives often paint him as a Neanderthal, out of touch, arguing for violence and against style, trying to defend a frontier that already has been opened wide to the arrival of international talent. Interest groups pick out one outrage after another, the shelves beginning to shake as soon as he speaks, carefully constructed politically correct ideas falling to the ground one after another as if they were so many pieces of cut glass or bone china. Oops, there goes another one.

None of this matters. The Canadian public simply can't get enough of him. He points. He shouts. He sneers. He laughs. His clothes come from the wardrobe of some road company of *Guys and Dolls*, flashy suits and fat-checked sport jackets, custom-tailored, elongated shirt collars starched to the consistency of vinyl siding, riding high above his Adam's apple. His head juts out like a hood ornament in search of a collision. Put on a small screen, he is a larger-than-life terror.

"My wife, Rose, wants me to quit," he says. "She stays home and just worries. She hates the show, hates it. She knows I'm going to say something sometime that's going to send every-thing up in flames. Probably some of the political stuff. She hates the political stuff. You know, though, she's my best critic. If I go home and she won't talk to me, that's when I know the show has been really good. The best ones are the ones she hates most."

It is a problem. The best things he says are the worst things he says. The danger is everything. The danger is the attraction for the public. What next? What will he do? He always is one F word, one outrage away from extinction. What will he do? He holds on to the stick of dynamite and watches the wick burn shorter and shorter. This is his eleventh season. He cannot let go as the inevitable approaches. *Ka-boom!*

THE FIRST TIME HE WAS PAID TO BE ON TELEVISION was during the 1980 Stanley Cup playoffs. He had been fired fol-lowing the regular season after a one-year run as coach of the now-defunct Colorado Rockies. His mouth had hastened his dismissal, an acrimonious ending. A year earlier he had resigned as coach of the Boston Bruins, another acrimonious ending, another problem with his mouth. He wasn't really looking for a job, but when the Canadian Broadcasting Company, the producers of *Hockey Night in Canada*, offered $1,500 a shot, plus expenses, he took a chance. Why not? He might as well make some money with his mouth instead of losing it because of his mouth.

He was on his way. His champion was Ralph Mellanby, then the executive producer of *Hockey Night*. Mellanby liked the way Cherry filled out a television screen, the way he talked in blunt terms, naming likes and dislikes, naming names. Cherry was different. He was a guy from the corner stool at the neighborhood bar, from the back room at the firehouse. His bad grammar was a plus, not a minus. His passion was a definite plus. He was people.

"I met him when he was in his last year as coach of the Bruins," Mellanby says. "That was when I first started thinking about him for TV. The Bruins were playing the Canadiens in the semifinals. He was coaching, and I was producing the games. After the second game he came up to me all mad. There had been a fight. Stan Jonathan of Boston had beaten up someone from Montreal. Cherry had seen a tape of the game and saw that we hadn't replayed the fight. He wanted to know if it was because a Bruin had won the fight. I told him it was our practice; we didn't replay fights. The Boston station did, but our policy was not to replay fights, to hold down the violence.

"During the fourth game there was another fight. This was at the Montreal Forum. Mario Tremblay won the fight. He beat up someone from the Bruins. We're doing the game from this little production room at the Forum, and suddenly we can see on one of the monitors that Cherry isn't behind the bench anymore. Where'd he go? This looks like it might be a story. Suddenly he's in the production room. In the middle of a Stanley Cup game. He's talking to me, telling me that we'd better not replay this fight either. He was worried because a Montreal guy had won. I remember thinking, The middle of a game. This guy is interesting."

The truth was that he always had been interesting, always had been flamboyant, wearing the flashy clothes and speaking his mind, but until he coached the Bruins, no one had noticed very much. He was a minor league guy, condemned to the back roads of hockey for most of his life. The logbook of former Montreal general manager Sam Pollock, filled with notations on every player ever under contract to the Canadiens, even listed him that way: "Confirmed minor-leaguer."

As a slug-it-out defenseman and high school dropout from Kingston, Ontario, he played sixteen years in the minors. He played in just about all the way stations to the top. His career ran from 1954 to 1972. This was the era of the old NHL: six teams, 120 players, everyone else locked into the netherworld at the bottom. The money in the minors was short, maybe $4,500 a year, the conditions awful. Cherry played in Hershey and Springfield and Sherbrooke and Spokane and Jacksonville and a long list of other places. He estimates now that he and Rose moved fifty-three times in the first twenty-six years of their marriage. For most of the time, they kept their possessions to a minimum. Unplug the stereo. Unplug the television. Put them in the backseat of the car next to Don's clothes. Gone. Don't mess up the clothes.

He played one game, total, in the NHL. It was a playoff game. He played for Boston, actually getting on the ice for a few minutes against the Canadiens in 1955. He thought then that he would be in the NHL forever. Alas, he separated a shoulder during the off-season, playing baseball, and never was in the big league again. His talent wasn't the greatest – and his mouth never helped.

"I guess I always had something to say," Cherry says. "I remember one time I was with Montreal in its camp. I was dressing with all of those great players. Jean Beliveau. Boom Boom Geoffrion. All of them. All the guys were complaining about the cab ride to the practice rink in Verdun. The club was picking up the cab fare, but the guys had to provide the tips. That was fifty cents each way, a buck round-trip. Everybody was complaining. Toe Blake, the coach, came in the locker room one day. Toe Blake won all those Stanley Cups. He asks if everything is all right. Not a word. I get up, a nobody. 'Well, Mr. Blake, all the guys have been wondering about the cabs. . . .' I was gone the next day."

He retired after the 1968–69 season, but two years later he started working out again and tried playing for one last season with the Rochester Americans. Midway through the season an amazing thing happened. Doug Adam, the Americans' coach, resigned. Cherry was named as Adam's replacement. Three years later he was in Boston, coaching Bobby Orr.

Rose remembers thinking, *How can we go to Boston? We're confirmed minor leaguers. I'm going to be sitting next to Bobby Orr's wife? I have nothing to wear.* Don didn't have that problem. He always had the good wardrobe. Now he finally had a proper place to wear it.

His five years with the Bruins were some of the happiest times of his life. His strategy called for simple, workmanlike hockey: throw the puck into a corner, beat up anyone in your path, get the puck out of the corner, shoot the puck at the goalie as hard as you can. He had a team of big players who could do that. The Big Bad Bruins. He was the ringmaster at their hockey circus but also a star performer. He walked the dasher as if it were a tight-rope, pumped on adrenaline, howling at all perceived injustices. He quoted Lord Nelson and Popeye to the press. He treated each game as if he were sending knights of honor off to an icy plain to defend the honor of the poor city of Boston. He had fun.

"I don't think any team had more fun than that one," he says. "I remember one night we're playing L.A., and Hilliard Graves hits Bobby Orr from behind. I went crazy. I grab a guy, Hank Nowak, send him over the boards, screaming, 'Get him, Get him, Get him.' Poor Nowak, he skates to the blue-line and turns around. 'Get who?' he asks."

There was the time when Stan Mikita of the Chicago Blackhawks committed some transgression. Cherry threatened to have the Bruins "send him back to Czechoslovakia in a pine box." Reporters wrote that down. Put it in the papers.

There was the time when Bruin winger Rick Middleton arrived at training camp overweight. Cherry said that Middleton "looked like Porky Pig." Reporters wrote that down, too. There was the time . . . there were a lot of times.

By the end, when he was feuding with then general manager Harry Sinden and assistant general manager Tom Johnson, calling them Ben and Willard, after the cinematic rodents; when he was decrying management for using "cheap pucks, no logo on the top, dime-store pucks that a rookie would be ashamed to keep if he scored his first goal in Boston Garden," he had developed a full-blown notoriety. His pet English bull terrier, Blue, subject of so many of his stories, had become famous. Blue was even doing commercials. The Bruins might not have won a Stanley Cup during his time, but they always were in the hunt, finishing first in the division four times.

Then Cherry was off to Colorado to coach the expansion Rockies. He was working with a ghostwriter on his autobiography. "Three years ago I couldn't spell *author*," he said on the first page when the book was published at the end of that expansion season. "Now I are one."

He was ready for television.

"There was controversy about him from the beginning," Mellanby says. "We decided that being a color commentator wasn't the right vehicle. He had too much force. It was too much of him. We came up with *Coach's Corner*. In and out. Don't overwork it. A lot of people didn't think he was right at all, wanted to get rid of him right away. Luckily, I was in a position to have some control. He stayed."

The first shows were scripted and rocky. Cherry soon threw away the scripts and simply talked. Another broadcaster at the anchor desk fed him straight lines and subjects. Cherry talked. Talked? Cherry shouted, ranted, commanded the screen. An interesting statistic evolved: CBC executives noticed that between the first and second periods of *Hockey Night* in French-speaking Quebec, the ratings were going down for the French version of the broadcast while the ratings for the English broadcast were going up. What was happening? People were switching channels. They wanted to hear Cherry.

"I GO WITH HIM TO MONTREAL," SAYS RON MACLEAN, the broadcaster who now shares the CBC anchor desk with Cherry. "This is 1986. I had just started. This is our first trip together. We come out of the airport to catch a cab to the city. The first cab in line is this little cab. It's one of those Russian cars. A Lada. The starter tells us to get in. Cherry looks at the cab and goes crazy. What kind of cab is this? He isn't going to ride in a cab like this . . . this Communist piece of crap. He is screaming. There's a whole big scene. We get a new cab. A bigger cab.

"Same trip," MacLean continues. "We're at the studio. Don likes to arrive late. He likes everything to be spontaneous. I'm doing some work, and I notice the director is speaking in French. He's counting down, '*dix, neuf, huit, sept*. . . .' O.K., we're in a place where the people speak French. Their language. No problem. Don comes in. The director starts the same thing. Cherry goes crazy. 'What is this einz-freinz crap? English! This is a program in English.' The director begins again: 'Ten, nine, eight.'"

The original four-and-a-half minutes have grown. They are still the foundation – four-and-a-half minutes every Saturday night, plus other nights during the playoffs – but now Cherry also does a weekly taped half-hour interview show on The Sports Network, the Canadian equivalent of ESPN, and a daily three-and-a-half minute radio show that is heard on more than 100 stations. He writes a monthly column, longhand, for twelve newspapers. He writes columns for two hockey magazines. He has done a commercial for a government-sponsored hockey lottery in three provinces.

The bars are another success. The set of a bar was used for the first season of the taped show. And someone suggested that maybe a real bar with Cherry's name on it would be a good business venture. There now are fifteen franchised Don Cherry's Grapevine bars across Canada, three more soon to open. Then there are the videos. For four years he has issued annual highlight videos, featuring KOs and random collisions. There have been more than half a million copies sold. Then there is the rap video. The rap video? Cherry did it for charity, wearing a red trench coat, black fedora and sunglasses, saying, among other things, "Probert, Probert, what a man; we see him, it's slam-bam. Let's go." Cherry wrote those words about Detroit Red Wing enforcer Bob Probert. The video was shown on MuchMusic, the Canadian equivalent of MTV.

"People always ask me what he's like off the air," MacLean says. "I tell them, he's no different. What is on the screen is what he is."

His passions are as visible as his neckties. That is his attraction. He is a neon light on a bland landscape. How many men say what they think, what they really think? How many are strong enough, maybe even crazy enough, to disregard possible consequences? How many are able to do it on TV? He is real, a real face from a real world. That is what makes him unique. He says what he thinks.

"I thought I'd do this two or three years, and then I'd fade away," Cherry says. "That's what happens to guys when they leave the game. Two, three years on television, then they're gone. This . . . I don't know. For some reason, people respond to me. I had a letter from the parents of this five-year-old girl who is hearing-impaired. She never had talked, never said a word. Every week, though, she watched the games, watched the show. One week, for some reason, I wasn't on. She turned to her parents and said, 'Where's Don?' The first words out of her mouth. 'Where's Don?'"

The essence of his blustery message is his love of tradition. Why can't things be the way they always were? Where is the honor? What has happened to the virtues of hard work? His is the voice calling for the return of Latin to the Sunday Mass, for the preservation of the neighborhood variety store, for the past against the troublesome future. If hockey is his country's national religion, then he is the keeper of the faith.

His two main crusades are for Canadian kids' keeping jobs in the NHL and for fighting to remain in the game. Keep everything the same. Why change something that has worked for all these years? Every week he talks about the increasing number of foreign players on the league rosters. Who needs them? Every week he talks about the people who would change the game to a wide-open, violence-free exhibition of skating and puck-handling skills. This is supposed to be hockey?

"They talk about all the things the foreign players have brought to the game," Cherry says. "Well, let's see, what have they brought? The helmet. The visor. The dive. Lying there and letting on that you're hurt, the way soccer players always do. I guess, you look at it that way, these people are right. The foreign players have brought a lot to the game."

What is better now? New NHL commercials are being filmed, backed by classical music, to portray "the majesty of the game." Cherry scoffs. What majesty? The game is hits and grunts and hard work. Majesty? How many touchdowns does the NFL show in its commercials in relation to hits and grunts? The game of hockey is a question of valor, of not being afraid. The majesty of the skating and the puck handling is that they are executed in an atmosphere of violence. This should be a man's world, men dealing with men. The new world is a world of parking tickets and regulations and show business.

"It used to be, you'd get cut, you'd finish your shift, no matter what," Cherry says. "A guy like Tim Horton of Toronto, the blood would be coming down his face, and he'd finish his shift. You'd want to get up there to the NHL to be like Tim Horton. Now, you have a guy like Jaromir Jagr of the Penguins. Jaromir Jagr [who not coincidentally is Czech] is everything that's wrong with the NHL. He gets hit, he goes down and stays there. Get up!"

Who are these people who would change the game? Cherry has called McNall, the Kings' owner, Bruce McNutt. He points out again and again that Gil Stein, the league's interim president from June 1992 until Gary Bettman became commissioner on February 1, instituted various rules changes in the past year but "never saw a hockey game until he was thirty-nine years old." Should someone who never saw the game until he was thirty-nine be allowed to tinker with something that has been a part of people's lives from birth? Is that right? These are people "who wouldn't know a hockey player if they slept with Bobby Orr." Bettman is a basketball man, the former senior vice-president and general counsel of the NBA. Cherry says he is withholding judgment on Bettman, but is there any doubt about which way he is leaning? He noticed that Bettman recently said he wants to "enhance the puck" so it can be seen better on television. What does that mean?

"They all want to change something," Cherry says. "They think if they change – if they take out the fights, do something different – hockey is going to become big in the U.S. The big TV contract. It just isn't going to happen. Face it, people in the U.S. would rather watch *The Rifleman* than a hockey game. It's almost sad the way our people try to market this game. Let it stand for itself. Let it be what it is."

The league boasts that fighting is down 33 percent this year and that the number of foreign players still is rising. As of last Friday a total of 767 players had appeared in at least one NHL game this season. There were 49 players from the former Soviet

Union on the list, 29 from the former Czechoslovakia, 24 from Sweden, nine from Finland and 13 from other countries out-side North America. The 508 Canadians and a surging group of 135 Americans – U.S. players are all right with Cherry because they grew up under a similar hockey system – still were in the majority, but the freedom-of-hockey movement clearly is in full force. There will be more Europeans before there will be fewer.

"Don Cherry is like Humphrey Bogart in the wrong movie," Winnipeg Jets' assistant coach Alpo Suhonen, a Finn, says. "He's real, but he doesn't fit in all the different situations he's in."

"He's a total idiot," Calgary Flame defenseman Frank Musil, a Czech, says. "He's a goof. I ignore him. He accuses all European players of not playing physically, but not all Canadian and U.S. players have the same skills as the Europeans. You can't criticize these players for not fighting, because they never did it back home. If they grew up here, maybe they would be more willing to do that. What can you say? He's a goof."

"I think Don is very predictable," says Stein, who is now the NHL's Number Two man. "I think he's fun, but he's always been who he is. I guess he likes goon hockey. Well, the public doesn't, and the league doesn't, and the people running the game don't. The league has a wonderful group of Europeans now, and an international character has already been established. That isn't going to change."

Cherry responds the way he always responds. Directly.

"That's really stupid," he says into the camera. "Isn't that stupid?

"The fans love fighting. The players don't mind. The coaches like the fights. What's the big deal? The players who don't want to fight don't have to fight. Do you ever see Wayne Gretzky in a fight? What's the big deal? I saw Winnipeg and New Jersey the other night, and they were just skating around. Skating around. It was like a tea party, like watching Sweden and Finland play."

Ka-boom! Ka-ka-ka-boom?

CHERRY'S FRIENDS WORRY ABOUT HIM. MELLANBY, now working with the planning committee for the 1996 Olympics in Atlanta, says he is glad he no longer is in charge at *Hockey Night in Canada.* He would not want to be the one who eventually will have to deal with Cherry's future. Cherry is beating on the two themes too much, the foreigners and the fighting. He is moving into politics too often. Something will happen. Cherry has a deal with MacLean. "I don't tell him [MacLean] what I'm going to say . . . I don't want him to go down with me when it all blows apart." This is all right with MacLean. He has his own career.

"I was thinking about Don the other night," MacLean said recently. "I went to the movies and saw *A Few Good Men.* Every time Jack Nicholson came onto the screen, I thought about Don. Nicholson's character was exactly the same. Rules didn't matter. Everything was the Code. When they were carrying Nicholson out at the end, kicking and fighting, that's how I always thought Don would go out. In a ball of fire."

Cherry mostly just keeps going. He would like to slow down, like to stop, as Rose wants him to do, but says he doesn't know how. He hasn't had a vacation in his adult life. He owns a cottage on Wolf Island in Ontario, but he was there for only two days last year. He owns a boat, but it hasn't been in the water in two years. The craziness keeps him too busy.

He sits in the basement den of his modest house in Mississauga, Ontario, a suburb of Toronto. Except for the money he spends on his clothes, he is not an extravagant man. He does have three Lincoln Mark VIs, but all of them are at least ten years old. He says he likes them because they are like him, "a little ostentatious, a little old, but still going." He says he doesn't do much, outside of the work. He sits here a lot, watching hockey games on the giant-screen TV. He has the satellite dish. He can watch a lot of games.

He is eating a tuna fish sandwich. At his feet is his dog. This is a new dog, Baby Blue. The original Blue, the beloved dog, died four years ago. The original Blue was a trusted warrior. Her blue eyes were supposed to be a defect, but Cherry always thought they were a sign of strength. The original Blue was the toughest, meanest, bravest dog a man could find. Cherry doesn't like this new dog very much. He says, "If an intruder came, Baby Blue probably would try to kiss him to death."

The new dog is trying to lick tuna fish from Cherry's plate. He shoos her away.

"This dog," he says. "We took her to the opening of one of the bars. In Oshawa. We're there a little while, and she's all tired. Falling asleep. We had to leave early, take her home."

"Don," Rose says. "The dog was walking on top of the bar. The people were feeding her drinks. Everyone was giving her beer. The dog was drunk."

"You think?" Cherry says.

Damned dog. Where will it all end? The old Blue wouldn't have gotten drunk. The old Blue could hold her liquor.

12. BORIS AND HIS BOYS PREPARE FOR A FEW FRIENDLIES

In a mission to Moscow's hockey factories the author learns why the Soviets' famed amateurs can challenge the best teams in the NHL

BY MARK MULVOY 5/1/1976

OFFICIALLY, CHIEF COACH BORIS KULAGIN'S
Moscow party line for the historic hockey games now under
way between club teams of the U.S.S.R.'s Major League and the
National Hockey League is that they are "true friendlies." No
way, Boris. The NHL does not pay you $200,000 and pick up
your expenses – including all those pre-and postgame vodka
toasts – just for some cozy games between buddies; there's the
little matter of an expected 130,824 paying guests and an inter-
continental television hookup involved with the socializing.

"Pro teams do not play friendlies," admits Russian star
Alexander Yakushev, Bobby Hull's choice as the best left wing
in the world and currently on loan from the Spartak team to
Krylya Sovetov (Wings of the Soviets) for its matches with
Pittsburgh, Buffalo, Chicago, and the New York Islanders. "We
have been told it would be very bad for us not to win," says
Valery Kharlamov, probably the number-two left wing in the
world – ahead of Mr. Hull – who is with his regular Central
Army Club mates for their games against the New York Rangers,
Montreal, Boston and Philadelphia.

Unofficially, the Central Army Club–Philadelphia "true
friendly" next Sunday at the unfriendly Spectrum should also
carry the title of Super Face-off I, because it will match the league
champions of hockey's two worlds for the first time. In that game
Kharlamov will once again meet old pal Bobby Clarke. At their
last meeting, in Moscow during the 1972 Team Canada–U.S.S.R.
series, Clarke "hunted me down," Kharlamov says, "and inten-
tionally put me out of the game." In fact, Clarke, painfully aware

PREVIOUS PAGE: **Bobby Clarke's series-ending slash against Valeri
Kharlamov of the USSR in the 1972 Summit series made him the least
popular hockey player when the Soviet team faced him again in the
mid seventies.** (*Photograph by John D. Hanlon*)

216

of the fact that it was the shifty Kharlamov who had skated the Soviets to a 3–1–1 lead in the series, cracked his stick across Kharlamov's ankle, sending the Soviet star to the sidelines where he watched Canada rally to win the last three games and the series.

"If you want the people here to be friendly, you will not mention the name of Boo-by Clarke," said Felix Rosenthal, the intrepid interpreter, as he guided a visitor on a hockey tour of Moscow recently. "Boo-by Clarke is what we call a no-no."

"HELLO AGAIN, HOCKEY FANS, THIS IS OZZIE OZEROV here at rinkside at the Dvorets Sporta in Luzhniki Sports Complex for tonight's game between the Central Army Club and Spartak." Yes, it is hockey night in Moscow, and when first-rank teams such as Yakushev's Spartak and Kharlamov's Central Army Club meet at the Palace of Sports, 14,000 seats are filled and the game is beamed across the U.S.S.R. in black and white. For games between the Army Club and, say, Torpedo of Gorky, though, the stands are less than half filled and only the last period or two will be shown on videotape.

Ozerov is the Russian Howard Cosell, with silver on top instead of a rug. He always wears a shiny, black-and-gray herringbone sport coat over a blue sweat suit, and he stations himself next to a monitor along the boards, remembering to duck whenever the action gets too close to his herringbones. Ozerov works alone, with no Alexander Karrasov for color, and he never has to "pause for this message" because Russian TV has yet to invent commercials. Nor does he analyze or criticize the play or the players; instead, he simply peels off names – "Yakushev . . .

Gusev . . . Kharlamov" – as a skater touches the puck. When there is a fight or an argument on the ice, the cameras automatically shift away from the action while Ozerov fills in with tidbits like "Moscow Dynamo defeated Lokomotiv 2–1 in a big soccer game two weeks ago."

There are ten teams in what the Soviet Hockey Federation calls the Major League of the U.S.S.R. Hockey Championship, with another fourteen in the First Division and twenty-eight more in the Second Division. Major League franchises cost exactly $6 million less than the $6 million that the Washington Capitals paid for the privilege of joining the NHL. And, in Russia, Washington might not always finish in last place; in fact, each season the worst team in the Major League is dropped to the minors and replaced by the champion of the First Division, while the ninth-place team remains in the Major only if it can survive a two-game, total-goals series with the First Division runner-up.

As in most Russian sports, the ten teams in the Major League represent various trade unions or arms of the Soviet military. For example, Spartak is sponsored by a union of textile and light-industry workers in combination with public servants such as the Moscow sanitation men. Dynamo has two clubs in the league – one from Moscow, the other from Riga in Latvia – and both operate under government subsidy as affiliates of the home affairs section, which includes the militia, the border guards, and the KGB. Dynamo fans are the cold-faced guys with the short hair and the green shoulder straps on their khaki uniforms. The Wings of the Soviets are the representatives of the civilian aircraft industry, while Khimik represents the chemical industries in Voskresnsk, Traktor the tractor factory in Chelyabinsk, Torpedo the automobile plant in Gorky, and Sibir the machine works in Novosibirsk.

Finally, there are two army teams: the Central Army Club in Moscow, which has won nineteen of the twenty-nine U.S.S.R. championships, and the Army Sports Club of Leningrad, which has never won a national title because, Muscovites joke, its best players always seem to be transferred to headquarters in Moscow. Although the Army Club players all hold rank, from private to major, they do not muster for 5:00 A.M. roll call, peel potatoes, or spit shine their skate boots. "When I'm not in training with my teams," says Lieutenant-and-Goaltender Vladislav Tretiak, "I help instruct the young recruits here at the Central Army Club."

The 1975–76 U.S.S.R. championship schedule began last September 6 and will conclude on March 17. Each team plays only thirty-six Major League games, meeting every opponent four times; however, there are long breaks in the schedule following each nine-game cycle so that the National Team – really the Major League all-stars – and/or individual clubs can compete in international events as well as those frequent financial "friendlies."

The city of Moscow's four Major League clubs – Central Army, Wings of the Soviets, Spartak, and Dynamo – all play their home games in the Palace of Sports, a cold, drab building with sight lines little better than Madison Square Garden's. However, reserved sideline bench seats cost only one ruble and twenty kopecks (approximately $1.50), compared to the $12 top charged by the Rangers. Sitting space in the end zones costs a single ruble, while youngsters pay only ten to fifty kopecks (15¢ to 75¢) for admission if they cannot sneak into the building. Weeknight games start at 7:30 and there are usually two games on Saturday and Sunday – the first at 1:00 P.M., the second at 4:00 P.M. "You're supposed to leave the building after the first game," says thirteen-year-old Oleeg Yegorov, a youth member of Spartak, "but we all know where to hide inside so we don't have to pay ten more kopecks to see the second game." One favorite hiding spot between games turns out to be First Secretary of the Communist Party Leonid Brezhnev's rarely used private box above the VIP section at center ice.

Program sheets are free, not $1.50 as they are in Montreal, and there are no air horns, organ grinders, banners and, best of all, no vendors bawling and blocking the aisles. Between periods the spectators line up at the concession counters, and for about fifty kopecks they can buy a small meal consisting of a *sosisky* (a kind of hot dog) or a sausage sandwich, an ice cream bar about twice the size of an Eskimo Pie, and either tea or coffee. After the game almost everyone piles into public buses for the trip home. Parking is free at the Palace of Sports, but only one of every twenty-five adults in Moscow owns an automobile, so there are never any parking problems or traffic jams. The handful of people who do drive to the games always remove their windshield-wiper blades and lock them inside their cars, because the Pep Boys haven't yet opened a branch in Moscow and parts are even more difficult to come by than the cars themselves.

The players dress for the contests in rooms that are sparsely equipped by North American professional standards, lacking such conveniences as wall-to-wall carpeting, stereos, television sets, and, of course, hair dryers. Exactly five minutes before the start of each game the players on both teams leave their dressing rooms, walk out to the hallway adjacent to the VIP tea-and-caviar area, shake hands with visiting dignitaries such as former chess champion Tigran Petrosian, and then line up alongside each other behind the game officials. A bell rings, massive curtains swing open, and the players march out onto the ice to the recorded accompaniment of a Russian song whose roughly translated title is "Cowards Don't Play Hockey."

Game time.

The match between Spartak and the Central Army Club was clearly superior to the other seven Major League games played at the Palace of Sports during a recent six-day period; in fact, it was so spectacular that it could easily have passed for one of those wide-open, speed-skating skirmishes typical of a Buffalo-Montreal matchup. The capacity crowd was at least 95 percent male and maybe 80 percent pro-Spartak – the cry of "Spar-tak, Spar-tak, Spar-tak" echoed through the arena all night. On the other hand, the Army Club's supporters, mostly military men dressed in khaki uniforms, rarely unfolded their arms, and never uttered a sound, unless it was a slow yawn.

With Yakushev, a powerful six-foot-three and 205 pounds, swooping around the ice and controlling the puck, Spartak surged to a 4–2 lead. Then, midway through the third period, the Spartak players seemed to become unsettled when the referee approved an Army Club goal that Boris Mikhailov had clearly kicked into the net. Seconds later, as the Spartak players were still directing words at the official, the Army Club tied the score.

Yakushev was mad. He took the puck in his own end, cruised up one side of the ice, held off two Army Club defenders with his right arm, controlled his stick and the puck with his left arm, and broke in on Tretiak in the goal. Three Army Club players were draped around Yakushev, and Tretiak was in the process of lunging at him, but Yakushev coolly rolled the puck into the net to give Spartak a 5–4 lead.

"Mol-od-tsy, mol-od-tsy, mol-od-tsy," the crowd roared. Good boys, good boys, good boys. Unfortunately for Yakushev and Spartak, the Army Club scored once more and managed to escape with a 5–5 tie. At the siren the teams lined up at their respective blue-lines and, following Russian tradition, exchanged overhead waves of their sticks before turning to salute the appreciative crowd. "The —— referee," complained Spartak Coach Nikolai Karpov – the George Allen of Moscow – outside the dressing room, "he personally cost us the game. The replay proved that Mikhailov's goal should never have counted. But what can we do?"

As Karpov suggested, Soviet referees, some of whom have attended NHL training camps and wear official NHL-issue black and white shirts with the NHL logo covered by a Soviet federation patch, generally proved to be inept; they skated straight-legged and slowly, stayed too far away from play, acted only with indecision, and, confirming rumors, tended to favor the Central Army Club at all times. All in all, the officials were so poor that they deserved the crowd's derisive jeer *"Sudya Na Mylo"* – Referee to the Soap Factory.

BORIS KULAGIN IS THE ORIGINAL RUSSIAN LOMBARDI. Around Moscow they call him "Chuckles," one of those irony-laden Slavic jokes prompted by the near-perpetual scowl on the coach's bearish face. Kulagin continually barks criticism at his Wings, often accentuating his remarks by sticking a finger into a player's face. What he seems to be telling them – or maybe what his glare tells them – is something like, "Do that again, you dumbkov, and I'll option you to Siberia on twenty-four-year recall."

On or off the ice, Soviet coaches, with the possible exception of Kulagin, who handles the National Team as well as the Wings, hardly think or act with independence. They have all been pro-grammed by the Hockey Federation and operate their training schedules and game plans with strict attention to the official federation-approved guidelines. A coach like Konstantin Loktev, for instance, would never dream of breaking up the Central Army Club's vaunted line of Kharlamov, Petrov, and Mikhailov unless ordered to do so by the federation. Nor would Karpov ever experiment with Yakushev at defense. And the coach who does not follow the unit system – that is, substituting one five-player unit for another – may not be a coach very long.

Consequently, Major League games, even a superior match such as the 5–5 tie between Spartak and the Army Club, tend to look the same. Except for Riga Dynamo, the major teams con-centrate on short, crisp passes to move the puck up the ice; then, once in the attacking end, they work what might be called perimeter pick plays, trying to isolate a man for one good shot at the goal. In essence, four players simply move the puck around while the fifth attempts to clear the route for that one good shot by picking some defenseman and removing him from the play. In the NHL, pick plays are called interference and earn the picking player two minutes in the penalty box. Riga Dynamo, the exception, plays the Westernized way, sta-tioning its centers Phil Esposito–style in the slot and trying to work the puck directly to them for quick shots at the goal. Riga also is the only Soviet league team with the names of its players sewn on the backs of their jerseys.

Defensively, all Soviet teams ignore the standard pro tactics of forechecking and back checking. The idea of defense never seems to enter a play until the puck-carrying team has crossed the red-line. Also, Soviet players never invade the corners in search-and-destroy missions for the puck. In fact, the referees are instructed to whistle play to a halt rather than let two players jostle for the puck against the boards.

Not surprisingly, this systematic sameness extends to the equipment worn by the Soviet players and also to their physical appearance on the ice. Except for the goaltenders, Soviet players generally use only one piece of Russian-made equipment: their dentures. Goaltenders do wear bulky Russian-made chest protectors, but everything else is imported. Jofa helmets are in now because the Hockey Federation recently worked out a "good deal," as Kulagin says, with the Swedish manufacturer. The players favor Canadian-made skates, particularly Super Tacks, and Victor Kuznetsov of the Wings wears a pair of green and gold skate boots that once belonged to the California Golden Seals. "One of the best things about this trip to North America," says one Army Club player, "is that we'll all come back with a couple of pairs of new skates, dozens of new hockey sticks, new sweat suits, new shoes, and a lot of other equipment – all compliments of the manufacturers."

Finally, although no Russian has a full Mountain Man beard like Atlanta's Bill Flett or a perm like Philadelphia's Don Saleski, there is one player who does sport a mustache: the iconoclastic Yuri Tjerhin of the Wings. "I do not believe he will have his mustache when we are in North America," Kulagin says. Or, as one of Tjerhin's teammates said, "He may have his mustache, but he won't have it in North America."

FELIX ARRIVED PROMPTLY AT FIVE O'CLOCK WITH the champagne, the beer, the bread, the Stolichnaya vodka, the red caviar, and, most important, the guest of honor – Alexander (Sasha) Yakushev, who was full of apologies. "I'm sorry that Tanya is not with me," he said, "but she could not get a baby-sitter for Katya. The best baby-sitter is *Babushka*, but Tanya's mother lives far from us and can't come on short notice."

Instead of the sweat suit and gym shoes that Soviet hockey players seem to wear wherever they go, Yakushev was mod-ishly attired in a blue-gray Glen plaid sport jacket with a pink shirt and a red silk tie, flared navy-blue slacks, laced-up hi-riser shoes, and a nasty gash under his right eye, compliments of an errant hockey stick. He was obviously stunned by the view from Room 1321 of the Intourist Hotel on Gorky Street in downtown Moscow. Red Square, the Kremlin, Lenin's tomb and the mas-sive GUM department store were dead ahead, while to the right, protruding above a dark panorama of the eastern sector of the city, were the Gothic spires of Moscow University and the cav-ernous Ukraine Hotel. "Do you mind if I have a look?" Yakushev asked. "I have never seen my city like this before."

Yakushev finally sat down on the hard couch, crossed his legs, then, in rapid order, politely declined the champagne, the beer, the bread, the Stolichnaya, and the red caviar. "Do you have any mineral water?" he said. Felix jumped to the phone and ordered some mineral water. "Grape, please," Yakushev requested. "I am in serious training." Oh? So he was not in serious training that night after an exhibition in Portland, Oregon, back in January 1974, when he spent an hour trying to persuade the bartender at the Holiday Inn to sell him an after-hours' fifth of vodka? Yakushev laughed. "Yes, I remember," he said. "I think we were celebrating someone's birthday or anniversary." He winked.

Growing up, Yakushev lived with his father, mother, and two brothers in a one-bedroom apartment that was within walking distance of the Iron-Steel Works Sports Stadium in east Moscow. His father worked at the iron-steel plant, so young Alexander was permitted to play for the various athletic teams sponsored by the plant's trade unions. In time Yakushev showed particular skill in hockey, having honed his abilities during endless games in the courtyard of his family's apartment complex, and at the age of twelve he was invited to play for the union's Hammer and Sickle team in the Moscow city championship. Although Yakushev was three years younger than most of the other skaters, he was named the most valuable player in the tournament and, consequently, became a red-chip prospect for the recruiters.

"I joined Spartak when I was fifteen," Yakushev said. "The main reason, I guess, was that Spartak also was the home club of my hockey heroes – the Mayorov brothers, Boris and Evgeny, and Vyacheslav Starshinov. Besides, Spartak is more liberal, more democratic than, say, the Central Army Club, which has a very stern regimen that I don't like."

During the next few years Yakushev frequently toured Europe and North America with the Soviet National junior team; then in 1968, at the age of twenty, he was selected for the regular National Team. Now twenty-eight, Yakushev has been a member of six world championship teams, and he led Russia to an Olympic gold medal at Sapporo in 1972. During this period he also completed his studies and received a bachelor's degree from the Moscow Institute of Physical Culture and Sport. For all his accomplishments, Yakushev officially ranks as a Merited Master of Sport in the U.S.S.R.

"What's your salary?" he was asked.

"Three hundred rubles [approximately $400] a month, paid by the Hockey Federation," he said. "Besides playing hockey, I also handle the admissions program for the youth hockey school at Spartak."

"Any bonus rubles?"

"Occasionally."

"Like 1,500 rubles for a world championship and 5,000 rubles for a gold medal in the Olympics?"

"No comment."

"You know, if you ever defected to North America and signed with one of the major professional leagues, like your friend Vaclav Nedomansky of Czechoslovakia did last season with the WHA, you could make 200,000 rubles a year."

"I've thought about it. The money, I mean, not leaving my country. I read about all those salaries, but I don't understand them. Why does someone *need* all that much money, anyway?"

By Russian standards, Yakushev lives the good life on his 300 rubles a month, which is about twice the salary of the average Soviet worker. "We have a big apartment out off the Leningrad Highway, with a bedroom, a living room and a kitchen," Yakushev said. "Tanya was a philologist when I met her on a cross-country skiing holiday, but now she stays home with Katya, our three-year-old daughter, and likes to do a lot of decorating." When Yakushev is home, he reads all the hockey and soccer magazines, dabbles in Tolstoi and Dostoevski, and listens to an eclectic mixture of music – Elton John and Khachaturian's ballet *Spartacus* – on a stereo he purchased in Sapporo.

Yakushev drives a new Volga, too, with the vanity license plate 00–15, his uniform number on the National Team. New Volgas cost some 9,000 rubles but like all Merited Masters of Sport Yakushev was permitted to buy his for the low, low, Duke of Discount price of about 5,000 rubles. And when the eleven-month hockey season ends each year, the Yakushevs spend the month of June on an all-expenses-paid vacation at the Spartak resort on the Black Sea.

"I pay 17 rubles a month for rent, 20 rubles for gas for the Volga, 150 rubles for food and about 30 rubles for taxes," Yakushev said. "I'd spend at least another 50 rubles on food, though, if I didn't live in camp with my hockey teams so much."

"What's this camp life you keep talking about?" Yakushev was asked.

"Oh," he said, "when the league schedule gets very difficult, with a lot of games to be played during a short period of time, all the teams move into their camps so they can concentrate on the games and keep in good training. When the National Team is together, we usually practice at the Army Club's rink and spend the rest of our time at a *dacha* out on the edge of the city."

"What happens if you miss curfew?"

"You don't miss curfew. Ever."

The Spartak resort camp is in the Serebryanyi Bor – the Silver Forest – on the northwest fringe of Moscow. "On game days," Yakushev said, "I get up at nine o'clock, then do about forty minutes of P.T. Breakfast is at ten o'clock: yogurt, fried or boiled eggs, a variety of meats, coffee or tea, bread, and mineral water. After breakfast the coaches meet for at least thirty minutes with

each five-man unit. At two o'clock we have a four-course lunch –
salad, soup, meat, and fruit, along with coffee or tea, bread and
mineral water. Then I try to take a nap. At five o'clock we have a
team meeting, and at 5:45 we take the bus to the rink. After the
game I see my wife, and sometimes I get permission to spend the
night at home if we don't have a game the next day. If we do
have another game, I ride the bus back to camp, eat supper –
salad, fish, meat, milk and, yes, mineral water – and go to bed.
Curfew is 2300 hours." He stopped for a moment.

"Do they have curfews in the pro leagues?" he asked.

"The pros prefer to call them bed checks," he was told.

"Bed checks?"

"Yes. The coach checks each player's room to see if the beds
are there. Bodies don't count. Just the beds."

He laughed. "Now let's get serious," he said. "You realize,
don't you, that I have been very fortunate. I am a member of
the third generation of Soviet hockey players, but I have
played against the elite of all three generations – Gordie Howe,
Bobby Hull, and Bobby Orr. I saw Howe play in 1964 when I
was in North America with the junior team. How old was
Howe that year?"

"Probably eighty-seven."

"No, he was thirty-five or thirty-six, wasn't he?"

"At least. He was just a kid."

"Incredible. I expect to retire in just a few more years, maybe
when I'm thirty-two, and now Howe's what? – forty-seven,
and playing on the same team with his two sons. On the basis
of my limited information, he must be the greatest player in
history."

It was 7:30 P.M., time for Yakushev to leave. "Tell me," he said, putting on his coat. "This Schultz I keep reading about, the guy who plays for Philadelphia. Is he really a good fighter?"

"Well, they call him the Hammer," he was told.

"So why don't they call him the Hammer and Sickle?"

He grinned. "Now we're even," he said. "You had your bed check, and I had my hammer and sickle."

"WOULD THE HONORABLE COACH OF THE NATIONAL Team and the Wings of the Soviets stop popping stomach pills and consent to a brief interview?"

"Of course," mumbled Kulagin, popping another pill. "You'd have a jumpy stomach and high blood pressure if you had my troubles. The Wings are only in fourth place now and have shown a bad performance. I've got five newly marrieds on the team, and they spend too much time with their wives and not enough time with their hockey. We have the games against the North American professionals, then the Olympics in February, and I only hope that my stomach and my blood pressure don't crack."

"Violence, Boris. Have there been any outbreaks of violence in your league?"

"It has been terrible. Since that 1972 series against Team Canada we have played more dirty in every game. The professional influence is hurting us. Sometimes we even have fights."

"Right, Boris, and didn't even the normally mild-mannered Mr. Yakushev recently get a five-minute major penalty for decking Yuri Shatalov of your Wings when Shatalov attempted to cross-check him for the second time in a game?"

"Yes, that happened. I saw it all myself. Yakushev was provoked."

"Boris, the people in North America always have thought that your guys play sneaky and do a lot of holding and hooking and even kicking when the referee is not looking."

"I am not going to answer that. However, we do a lot more hooking and use our sticks a lot more now than we did before that 1972 series. Our games are much rougher. Much too rough now."

"According to the statistics, your Wings are the most penalized team in the league with 8.3 penalty minutes per game."

"What can I do? My players are very young, and it is very difficult to reach the young minds."

"The Philadelphia Flyers average a little more than twenty-five penalty minutes a game. In fact, any of your Wings would win the Lady Byng award for clean play if they were in the NHL. Do you know Dave Schultz?"

"I've heard of him."

"Sergei Kapustin is Dave Schultz, you know, because he is the most penalized player in the Soviet league."

"Ridiculous."

"Well, he does have 24 minutes in 18 games with your Wings. Of course, Schultz sometimes gets 24 minutes a game."

"A game?"

"Sometimes, yes."

"Whew!"

"Valery Vasiliev says that he is a fan of roughness himself and knows all about Schultz. Is that why you've added Vasiliev to the Army Club's roster?"

"What do you mean?"

"The Army Club plays Philadelphia."

"No, I never think that way."

"Oh?"

"These games are friendlies for us."

"Bobby Clarke's team does not play friendlies with anyone."

"Ah, excuse me, please. I've got to see the trainer. I must get some more little pills."

WHEN BRAD PARK AND JEAN RATELLE JOINED BOSTON recently, veteran Bruin forward Wayne Cashman graciously gave them a guided tour of their new quarters at the Boston Garden. Coming to the trainer's room, Cashman told his new teammates, "This is where we hide from the writers after the game." In Moscow, the sportswriters hide from the players. They talk only with the coaches, and even then the coaches ignore all questions and simply issue a few terse sentences on how they saw the game, never mentioning the name of any individual player. Game stories are direct from Journalism One, long verbal replays of each goal but little analysis or criticism.

Occasionally, however, the Soviet sports hierarchy uses the press to censure players and coaches for excesses, all of which occur, it seems, when a player or a team has performed poorly. When the National Team lost several hockey games in Sweden a few years ago, the Moscow press reported that the Soviet players were detained at the airport while officials confiscated the "contraband" – clothes, stereos, records – they had stashed in their luggage. Despite having guided the National Team to European and World titles, coach Vsevolod Bobrov was criticized in the media for buying too many foreign gadgets for his Volga when the team seemed to be slumping; indeed, few Muscovites were surprised when he was demoted to a minor soccer job a few months later.

Komsomolskaya Pravda, the youth paper, recently attacked Alexander Maltsev, the captain of Dynamo and a regular on the National Team, with a stinging editorial broadside in the form of an open letter, written, undoubtedly, by someone from the Hockey Federation. The letter itemized Maltsev's alleged sins: "1) He missed the National Team's plane from Moscow to Sweden because his alarm clock failed; 2) He has been boozing with well-wishers; 3) He has been bragging of his successes; 4) He has constantly violated training schedules." Continuing, the letter said, "Maltsev has become affected by a star disease. Glory has made his head spin. Maltsev should think about his responsibility to himself, his teammates, his club, and hockey. He should not wait until the alarm clock goes off."

The next day *K-Pravda* printed coach Anatoly Tarasov's reported reaction to the criticism of Maltsev. "It was timely," Tarasov said, "and it should have a sobering effect, like a cold shower, on all those who lack culture, modesty, and the patience to carry the lofty name of sportsman. Our society, unlike the capitalist world, does not need supermen, but, rather, human beings with all-round development."

Seated at a table in the VIP section at the Palace of Sports, Maltsev sounded contrite when questioned about the printed criticism. "I was embarrassed," he admitted, "but I also realized why it was done. I was becoming a hockey bum and I had to change my approach before it was too late."

Chastened, the new Maltsev has lost ten pounds, one extra chin, and a few inches around the waist. He also has been the leading scorer in the Major League and has helped keep the surprising Dynamo club in first place. "I have found a new life," he said. He also bought a new alarm clock.

OFF THE ICE, VALERY KHARLAMOV IS RUSSIA'S answer to Derek Sanderson: a well-heeled bachelor who squires only chic young ladies to the best Moscow discos in his luxurious Volga, which is equipped with a stereo tape deck, dual rear-seat speakers, reclining bucket seats, and a large pocket on the front right-side door for parking tickets.

"Valery will be a little late," said Anatoly Firsov, the assistant coach of the Central Army Club team. "It was a long game last night, and he was very tired at the end. He will be here in about an hour." Firsov was sitting in a small room across the hall from the dressing quarters at the Army Club's athletic complex on the northwest side of Moscow. Out on the ice, Irina Rodnina and Alexander Zaitaev, the world pairs figure-skating champions, were practicing. In the other buildings and on the dozens of outdoor athletic fields, youngsters from five to eighteen were kicking soccer balls, shooting basketballs, firing pistols, spiking volleyballs, balancing on parallel bars, playing street hockey, and working on tennis backhands.

"When you come here," Firsov said, "you see why the Army Club is such a dynasty in all the sports. We have a system of training. In hockey we hold the first tryouts when the kids are almost six years old. Then we select the best forty of the players and submit them to our training regimen. Vladislav Tretiak, Alexander Gusev, Vladimir Lutchenko – some of our best hockey players – have been working with us since they were little tots."

For years Firsov was considered the U.S.S.R.'s best hockey player. Now, at the age of thirty-four, he is Major Anatoly Firsov and working on the third season of his retirement. "Yes, I know that I am still very young by the standards in North

America," he said, "but I played at the top level for fifteen years and got fed up. I never saw my wife or my children. Our constitution provides for only one month's vacation each year, while the North American pros get about four months. Also, glory can have a negative effect on your head, you know. When you are six times the world champion and win a couple of Olympic gold medals, it's hard to keep pulling yourself up to meet the next challenge."

Kharlamov finally walked into the room. "My son Anatoly is five years old," Firsov said, "and he believes he is Yakushev when he plays hockey with his friends. I've told him a million times to forget Yakushev, that Kharlamov is our pet here at the Army Club." Pause. "Oh, excuse me, Valery, I didn't know you were here."

Kharlamov smiled as he sat down on a bench underneath a 1971 Toronto Maple Leafs calendar and began to pick through the Army Club's fan letters. "Listen to this," he said, reading from a card. "'Hello, guys. I can't recognize you. Your team should be at the top of the placing table, not behind a Dynamo. You should shoot more at the opponent's goal from any position.' It's signed Vera from Donetsk."

Unlike the NHL's garrulous Sanderson, Kharlamov is normally very close-mouthed. "I am twenty-seven years old and single," he said in a rapid monotone, "and I will not get married until my career as a player is finished. Some girls may have selected me, but I have not yet selected a favorite girl."

Kharlamov still is a student at the State Institute of Physical Culture and Sport and, like Yakushev, he hopes to be a coach at the end of his playing career. "Yes, I remember Boo-by Clarke," he said. "Anything can happen in a game, but I try to keep no grudge. He was not a sportsman in that game, but it is over now." With that, Kharlamov stood up, shook hands and bolted for the dressing room. "I am late for the workout," he said.

On the ice, Loktev had finished putting his players through their prescribed numbers of sit-ups, push-ups, knee lifts, toe touches, and deep knee bends, and now he called for a series of three-on-two line rushes. The Kharlamov line, with Vladimir Petrov at center and Boris Mikhailov at right wing, headed up the ice, moving the puck with the instinct acquired during six seasons of total togetherness. This time, though, a defenseman broke up the play. Loktev was mad, particularly at Kharlamov, who had messed up the maneuver with a fancy but unrequired behind-the-back pass to Petrov. So, at Loktev's command, there was the Soviet Sanderson contritely doing a dozen push-ups.

"Was that the way for a coach to treat his star?" Kharlamov was asked later.

"If we had lost the game last night," he said, "I might have had to do two dozen."

THE SPRAWLING NEW CAMPUS OF THE STATE Institute of Physical Culture and Sport is located on Moscow's eastern edge, not far from the Lokomotiv Stadium, where, Felix had joked, "The big cheer goes 'puff-puff.'" The institute's uniquely trained faculty prepares high school and university instructors in all sports while its scientific branch designs the training regimens for Soviet national teams.

Fred Shero attended the institute's summer hockey clinics in 1973 and 1974, then coached the Philadelphia Flyers to two consecutive Stanley Cup championships. John MacInnes attended the 1974 clinic, then coached Michigan Tech to the

NCAA championship. On the other hand, recently-fired coach of the St. Louis Blues, Garry Young, said the only thing he had learned was "something about the power play that I haven't had time to put into our system."

Valery Kharlamov is enrolled in the institute's four-year program for hockey instructors. Anatoly Firsov is taking a one-year refresher course. Alexander Yakushev already has graduated from a similar institute. And there are several players on teams in Leningrad and Chelyabinsk who are taking the institute's five-year correspondence course. Before they graduate, students spend a minimum of 1,600 hours immersed in the study of their sport.

Tuition is free. In fact, each of the 8,000 regular students is paid a monthly stipend of fifty rubles to cover bus and subway expenses, laundry, and other incidentals. One five-story wing of the main building houses the institute's administration offices, dozens of classrooms with tiered seating, study halls, lecture rooms, and libraries. On the walls are pictures of former Olympic champions, including such gold medalists as Sonja Henie, Jesse Owens, and an old Yale track star named Richard Sheldon. There are also two wings of sports halls – every sport, it seems, from archery to yachting, has its own facility, complete with videotape equipment to analyze the finest points. There are also a number of what Dean Vyacheslav Varjushin called "relaxing parlors to get one's head back in place after a hard day's work." Two hockey arenas and a grass tennis court are under construction.

"There is nothing we don't teach the students about their sports," said Varjushin, who prefers soccer to all others and dispels any Jack LaLanne–style zealotry on the subject of physical fitness by chain-smoking filter-tip cigarettes. "At present the institute's emphasis is on hockey, particularly the kinesiology of hockey. Vyacheslav Kolosov, the head of the Hockey Federation, wrote his doctoral thesis on the kinesiology of hockey players here. We are very concerned about physiology: anatomical rehabilitation after practices and games, diet, sleeping habits, *everything*. What we want to do is make a model for the teams in all the hockey programs."

Varjushin opened his desk. "It's cold outside," he said, taking out a welcoming bottle of vodka and some goblets. Then he picked up the telephone, mumbled a few commands and, presto, a matron appeared with a platter of bread and caviar. "It's a Russian tradition," Varjushin said, hoisting his goblet. "Bottoms up."

The scientists at the institute have been using the Moscow Dynamo team in their kinesiological studies. "Nothing is official yet," Varjushin said. "The scientists have examined the players very frequently during the schedule, and they have been putting the results into the computers for estimation. We have given each Dynamo player a printout of his physical and psychological ratings, and we have recommended methods of training for each. Dynamo is now at the top of the placing table, so the programs we have devised must be working. One thing we discovered is that a glass of dry wine after competition is better than a glass of beer. We have found that at the top level the best sportsmen use liquor to kill the shock of hard training. The best thing to drink after a game, though, is mineral water. Grape mineral water."

Before the last few words were out of his mouth, Varjushin was refilling the goblets with vodka – not grape mineral water. "We must be doing something right," he said. "Bottoms up."

13. THE WORST JOB IN SPORTS

While some NHL enforcers like to brawl, many members of the fraternity of fighters find it dangerous and demeaning, an ugly way to earn a handsome living

BY MICHAEL FARBER 24/3/1997

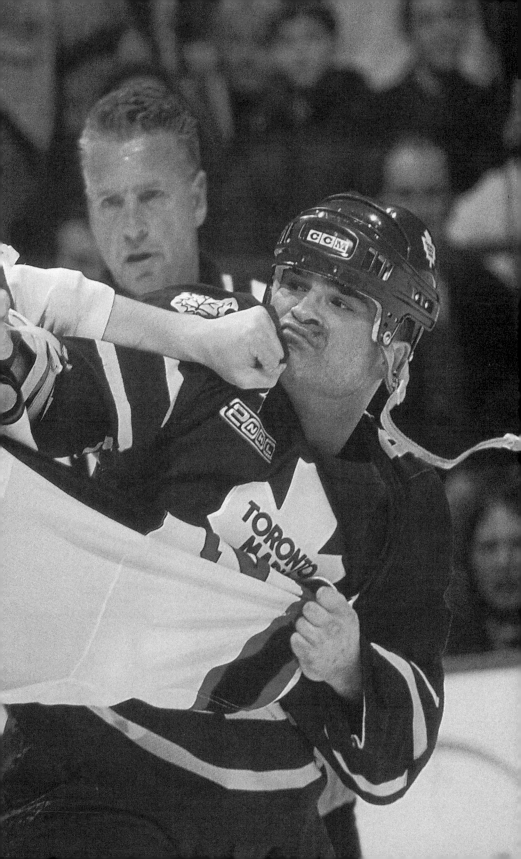

> "Came in as a crusher. Now thinks he's a rusher. Will soon
> be an usher."
>
> — NHL ADAGE

LOUIE DEBRUSK HAS NOT BEEN REDUCED TO AN usher, although on this February night he does have an excellent seat on the Edmonton Oilers' bench. He is far enough from the gate not to have to open it for teammates. He had a couple of shifts in the first period against the Toronto Maple Leafs, skating his wing, banging opponents, but the Oilers are up 6–1 in the second period, and DeBrusk looks as if he has been glued to the bench. There is another NHL adage, not as catchy as the one about the crusher-rusher-usher devolution of a hockey fighter, but just as poignant: If you can't play in a 6–1 game, you can't play.

DeBrusk is supposed to be the Oilers' enforcer – or cop or tough guy or, if you prefer the G word, goon – but the skin on his knuckles is hardly marked. Edmonton coach Ron Low declines to discuss DeBrusk's job performance, but not dressing him for eighteen consecutive games earlier this season and burying him on the bench during the Toronto blowout are eloquent enough.

"It's not that Louie is chicken," an Edmonton executive says. "Not at all." But sometimes the nuances of DeBrusk's role escape him. Example: If an opposing player takes a cheap shot at Oilers' star center Doug Weight and Weight responds with a cross-check of his own, then the six-foot-two, 215-pound DeBrusk sees the

PREVIOUS PAGE: Tie Domi reveled in being an enforcer, while many others were less enthusiastic about the expectations of the job. *(Photograph by Damian Strohmeyer)*

affair as closed, or at least not requiring his intervention. An enforcer, however, is expected to take everything personally – and to respond personally.

DeBrusk, who turns twenty-six this week, is still trying to come to terms with that reality. Being an enforcer has never been easy for him, but he is adjusting. He hasn't had a drink since the summer of 1995, a year after his second stay at the Betty Ford Clinic. "I can look back and say fighting's pretty much given me a life, but it's also kind of destroyed my life," DeBrusk says the morning after the Leafs game. "The fact that I am a fighter on the ice and the difficulties I've had with that job definitely brought me to drink a few times. I'd go out after a game, and all I could think of was the pressure I had on me during the game. Maybe I didn't fight. There'd be the guilt that I didn't fight, the feeling of worthlessness, I guess. Then I'd go out and drink myself into oblivion, and maybe I'd get into a fight later. I've been advised by people who have helped me in rehab not to go back to my job."

A sixth-year veteran with 19 goals, 12 assists, and 792 penalty minutes over his career, DeBrusk earns $350,000 a year, and while that isn't exactly Mike Tyson money, fighting pays. If you prorate DeBrusk's salary over his ice time, he probably earns almost as much per minute as the Pittsburgh Penguins' Mario Lemieux, who makes $11 million a year. DeBrusk has a high school equivalency diploma. He doesn't have many career options.

"I love this job, but at times I almost hate this job," DeBrusk says. "There are times you don't feel like going out there and fighting. If someone does something to me on the ice, it's not difficult for me to flip the switch. Sometimes when I'm sitting on the bench for the whole game, though, and someone does something to a teammate, I don't necessarily feel great about having to go out and fight. Unfortunately, that's my job."

That job is the worst in sports.

THEY THROW DOWN THE GAUNTLET AND THEN THROW down the gloves, and for the next 20, 30, or even 45 seconds, until exhaustion or a linesman intercedes, two guys throw punches. They do it while holding on to each other's sweaters and balancing themselves on one-eighth-inch-thick blades. They are not punching with those cute ten-ounce gloves Iron Mike wears but with their bare fists, and they are connecting with skulls or the plastic helmets that cover them, usually while getting socked in the head themselves. "It's like punching a wall every night," Florida Panthers defenseman and enforcer Paul Laus says.

Some players, such as Tie Domi of Toronto, relish fighting – Domi claims he has started 90 percent of his twenty-three fights this season – but most do it without any sense of joy. The job certainly isn't thankless; 18,000 fans will roar their approval and teammates will bang their sticks against the boards if you win a scrap. But the physical and psychological toll can be staggering.

If you are a member of the fighters' fraternity, you are going to get hurt; Todd Ewen of the San Jose Sharks, for example, has had four hand operations. If you don't fulfill your pugilistic obligations, you might get blackballed, as forward Paul Mulvey found out fifteen years ago. You do not necessarily fight on your own terms. You cannot always pick your spots. Maybe you are married and have kids, and your wife thinks you're setting a terrible example for Junior. Maybe you are not as tired of fighting as you are tired of *thinking* about fighting.

"We've all had that oh-I-think-my-girlfriend's-pregnant feeling, that sick-to-your-stomach feeling when you have to do something you don't want to do," says Kelly Chase, the rambunctious Hartford Whalers winger who has averaged 4.7 penalty minutes per game while stirring pots and throwing rights since the 1989–90 season. "It's like when you've had somebody in school organize a fight for you. You know that at 3:30 you've got to go out and have that fight. That's how I feel every game and probably how I've felt since junior hockey. Eventually that's what chases a lot of guys away from the game."

They didn't start out to be fighters. None of them. When their parents woke them at 5:00 A.M. and helped them into shoulder pads in the dead of January, when they spent summers at hockey camp instead of at the lake, they weren't learning how to fight. They were playing hockey because they liked playing hockey. By the time they were in juniors, though, they probably knew what their role was. And they learned a cruel fact: If you're a fighter, you don't spend much time actually playing hockey.

"The worst part for a fighter is that when hockey matters most, you become irrelevant," New York Islanders general manager Mike Milbury says. "In Game 7 of a Stanley Cup series, chances are you won't play or maybe even dress." There have been only 15 fights in the 65 seventh games played since 1969, and none since 1991. "A hockey player wants to play Game 7," Milbury says. "That's what he lives for. Everyone wants to matter."

But many fighters never get a chance to develop beyond the goon stage. If a guy has some skills and gets ice time, the opportunity to develop, he could end up on a regular shift, as did Chris Nilan, the fourth-most-penalized player in NHL history, who earned a spot on a checking line with the Montreal Canadiens after four years in the league. Or he might wind up like Marty McSorley, who went from being Wayne Gretzky's bodyguard with the Oilers and Los Angeles Kings to a solid defenseman, now with the San Jose Sharks. Nilan and McSorley are the idols of every roughneck who dreams of attaining a Gordie Howe hat trick: a goal, an assist, and a fight in the same game.

"You go to war for your teammates, you expect to be rewarded with an opportunity to play," Florida general manager Bryan Murray says. "That's the only way you can develop as a player. [Enforcers] all say, 'Give me a chance to show what I can do.' To make money, to stick around a long time, you need ice time to develop."

But the enforcer's job more likely will bury him. If a coach allows a player's skills to rot, that player could end up like Willi Plett, the 1976–77 rookie of the year with the Atlanta Flames. When Plett came up he was a talented power forward who was also adept with his fists. After thirteen seasons with three teams, however, he retired prematurely because he felt he was being turned into a full-time thug. He finished with 222 goals and 2,574 penalty minutes. "As my career went on, my toughness was more important to the team than my goal scoring," Plett says. "And that pissed me off. I was tough and I could play, but it turned on me."

The ultimate cautionary tale of a crusher turned rusher was that of the Boston Bruins' John Wensink, who had 20 goals after 28 games of the 1978–79 season but was bumped to the fourth line by coach Don Cherry because Cherry thought all that scoring was turning the six-foot, 200-pound Wensink soft. Wensink finished the season with 28 goals and went on to play for five

NHL teams over parts of eight seasons. He gained his greatest fame for standing in front of the Minnesota North Stars bench in 1978 and challenging anyone who would oblige him to a fight. Nobody did.

And if a coach puts a player in a little box, why shouldn't fans? "Nobody expects Arnold Schwarzenegger to be firing a machine gun when he walks into a restaurant," says Ewen, who once asked his wife, Kelli, a model, to turn down a chance to pose for the cover of *Playboy* because he figured if she posed, he would have to fight on every shift he took. "People who know me kind of think I'm a Renaissance man" – Ewen has written and illustrated a children's book – "but most people assume when I walk into a restaurant that I'll break down the door, slap a head, order raw meat, and then gnaw on the bone. That's the weird part. So many people live through fighters. After a game they'll say, 'Yeah, you smacked that guy's face; you killed him.' But once you don't do well, they're the first to call you a bum and say you're too old. You get labeled for life."

In the 1978 playoffs, six-foot-two, 205-pound Pierre Bouchard was branded by a punch to the nose thrown by Boston's Stan Jonathan, a small (five-eight, 175 pounds) but fierce man who left Bouchard, then the Canadiens' enforcer, a pulpy mess. The memory of Montreal's Stanley Cup–winning goal that year has faded, but Bouchard's blood still flows bright crimson in fans' minds.

"Goliath was also remembered for his defeat," says Bouchard, now a Canadiens television analyst. Even today an occasional wise guy will spot Bouchard and sing out, "How's Jonathan?"

THE FIRST MYTH ABOUT HOCKEY FIGHTS IS THAT

they start spontaneously. They almost never do. They start because of a cheap shot, a team's need for an emotional lift or the mere proximity of two thugs on the ice. When opposing enforcers are sent out at the same time, a fight is going to break out.

"Most fights are caused by coaches," Philadelphia Flyers general manager Bob Clarke says. "If a team's getting beat, the response is, Let's have a fight. The coaches don't have to tell the players to fight. The players aren't dumb."

No. The fighters understand what they're supposed to do. The standard invitation to an NHL bout is, *Want to go?* The "regulars," as Ewen calls them, even have a code of ethics: no sucker punches, just square-up matches. "Everyone accepts that," Ewen says.

What tough guys have trouble accepting is being ordered onto the ice to fight, as almost every enforcer has been at least once in his career. That slap in the face is almost as hard to take as a haymaker. Says veteran enforcer Stu (the Grim Reaper) Grimson of the Whalers, "Nobody wants to sit for two-and-a-half periods, have your team down three or four goals, and have the coach send you out there and expect you to make it all right. That's demeaning and dehumanizing. I've gone, but after the game I've told coaches, 'Don't *ask* me to do my job. I know what's expected of me.' You don't order a goal scorer to go out and score a goal. I don't need someone tapping me on a shoulder, winding me up like a robot."

"One time it happened to me," says Ewen. "Our coach yelled at one of their players, and the player skated by the bench and shouted an obscenity at our coach. He tapped me and said, 'Go get him.' I thought, *You* go get him. The coach tapped me three times, and I didn't go. We yelled and screamed about it later. I wound up on the bench for a week and a half."

"One coach ordered me out with twenty seconds left, we're losing by three goals, they've got their three toughest guys out there, and I haven't played a shift all night," Chase says. "I didn't think he was sending me out there to tie the game. I mean, don't embarrass me. I went straight to the locker room and got undressed, and when he came in, we had a big shouting match. We settled it all the next day – out of court."

Ultimately, Paul Mulvey did too.

ON A FRIDAY NIGHT LAST MONTH, AT THE RESTON Ice Forum in northern Virginia, scores of young hockey players were on the two rinks, a mob of hockey moms were in the lobby, and the noise from a kids' birthday party blared incessantly from the second floor. The tootling of the party horns filtered through the closed office door of Mulvey, who is part owner of the facility. The office is tiny, but it seems even smaller when the six-foot-four Mulvey rises from his chair. There are mementos of his pro career – a *Goal* magazine cover and a grip-and-grin photo of Paul with his father, John, and his brother Grant, who played ten NHL seasons – but the most prominently displayed souvenir is from Mulvey's posthockey days. Behind his desk is a framed copy of a May 9, 1982, *Parade* magazine story that lauded his courage for having taken a stand. Mulvey was, as the headline says, THE MAN WHO WOULD NOT FIGHT.

Mulvey was one of those quirky characters of the 1980s who, like Joe Piscopo, came and went. He represented a *cause*; he was the poster boy against hockey violence. Mulvey had been a heavyweight with the Washington Capitals, the Penguins, and the Kings, snacking on Tagamet and Tums to calm his nerves before doing his duty on the ice: squaring off with the Flyers' Behn Wilson and Paul Holmgren and the other toughs of his generation. In 1980–81 Mulvey jumped into the penalty box and swung his stick at the Quebec Nordiques' Kim Clackson in retaliation for Clackson's having crushed Mulvey's vertebra when they were juniors six years earlier. "If a guy like Holmgren needed to be settled down – no problem," Mulvey says.

But Mulvey did have a problem on January 24, 1982. The Kings were on a power play, with five skaters to the Vancouver Canucks' four, when Vancouver's Tiger Williams, the NHL's all-time penalty leader, began roughhousing. Los Angeles coach Don Perry tapped Mulvey on the left shoulder and, according to Mulvey, said, "Go – and I don't want you to dance." Mulvey didn't move. Not right away, anyway. The Kings already had the Canucks outnumbered, and Mulvey didn't see the point. Only after Vancouver's Stan Smyl left the bench and a general melee broke out did Mulvey get up. He estimates the gap between the time Perry tapped him and the point at which he went onto the ice as twenty seconds.

Between periods Perry sidled up to Mulvey and said, "When I tell you to go, I expect you to go."

Mulvey replied, "Absolutely not. You got the wrong guy, Don, if you expect me to do that for you." Perry, a legendary fighter from the now defunct Eastern League, started screaming that Mulvey wouldn't stick up for his teammates. Mulvey got undressed – and never again put on an NHL uniform. "Those twenty seconds," Mulvey says, "probably cost me a million dollars."

League president John Ziegler immediately suspended Perry

for fifteen days and fined the Kings $5,000 for instructing a player to join an altercation, but Mulvey paid the heaviest price. For his momentary crisis of conscience he was forced to trade the neon of Los Angeles for the fifty-watt frosted bulbs of New Haven, Connecticut, where the Kings banished him. Los Angeles released Mulvey after the season, and he spent 1982–83 with Edmonton's farm club in Moncton, New Brunswick. Worse, Mulvey grew depressed, losing thirty pounds and feeling alone and scared, wondering why even his best friends in the NHL would not support him publicly.

"There was no doubt in my mind I was blackballed," Mulvey says. "I was marked. I wasn't a game breaker, not a top-10-per-center, not a guy who made the difference, and this incident was baggage." Mulvey quit hockey after the 1982–83 season, done at twenty-four. He'd had his first upper G.I. series at age fourteen, been in and out of hospitals starting in juniors, because of nerves. The moment he quit, he started to get better.

Mulvey sued the Kings – "I guess you'd call it for loss of career," he says – and in 1986 he received an undisclosed cash settlement. The money represented closure, easing the bitterness toward a game that had, perversely, turned him into a hero when all he wanted to be was a player. He is remembered fondly, if at all, for refusing to goon it up, and he says he wouldn't have honored Perry's request even if he'd had a year to reflect on it. "I coach teams, and I teach five-year-olds up to twenty-year-olds," Mulvey says. "I try to teach the values my father taught me about sportsmanship and respect for others."

And yet. . . .

"I was the guy who wouldn't protect my teammates, right?" Mulvey says. "Let me tell you about the last game I played in my life. I was with Moncton, and we were in Baltimore. Billy Riley, the black guy who'd been my teammate in Washington, was being harassed by three guys. I was in the penalty box, but I jumped out and chased those three guys back to their bench. Of course I was suspended, and that was it. To protect a teammate, I went. No tap. No nothing."

LOUIE DEBRUSK IS GOING TO GET THIS THING figured out. Maybe he will start running little guys even though his skewed notion of sportsmanship says you pick on players your own size. When Craig MacTavish was the Oilers' captain, he once upbraided DeBrusk for going easy on six-foot, 195-pound Kings defenseman Darryl Sydor in a fight that started when Sydor took exception to DeBrusk's hit on another L.A. player. "Mac-T said, 'If a guy comes at you like that, kick his ass,'" DeBrusk says. "He said, 'It doesn't matter if the guy's four-foot-two. In a heartbeat he'd go around you one-on-one, abusing you in his way. Why not abuse him in your way?' I was angry, because Mac-T was right. I'm learning."

No one said it would be easy.

14. SUPER CONDUCTOR

*Scotty Bowman – the NHL's winningest coach – and his Pittsburgh
Penguins are on track to win a third straight Stanley Cup*

BY E.M. SWIFT 10/5/1993

Abrupt, straightforward, without flair or charm, he seems cold and abrasive, sometimes obnoxious, controversial but never colorful. He is not Vince Lombardi, tough and gruff with a heart of gold. His players don't sit around telling hateful-affectionate stories about him. . . . He is complex, confusing, misunderstood, unclear in every way but one. He is a brilliant coach, the best of his time.

— KEN DRYDEN, 1983, THE GAME

The players are different now. And I found out you can do things differently.

— SCOTTY BOWMAN, 1993

THIS STORY MIGHT HAVE BEEN SUBTITLED "THE mellowing of hockey's winningest coach." Might have been, if fifty-nine-year-old William Scott Bowman had cooperated and mellowed to any appreciable degree. He hasn't. Oh, he has smoothed out some of the renowned rough edges he featured in the 1960s, when as a young up-and-comer he cajoled and browbeat the expansion St. Louis Blues into overachieving their way into three straight Stanley Cup finals.

He has tempered the unpredictable, intimidating style he used in the 1970s, when, chin distinctively thrust out, he drove the fire-wagon-style Montreal Canadiens to five Stanley Cups in eight years. Recently he has even shown himself to be human

PREVIOUS PAGE: Scotty Bowman, one of the greatest coaches of all time, pictured here with one of the greatest teams of all time, the Canadiens of the late 1970s. *(Photograph by Manny Millan)*

now and again, shucking the brusque armor he wore during the 1980s, when, as full-time general manager and sometime coach, he steered the Buffalo Sabres to, on average, ninety-five points per season, falling short of his ultimate goal: winning a sixth Stanley Cup. But you wouldn't say the coach of the Stanley Cup champion Pittsburgh Penguins has mellowed.

Any temptation to think so is laid to rest by a chance meeting with a taxi driver who regularly services the downtown hotel in Pittsburgh that Bowman calls home during the hockey season. (Bowman still lives in Buffalo, where he commutes once every two weeks during the season, schedule permitting.) "I almost got in a fight with him last year," says the cabbie, some thirty years Bowman's junior. "I was parked where he couldn't get past me in the garage, and he wasn't any too subtle telling me to move. He's definitely got an attitude. I finally told him to relax or he was going to have a heart attack."

Tact has never been a Bowman trademark. As for subtlety, it is surely no coincidence that Bowman's father, John, who died last December at the age of ninety, spent thirty-one years toiling as a blacksmith. Like father, like son. Only Bowman's hammer is his tongue, his anvil is his certitude, and pity the person whose ego gets caught between them. Bowman is a bottom-line guy – high on results, low on posturing. At the end of the day he's interested in two things: Did we win? and, What can I do to help us win tomorrow? Some coaches teach; others inspire. Bowman wins. It's his nature.

Bowman traces his competitiveness to his eighty-six-year-old mother, Jean, who to this day will throw her cards in the fire if she loses at euchre. "If you like the game, Scott, why lose at it?" she once said to him, and that advice would look good as his epitaph. Bowman has been hockey's all-time winningest coach since December 1984, when his Sabres beat the Chicago Blackhawks for his 691st career win, eclipsing the mark of one of his mentors, Montreal's Dick Irvin.

Today, in his twenty-first season coaching in the NHL, Bowman's regular-season record stands at 834–380–226, a winning percentage of .657, easily the highest of anyone who has coached more than 600 games. Bowman, who at week's end was 134–79 in the postseason, also has more playoff wins than any other coach. His teams have been winning for so long that the NHL's second-winningest coach, Al Arbour of the New York Islanders, who has 745 regular-season victories, *played* for Bowman in St. Louis. Heck, it was Bowman who first put Arbour behind the bench twenty-three seasons ago, and they're both still going strong. "In the back of my mind, I'd like to get 1,000 wins, including playoffs," Bowman says. "It would take another good season, but I'm charged up because we have a good team."

A great team is more like it. The Penguins, who beat the New Jersey Devils in five games in the opening round of the playoffs and who at week's end trail the Islanders one game to none in the Patrick Division finals, have won two straight Stanley Cups and are odds-on favorites for a third. This season the Penguins had the league's best record, 56–21–7, reeling off a seventeen-game winning streak in March and April that broke the NHL record.

And if Bowman is kinder and gentler with the Penguins than he was with the Blues, the Canadiens, and the Sabres – and he is – it's not because he has mellowed. It's because he has discovered that to win in Pittsburgh in the 1990s requires a different formula than was needed in Montreal in the 1970s. "I don't think Scotty could do the things now that he did years ago," says Mario Lemieux, whom Bowman calls the greatest player he has seen in his twenty-six years in the league. "Not with the kind of team we have in Pittsburgh."

"Scotty still has that intensity, but it's somewhat softened," says Penguin general manager Craig Patrick, who brought an element of generational symmetry to Bowman's coaching career when he offered him the Penguin job. Bowman's first NHL coaching position was offered to him by the late Lynn Patrick, Craig's father. "He's still driven," Patrick says. "I think he wants to be the winningest coach ever."

But isn't he already?

Says Patrick, "I don't think he wants anyone ever to touch him."

BOWMAN, THE SECOND-OLDEST OF FOUR CHILDREN, grew up in Verdun, a working-class suburb of Montreal. His parents were Scottish immigrants, and if he learned competitiveness from his mother, Bowman learned the value of hard work from his father, who in thirty-one years of pounding sheet metal for the railway never took a sick day. The Bowmans lived on a street lined by twenty-six tenements, thirteen on each side, six families per tenement, more than 150 families on the block. Bowman rattles off these numbers as if he had visited that street yesterday. He is comfortable with numbers, more comfortable with numbers than he is with people. One thousand wins. Six Cups. Twenty-six tenements. He has such a precise mind that some of his Penguin players refer to him as Rainman.

As a lad Bowman could strap on his blades in front of his apartment and skate down snow-covered 5th Avenue, through the back alleys, to the city rinks where he learned to play hockey. Verdun had dozens of rinks. By March 1951 Bowman was a pro prospect. He was seventeen years old, a small, quick, talented forward for the respected Junior Canadiens. Then, almost as soon as his playing career had started, it was over. In the final minutes of a Junior A playoff game at the Montreal Forum, Bowman broke in alone on goal, chased by a defenseman named Jean-Guy Talbot, whose team, Trois-Rivières, was on the verge of being eliminated. Out of pure frustration Talbot swung his stick at Bowman once, twice, striking him in the shoulder and then the head. Bowman, like every player back then, wasn't wearing a helmet. He went down like a tree. "Scott put his hand up," Jean Bowman recalled not long ago, "and a piece of his skull came off of his head."

"It was like being scalped," Bowman says.

Talbot was suspended from hockey for a year, a suspension that was lifted eight months later. He went on to play seventeen years in the NHL. Bowman, his skull fractured, hung up his blades at eighteen.

Did he ever forgive Talbot? Did he ever *speak* to the so-and-so again? "It was in the heat of the game, eh?" Bowman says matter-of-factly. "He just totally lost it. It was his fifth penalty of the game. We picked him up on waivers, and he played for me three years in St. Louis."

Classic Bowman. He doesn't hold grudges. Grudges can't help you win hockey games. But he learned something about hockey players from his own misfortune, something he would always remember, a motivational tool he would employ throughout his coaching career. There is no greater punishment a coach can inflict on a hockey player than to not let him play.

His playing career over, Bowman turned to coaching. First twelve- and thirteen-year-olds, then fourteen and fifteen. By the time he was twenty-two, Bowman was coaching twenty-year-olds at the Junior B level. It paid him $250 a year, so to make a living he took a job at a paint company five minutes from the Forum. Every day he took an early lunch, 11:00 A.M. to noon, so he could walk down and watch Dick Irvin's Canadiens practice.

Irvin used to say that if you could get your team to laugh before a big game, you had an edge. Bowman watched, learned, absorbed. People noticed him, marveled at how Bowman commanded respect from players nearly his own age. In 1956 the Junior Canadiens moved from Montreal to Ottawa, and the team's coach and general manager, Sam Pollock, asked the twenty-three-year-old Bowman to be his assistant. "Pollock was a very demanding coach," says Bowman. "His philosophy was, You go with your best players as much as you can. I learned that from him."

Pollock was also aloof, private, intimidating. Bowman would later display all those traits. After the team won the 1958 Memorial Cup, the top prize in junior hockey, Bowman took over his own Junior A team in Peterborough, Ontario. He coached there for three seasons, then became the Montreal Canadiens' head scout for eastern Canada. But he missed coaching, missed being with a team and moved back behind the bench of the Junior Canadiens in 1963–64.

It was then that he met Montreal's Toe Blake, the only man to coach more Cup winners (eight) than Bowman. "I used to go into his office a lot," says Bowman. "And he might say something like, 'I'll let you in on a tip. Your friend Terry Harper's not going to play much tonight.' He knew how each of his players did against everyone else. Certain guys do well against one team but not another. He was a good strategist and a good match-up man and wasn't afraid to sit guys out to change his ammunition."

When Bowman's Junior Canadiens were matched up against a superior opponent in the playoffs, Blake called him in and drew up three radically different forechecking schemes for Bowman to try. All of them worked, and Bowman learned another lesson: If you threw something different at a team, almost anything, it got the players out of rhythm, slowed them down, kept them off balance. No matter how clever the opposing coach was, it took his team some time to react to the changes. And by that time Bowman, always a step ahead, might have altered his strategy again. It was a good way to play when you were outmanned. "I found out that if you're going to win games, you had better be ready to adapt," he says.

"When the puck is dropped, there has never been anyone who could run a bench better than Scotty," Toronto general manager Cliff Fletcher, an assistant general manager in St. Louis during the Bowman years, once said. "He was always three or four moves ahead of the opposition. So his players knew they only had to be as good as the other team. Scotty would make the difference."

Bowman was just thirty-three when Lynn Patrick, the expansion Blues' first coach and general manager, hired him as assistant coach for the 1967–68 season. Craig Patrick had played for Bowman with the Junior Canadiens and described Bowman to his father as "very stern, but fair." On more than one occasion, Craig Patrick recalls, Bowman made him and his teammates hold a practice before school, at five or six in the morning, after they had just spent all night on a bus returning from a game. He insisted his players keep their own plus-minus records in a notebook – this is some twenty years before the NHL began keeping that statistic – and occasionally checked to see if the notebooks were up to date. "He was known then as a very bright, innovative young hockey man," Craig says, "and he was the first guy my dad hired."

Lynn Patrick put Bowman in charge of the Blues' defensemen. The team won just four of its first fifteen games but was leading the Philadelphia Flyers by a goal in its next outing when Bowman advised Patrick to have a certain player skip a shift. Patrick ignored the advice, and with that player on the ice the Flyers scored and went on to win the game. At two o'clock the next morning Bowman got a call from Patrick. "I've always prided myself in having the right players on the ice at the right time," Lynn said. "I think this coaching business has passed me by."

Bowman took over behind the bench the next game, and under his guidance the Blues went 23–21–14 the rest of the way to finish third in the Western Division. In the playoffs they pulled off two seven-game upsets to advance to the 1968 Cup finals, where they lost to Blake's powerful Canadiens, four games to none, each game decided by a single goal.

That was the start. Each of the next two seasons the Blues won the Western Division and advanced to the Stanley Cup finals. They had limited talent but an outstanding, experienced defense that thrived under Bowman's system. In 1968–69, with Glenn Hall and Jacques Plante in goal, the Blues posted thirteen shutouts and a goals-against average of 2.07, the lowest ever by a team in the post-expansion era. "People didn't know how good Bowman was," the late Dan Kelly, the team's broadcaster, once recounted. "He was the first guy to use videotape to scout other teams. He knew more about the other team than the guy coaching them. That was a secret to his success."

Another reason for Bowman's success was his unpredictability, a trait he felt gave him an edge, both with the opposition and with his own players. "We did a lot of crazy things back then," Bowman says. One week he made the Blues practice at 8:00 A.M., then again at 4:00 P.M., so they had to commute to and from the rink during rush hour like the rest of the working world. "They were ready to play hockey at the end of that week," Bowman says.

Another time, in a story Bowman denies, he told Bob Plager, who now scouts for the Blues, to pack his bags and go to the airport because he was being traded. Plager, who had two brothers on the Blues, was to call Bowman from the airport to find out which team to report to. When Plager called, Bowman told him to come back, that he had decided not to trade him.

The Blues fell to second place in 1970–71, Bowman's fourth year, when he resumed the coaching duties after Arbour, who had succeeded him, returned to the active roster in February. The year before, Bowman had also become the team's general manager. In the first round of the 1971 playoffs, the Blues were ousted by the Minnesota North Stars. The next day the owner's son, Sid Salomon III, informed Bowman that he wanted neither Arbour nor Fletcher back the next season. Bowman replied that if they were leaving, he was too, and he resigned. In retrospect Salomon's gaffe may have been the worst front-office move in hockey history. Twenty-three years later St. Louis is still awaiting its first Stanley Cup, while Fletcher, Arbour, and Bowman have, among them, been associated with twelve Cup champions on four different teams. And counting.

Bowman's other mentor, Pollock, had become the Canadiens' general manager, so it was no surprise when, in 1971, he hired the thirty-seven-year-old Bowman as coach, a position he had been destined to fill since his skull had been fractured on the Forum ice twenty years earlier. Thus began Bowman's Montreal era, an eight-year span during which his teams won five Cups and had an amazing 419–110–105 record, a .742 winning percentage. They had seasons of 60, 59, and 58 wins, the three highest victory totals in NHL history. The best year, 1976–77, the Canadiens had 132 points. "That record is pretty safe," Bowman says. "With today's payrolls, I don't know if you can keep that many good players on one team anymore."

"He was an intense, intense individual," says Doug Risebrough, a forward on those Montreal teams and now general manager of the Calgary Flames. "He treated every game as if it was the most important game of the year, and he expected everyone to treat it the same way."

If you like the game, Scott, why lose at it?

The funny thing was, the better the Canadiens played and the more they won, the harder Bowman tried to find fault with them. "If you were playing well and winning hockey games, he got more . . . I shouldn't say irritable, but the higher his intensity grew," says former Canadien winger Pete Mahovlich. "We'd get to a certain point, and he'd say, 'O.K., let's cut the goals-against down – never mind scoring a whole bunch of goals.' There was no such thing as an easy game to Scotty Bowman."

Once a game started Bowman was utterly in control and absolutely unpredictable. Some games he used four lines, double-shifting All-Star Guy Lafleur to prevent opponents from shadowing him. Other games he went exclusively with his big-three defensemen, Serge Savard, Larry Robinson, and Guy Lapointe. With a lead, his defensive specialists – Risebrough, Bob Gainey, Doug Jarvis, Yvon Lambert – saw the bulk of the ice time.

When the Canadiens trailed, players like Lafleur, Mahovlich, Yvon Cournoyer, Pierre Larouche, and Steve Shutt carried the load. "A lot of coaches back then thought their job was just to open the door and change lines," says Shutt. "Scotty changed all that. I remember one game at the Forum, the ref made a bad call, really obvious. Scotty didn't even yell at the ref. He went right around the rink and started yelling at [then NHL executive vice-president] Brian O'Neill. That's intimidating to a ref. Scotty doesn't just fly off the handle. He knows what he's doing. It's all premeditated."

To a man, the Canadiens respected him. But very few admitted to liking him. Ken Dryden, one player who did, wrote in his marvelous book, *The Game:* "Scotty Bowman is not someone who is easy to like. He has no coach's con about him. He does not slap backs, punch arms, or grab elbows. He doesn't search eyes, spew out ingratiating blarney, or disarm with faint enervating praise. He is shy and not very friendly."

By design the Canadiens had an overabundance of specialty players – tough guys, speedy guys, emotional guys – each of whom might or might not be dressed, depending on the nature of that night's opponent. When Bowman did sit a guy out, he seldom explained the move to the player. "All he was thinking about was winning games," Shutt says. "He didn't care if he hurt feelings. He was going to do what he had to do, and personalities weren't going to get in the way."

In short he treated his players as professionals. Not as friends, and certainly not as needy, insecure youths, which many of them were. He allowed beer on charter flights and buses. He seldom checked on curfew. Glen Sather, who played for Bowman's Canadiens in 1974–75, remembers skiing right past Bowman one time in Lake Tahoe during an off day on the road, a direct violation of team rules. Bowman never said a word. All Bowman cared about was a player's performance on the ice.

He left the Canadiens in 1979, shortly after Montreal had won its fourth straight Cup. Bypassed for Montreal's general manager position, Bowman accepted an offer to be coach and general manager of the Sabres, and for the next seven-plus seasons his Buffalo teams had a 210–134–60 record with him behind the bench. But the Sabres were perennial disappointments in the playoffs, never advancing beyond the conference finals. Critics said that his caustic, impersonal style, so successful at spurring his veteran players in Montreal and St. Louis, was ill-suited for the young, inexperienced Buffalo players.

"I can remember him yelling, 'Patrick, you're nothing but an underachiever,'" said Steve Patrick, Bowman's first-round draft pick in 1980, after he was traded to the New York Rangers in 1984. "Once I had a chance to score in Philly, the goalie was down, and I couldn't get the puck up. Afterwards Scotty walked by me, and no eye contact. Nothing. He was like that. Then we walked by each other again, and he sort of stopped in his tracks and said, 'Steve, you had the whole net open, and you couldn't even put the puck in it?' Then he just walked away."

"Off the ice, away from hockey, he's as good a guy as you'd ever hope to meet," says Roger Neilson, who was Bowman's assistant in Buffalo in 1979–80 and the team's head coach in 1980–81. "Around hockey he's very demanding. He motivates by fear. Players are never quite sure where they stand."

Bowman certainly kept Tom Barrasso guessing. He made Barrasso Buffalo's first-round draft choice in 1983, a gutsy selection considering that no goalie from a U.S. high school had ever been taken that early. But Barrasso made him look pretty smart. In 1983–84 he was Rookie of the Year and a first-team All-Star and won the Vezina Trophy as the league's top netminder. When Barrasso and the team got off to a slow start the next season, Bowman dispatched him to the minor leagues after just six starts with nary an encouraging word. "I wanted to beat the s—— out of somebody," Barrasso said at the time. "It was humiliating."

Bowman ignored the carping, but no amount of badgering or mind games could overcome the Sabres' fundamental shortcoming: They didn't have the horses. In the NHL the Stanley Cup tends to follow the league's best player, and Buffalo's best player in the Bowman years, whoever he might have been, was not among the league's top ten. Bowman began to lose his appetite for coaching. Problem was, Bowman the general manager couldn't hire a coach who was his equal behind the bench. Bowman hired and then personally replaced Neilson (in 1981), Jimmy Roberts (in 1982), and Jim Schoenfeld (in 1986). "I was spread too thin doing the two jobs," Bowman says. "Looking back I should have been in the trade market more the last two years, but if the same man is coaching and managing, he ends up juggling one job or the other."

In November 1986, with the Sabres off to a poor start, Bowman stepped down as coach for a fourth time to concentrate on his general manager duties. The team, however, continued to struggle. Less than a month later he was fired.

Bowman is, by all accounts, devoted to his family. It's difficult to know when to insert that information into this story, because he keeps the two – hockey and family – distinctly separate. He has a wife, Suella, and five kids: Alicia, 22; David, 20; Stanley, 19;

and 16-year-old twins, Nancy and Bob. David, blind and born with hydrocephalus, also known as water on the brain, has spent most of his life in an institution for the mentally handicapped.

The twins are seniors at Buffalo-area high schools, and Bob plays varsity hockey. Bowman used to make a backyard rink for the kids – boards, lights, the whole bit – and found it unbelievably therapeutic, after a Sabres' game, to go there with a hose and resurface the ice late at night. It brought back memories of his childhood in Verdun. Or he would relax by running his model train set. It would probably surprise a lot of people to know that Scotty Bowman likes to play with a model train set, that he takes great pride in its extensive layout. But he is a man of many layers and surprises.

"That's been the toughest part," he says of living in the Pittsburgh hotel, away from his wife and kids. But Bowman had made a deal with his family: Once the twins started high school, he wouldn't ask them to move. They could finish school in Buffalo, regardless of where he might be working. "Kids change so much when they're in high school," he says. "So much happens to them that you're not part of."

After leaving the Sabres, Bowman spent three years as an analyst for _Hockey Night in Canada_, but as had happened years before, he missed being part of a team. When Craig Patrick offered him the job as the Penguins' director of player personnel in 1990, Bowman jumped at it. It was a good fit for everyone. Bowman could remain in Buffalo with his family, scout teams for Bob Johnson, then the Penguin coach, and occasionally commute to Pittsburgh for consultations.

As a coach Badger Bob was as different from Bowman in style as one could imagine – garrulous, cheerful, an incessant communicator, nonconfrontational, paternal. But they shared a deep mutual respect and had much in common. (Johnson, too, had a mentally handicapped child who lived away from home.) After watching Lemieux get shadowed one game, Bowman made a suggestion to Johnson: Tell Mario to pick up an opposing player on the ice when he's being shadowed, so he'll have two guys on him. It was a tactic Bowman sometimes had used with Lafleur. Johnson liked the idea but asked Bowman to present it to Mario himself. "He made me feel I was part of the coaching staff, and I wasn't," Bowman says.

The Penguins were a relaxed outfit under Johnson and led by the unstoppable Lemieux went on to win the 1991 Stanley Cup. That summer the hockey world was stunned when Johnson was stricken with brain cancer. Patrick appointed Bowman, who had traveled with the team throughout the playoffs, the interim coach. "It wasn't like Craig said, 'Come in and coach for the year,'" Bowman recalls. "It was, 'Keep the job until Bob comes back.' We hung on to the hope that a miracle would happen. But a month into the season, we knew he wasn't coming back."

Johnson died in November 1991, and Patrick, believing the team had gone through enough changes, asked Bowman to finish the year. The Penguins didn't play as soundly on defense as he liked, but Bowman was reluctant to tamper too much with a style that had won them the Cup. There was also the matter of changing his temperament. "I was aware that if I coached the way I did in the past," Bowman says, "it wouldn't have brought the same results. I knew I had to be different. If you're critical of a player today, especially openly, it's perceived as being negative. Bob Johnson was so positive. You have to stroke them more."

It wasn't an easy thing to radically alter a coaching style that had made him so successful. And the transition didn't happen overnight. "He was such a hard-line coach in the past," says Barrasso, who ironically now tends goal for the Penguins, "and we were such a relaxed team, that there was a period of adjustment. It was February or March until he was comfortable."

Bowman chose not to run the Penguins' practices, delegating that responsibility to Johnson's – now his – assistants, Barry Smith and Rick Kehoe. He kept a wary distance from the team, and the team muddled along with a 39–32–9 regular-season record. "Scotty, especially at first, was not as available as Badger," says Lemieux. "He's changed a lot since then. He's become a little closer to the players. With the type of team we have, it's important for the coach to be close."

The turning point may have come in the opening round of last year's playoffs, after the Penguins fell behind the Washington Capitals three games to one. Pittsburgh had been unable to control the Capitals' offense, particularly the role Washington's defensemen played in the offense. Lemieux, of all people, came up with a defensive plan. "He came to me the morning of the fifth game and said, 'Why don't we surprise them and play the game close to the vest. Tight, tight, tight,'" Bowman recalls. "I'd never pushed a lot of defensive hockey on this team, but since it was Mario who suggested it. . . ."

They cooked up a forechecking system called the 1–4 delay, in which the Penguins didn't chase the puck in the offensive zone but stacked the neutral zone with players and thought of the blue-line as a battleground. It was remarkably similar to one of the forechecking systems Blake had drawn up for Bowman thirty years earlier, when he was coaching the Junior

Canadiens. At the Penguins' morning meeting, it was introduced to the rest of the team. Kehoe started to explain it, when Bowman interrupted.

"Fellas, this idea came from Mario," he said. Then he asked Lemieux to explain the 1–4 delay. "Go ahead, Mario."

Lemieux, embarrassed, said no, thank you, that Kehoe was doing just fine. "The team laughed," Bowman remembers. "They got a big kick out of that." He also remembered what Irvin had said so many years before: If you could get your team to laugh before a big game, it gave you an edge. The Penguins, of course, swept the next three games to eliminate the Caps. They then defeated the Rangers, who had been the NHL's top team in the regular season; then the Boston Bruins; and then the Blackhawks, reeling off eleven straight playoff wins, a record, en route to their second – and Bowman's sixth – Stanley Cup. Says Bowman, "As great as our teams were in Montreal, we never won eleven straight. We got on a roll and never looked back."

Nor have the Penguins looked back this season. It is a trademark of Bowman's teams – never look back, never be satisfied. If tonight's game is important enough to play, it's important enough to win. "Scotty's underlying persona hasn't changed," says Barrasso. "He still wants to be the best coach in the game. He's still the same in the locker room and the best bench coach ever. It's almost unthinkable that he would have the wrong players on the ice at the wrong time. What has changed tremendously is his mental approach to players. In the past you could walk right by him and it was like you weren't there. It was impossible to show any friendliness toward him. Now he might speak to you about your family or the weather. He's a more open person."

"I have more experience, more patience," Bowman says. "Players are much more sensitive today. It used to be, if a guy's unhappy, so what? Now it might disturb the chemistry of the team. You take players off the ice, and you see they have the big lip on. So you have to explain they missed a few shifts because we needed more offense. You hope they accept it. Ten years ago I wouldn't have bothered. That's the reality of team sports today." He shrugs. "In many ways, it's more intriguing now."

In many ways, so is he.

15. **TO PICK A GOLDEN FLOWER**

They cannot finish in first place, but the Canadiens are fighting to be first in line for the rights to a blooming Guy from Quebec

BY MARK MULVOY 1/3/1971

FOR YEARS, WHILE THEY FINISHED FIRST, ALL THAT
the Montreal Canadiens watched was the top of the NHL stand-
ings. But this season the Canadiens are skating along in third
place with no hope of catching the Boston Bruins, and their eyes
are directed down – way down. The goal in Montreal is this: to
make sure the California Golden Seals finish *last*.

To that end – and to that end alone – the Canadiens traded
Ralph Backstrom to Los Angeles a few weeks ago, when the
Kings began a dangerous slide toward the cellar. For that reason
and no other the Canadiens gave center Gordon Labossiere to
the Minnesota North Stars when the fading Stars were desperate
for goals. The very next time the North Stars met the Seals they
beat them 7–1, and three of the seven were scored by Labossiere.
Smart trade, noted all of Montreal.

There are those in the know who say that if any team in the
NHL should show signs of displacing the Seals at the bottom
of the combined East–West rankings, Montreal general manager
Sammy Pollock would show up at rinkside offering a Beliveau
or Cournoyer to pull them out of the slump.

Why?

The reason is the latest flower of Canada's junior hockey program, Guy Lafleur.

There was a time when the two Canadian members of the NHL
– Montreal and Toronto – did not have to concern themselves
much over acquiring top junior hockey players; they owned
them practically from birth. But new draft rules adopted some
years back changed matters to give the Canadiens and the Maple

PREVIOUS PAGE: Guy Lafleur led the Canadiens though the 1970s,
winning five Stanley Cups and establishing a team record for points,
with 1, 246. *(Photograph by Tony Triolo)*

Leafs only a slight preference in choosing young players, and three years ago even that advantage was taken away. Now the Canadian teams must compete in the draft on equal terms with everyone else. And everyone else has his eye on Guy Lafleur.

Last season the flashing right wing of the Quebec Remparts scored 146 goals in eighty-three games. Already this season this nineteen-year-old six-footer, who is cast in the mold of Rocket Richard, has scored more than 100 goals, and only recently he helped his team beat Rosemont by making seven goals himself and assisting on four others. It is obvious to every scout in the league that young Lafleur could play as important a part in the Canadiens' future as his idol, Jean Beliveau, who also played in Quebec, did in their past. It is obvious, too, that the Canadiens will do everything in their power to sign him up. The first and best way to do that is to keep the California Seals in last place, for the Seals, you see, traded their first draft pick to Montreal last year.

When and if the Canadiens get Guy Lafleur, sportswriters on this side of the border will surely begin calling him "another Orr." But in French-speaking Quebec they have long been calling him something like that. "*Il est en or*," the Quebecois say of Guy, meaning that he is their Golden Boy.

When Jean Beliveau left their city some seventeen years ago to play for the Canadiens, the Quebecois began to lose interest in Canada's national sport. Over the years the city's team, the Aces, averaged barely 1,000 customers a game at the arena they built for Beliveau. Then came Lafleur and later a new name for the team: the Quebec Remparts. Suddenly the box office at the 10,000-seat Coliseum began to hum again. "Everyone is coming to see *Les Remparts*," crowed one official of the team. "Ah, no,"

Roland Mercier, who once signed Beliveau for the Aces, corrected him. "They come to see Guy Lafleur."

Like most Canadian boys Lafleur grew up with his eye on a puck. His family lived in Thurso, a lumbering town about twenty-five miles from Ottawa. "My father is a welder, and he took me out to play hockey for the first time when I was four years old," says Guy. "I played in all the various leagues – Mosquito, Peewee, Bantam, and Midget – and when I was fourteen I received a letter from a Paul Dumont asking me if I'd come to Quebec City and play hockey in the junior program there."

Guy's father rebelled at the thought of his fourteen-year-old son living with a strange family in Quebec City and declined the offer. But when Dumont wrote again a year later the answer was yes.

As Guy soon discovered, junior hockey is a lonely life for a boy. Each year he was placed with a different family living near the Coliseum. "The first year was the worst," he says. "I was only fifteen, and most of my teammates were eighteen and nineteen. I was too young to go out with them, and I didn't know too many other people in the city. It was pretty terrible at times."

"We look after everything for our boys," says Paul Dumont. "We give them pocket money, get them a room, see that they go to school and, of course, let them play hockey. It is a tough life, sure. But it also is a very rewarding life."

Now Lafleur has finished his schooling, something many junior players never do, and he has his own quarters close to the Coliseum. Guy probably earns somewhere between $12,500 and $20,000 for playing amateur hockey with the Remparts. He won't discuss the total, but of money in general he says, "I buy lots of clothes and I put the rest in the bank. For now that is the best place."

For Guy Lafleur a game day in Quebec City means that he will be Exhibit A once more, and he generally arrives at the Coliseum at 3:30 for an 8:15 contest. "I like to sit in the Coliseum by myself and think about the game," he says. "I play over in my mind what I think the game will be like, and I always see myself scoring between three and six goals." All afternoon the phone rings in the Remparts office. Suzanne Belanger, the petite secretary, writes down names and hands them to Jean Sawyer, the publicist, who later will give them to Maurice Filion, coach of the Remparts. "Scouts," Sawyer explains, using one of his few English words.

After his "psych session," as he calls it, Guy walks down to the Remparts' dressing room to check his skates and his sticks. Alongside his locker stall, taped to a wall, is a large color picture of Jean Beliveau in his Canadiens uniform. "That man is my hero," Guy says. "I may never be able to play hockey like him but I'd like to be the man he is." Guy's fingers go down the blades of his skates. His hands are enormous.

"I used to milk cows and rake hay during the summers when I was young," he continues. "I've always had big hands because of that. In hockey big hands are very important." Some of the other Remparts drop into the room, and they start to kid Lafleur about something. "Go ahead, tell him," they say. Guy remains silent, so one of his teammates tells a story.

"One night Guy has four goals after the second period at Cornwall," the player says, "and a photographer asks him if he's going to score again. Guy says yes, and the photographer asks him how? So Guy says he will skate behind the net, come out in front and shoot from twenty feet – face-on at the camera – in the first minute of play. Darned if he doesn't, and he scored the goal, too."

Before one recent game Bernie Geoffrion, now a scout for the New York Rangers, brought Jeep George, another Ranger scout, into the Remparts' dressing room to see Lafleur. Then Boom Boom talked with Claude Dolbec, the coach of the Shawinigan Bruins, Lafleur's opposition that night. Both Geoffrion and Dolbec agreed that, among other things, Lafleur is too strong for the Junior A, that he should be in the NHL now. Indeed, he has scored almost twice as many goals as any other player in the league.

There are three Junior A leagues in Canada – the Quebec League containing the Remparts, the Ontario Hockey Association, and the Western League. Of the three the Ontario League is rated the strongest by far, with the Western League second, and the Quebec League third. "Maybe I'm not getting the opposition I should have," Guy says, "but I don't think it's hurting me. I keep working on my whole game, not just scoring."

At precisely 8:15 P.M. the Remparts skated onto the ice to a musical chorus rivaled only by the sing-along atmosphere of the St. Louis Blues' arena. The people were standing four deep in many places, even though there were a few empty seats high in the end balconies. "They want to see Lafleur up close," a local broadcaster explained. It was not a good game, and the crowd was silent throughout the first period. Then, in the second period Lafleur, back checking tenaciously, stole the puck at center ice and started to skate swiftly down the right wing. The whole Coliseum was electrified.

Ten feet inside the blue-line Guy shifted toward the center, almost forcing the defensemen to collide. He dropped his left shoulder, then wiggled his head half a dozen times, faking both defensemen to their knees. Instead of shooting, though, he veered sharply to his right. "That kid," said an awed Lynn

Patrick of the St. Louis Blues, "has more moves than a monkey on a mile of vine."

Seconds later Lafleur had a clear shot on the goaltender, who suddenly seemed uncertain. "Slap shot. Wrist shot. Backhander. He has all the shots and he always uses the right one," murmured Al Millar of the Buffalo Sabres. This time it was the wrist shot, safer than the slap shot under the conditions. Flash. The red light was on. Lafleur had scored again, and the people in the Coliseum started their sing-along: "*Il est en or*," they chanted. "*Il est en or.*"

Lafleur scored another goal that night, and also got an assist. He played a very disciplined game – the type of game NHL coaches prefer – and rarely strayed away from his right wing. "Very professional," said Geoffrion.

But Lafleur, like all good players, also can play it rough if necessary. "When there's a fight," Geoffrion said later, "he does not look at the clock." "They call him chicken sometimes," added Coach Filion, "because he won't fight everyone who wants to fight him. But I want him on the ice, not in the penalty box. And when he does fight it's a one-punch knockout."

One thing Lafleur did against Shawinigan that escaped general attention but caught the eyes of the scouts was the manner in which he handled a Shawinigan defenseman, Ghislain Boisvert, after Boisvert had illegally manhandled him near the goal. When the action turned back up ice Lafleur retaliated swiftly. Boisvert suddenly was on the ice, and the referee, who missed the incident, had to call time out while the Shawinigan trainer attended to the defenseman. "Lafleur's already learned some of Gordie Howe's old tricks," said Roland Mercier.

Lafleur and the Remparts lost to Shawinigan 5–4 that night, only their third loss all year. Before their next game Lafleur and his coach flew to Montreal, where Guy received a plaque from the Club Medaille d'Or as the outstanding French-Canadian athlete of the month. Of course, someone asked him if he would like to play for the Canadiens? Guy only smiled.

Playing for *Les Canadiens* in The forum at Montreal is supposed to be the dream of every French-Canadian youngster, but Guy Lafleur is not thoroughly convinced Montreal is the right place for him next year. "I want to get a lot of ice time," he said last week, "and I'm afraid Montreal will keep me on the bench or send me to the minor leagues. I see what Gilbert Perreault is doing for Buffalo [29 goals so far as a rookie] and I want to get a chance like him. You know, I would not hate Buffalo myself."

How about that, Canadiens?

6. THE DOGHOUSE DIARIES

Benched, berated, bullied, and beaten up in the film room. For many NHL players,
learning to survive a coach's wrath is the key to surviving in the league at all

BY MICHAEL FARBER 11/1/2010

ALEXANDER FROLOV, A GIFTED KINGS WINGER, seemed to be one of those rare hockey breeds, a two-time thirty-plus goal scorer with a smooth stride, a snappy wrist shot and the ability to play keep-away with the puck in traffic: Could that be a Schnauzer?

The turnover that led directly to a goal in an October game against Columbus wasn't what dogged Frolov. Los Angeles coach Terry Murray, among the NHL's least combustible, knows that mistakes are inherent in the game. (In hockey, shifts happen.) But to Murray's critical eye, Frolov seemed to be floating, immersed in a private game of shinny instead of viscerally competing in the red-meat world of the NHL. Murray was at the end of his rope, which meant Frolov was going on a leash.

First Murray dressed him down in an interview with the team-run LAKingsinsider.com, saying he was not the first coach to be exasperated with Frolov's lollygagging during the forward's seven years with the team. Then he didn't dress him at all, scratching Frolov for a game two nights later in Dallas. (Meanwhile rumors swirled in Montreal that the Kings wanted to trade Frolov to the Canadiens in a deal involving Andrei Kostitsyn, who had fallen out of coach Jacques Martin's favor and been dropped to the fourth line.) Frolov had two assists in his return from the one-game timeout, the start of a spurt in which he put up seven points in four games.

"It's not like you enjoy taking your top players out," Murray says. "But they can get in the doghouse."

Despite occasional denials that hockey coaches even have a doghouse – the concept is "media driven," Canucks coach Alain Vigneault says – there is irrefutable proof that, like the Mafia, it really does exist. (In an e-mail Blackhawks senior adviser Scotty Bowman, the most successful coach in NHL history, joked, "I don't know if I had a doghouse but will admit I had a Scotty Bowman Burial Program, which probably had more permanence.") Coach Claude Julien of the Bruins does not equivocate. He says, "My doghouse comes in different sizes. Some are small, so that you're always near the door. Some are so big that you can get lost in 'em."

"Doghouse," Maple Leafs coach Ron Wilson says, "is a metaphor for ice time."

Certainly diminished ice time – in Frolov's case, zero – is a leading indicator that a player has been relegated to what Blues president and former TV analyst John Davidson calls the Château Bow Wow, but the doghouse neither begins nor ends there. The player in the doghouse also becomes the reluctant star of daily video sessions, his flaws exposed frame by frame in front of teammates. Recalls Lightning captain Vincent Lecavalier, who was billeted in former coach John Tortorella's doghouse so often he had a personalized chew toy, "You'd be on the ice in a game and make a mistake that you might've made before and your first thought was, I just know tomorrow morning I'm in the video. I'm gonna get talked about."

There is also an excellent chance you'll be talked *to*. Murray said he had more than a handful of meetings with Frolov before going public with his displeasure. In November, Flames coach Brent Sutter ordered left wing Curtis Glencross to skate around the center-ice circle during practice because that is what Sutter said the forward had done in the previous game – skate in circles. Then there is the Oilers' twenty-seven-year-old winger Dustin Penner, who over the past few seasons has endured gruff handling as perhaps the NHL's most kennelized player but now can look back at those times and laugh. Why not? This year he's been one of the best in show.

WHEN ASKED DURING ANAHEIM'S 2007 PLAYOFF run if he was coach Randy Carlyle's favorite whipping boy, the sly and self-aware Penner considered the question and replied, "Nine out of ten dentists would agree." Carlyle, a Norris Trophy–winning defenseman who was not exactly Jack LaLanne in his playing days, continually rode Penner about his fitness. After the Oilers signed the left wing that summer – coming off a twenty-nine-goal season, Penner received an offer sheet from Edmonton that the Ducks' general manager, Brian Burke, declined to match – he fell to the care of a coach, Craig MacTavish, who was no more tolerant of the player's spare suet or seeming lack of commitment than the caustic Carlyle had been. "When I was in the House of Dog in Anaheim," Penner says, "[Carlyle] was constantly poking and prodding, but he was also on young guys like [Ryan Getzlaf and Corey Perry]. He was just trying to make me the player I wanted to become. With MacTavish, it seemed more personal. It was the difference between how I was being treated and the rest of the team, what was being said about me in the media. You pick up on it."

So did fans. The winger was dubbed Dustin Penne on Edmonton talk shows, the implication being Penner was a carbo load.

The six-foot-four Penner now weighs about 240 pounds, just four or five pounds less than he did in 2008–09, though he looks noticeably sleeker. Probably not coincidentally, he is on a seventy-four-point pace under new coach Pat Quinn, a dramatic uptick after two MacTavish seasons in which he averaged forty-two. MacTavish, who was fired after last season and now works as a studio analyst for TSN in Canada, says any disagreements with Penner were professional, never personal. "I'm happy for him," he says. "He's figured out a comfort zone and a way he needed to play. I just had a great degree of difficulty getting him to the level I knew he could play at."

With MacTavish gone, Penner's remedial work in the gym is over. "On the bike I'd have to burn 1,000 calories before practice and 500 calories after practice," Penner recalls. "Did it make me a better player? It made me tired. But it also gave me a new passion for the Tour de France." His ice time has also shot up by 28 percent under Quinn, to nearly twenty minutes a game.

"You look at Penner now, and a change of coach is being credited for the way he's playing," says Vigneault, who last season was publicly and pointedly critical of the conditioning level of Vancouver center Kyle Wellwood, who was cruelly nicknamed Wellfed. "My guess is it's a change in work ethic. For guys like Penner and Wellwood, it's about attitude. They found out what they needed to do to be successful."

"You have to read between the lines in what a coach is saying," Penner says. "Sometimes there's swearing or demeaning stuff, but I've always had a pretty good filter. I'm like, What is it he's really trying to say to me? So, 'You're a f——ing idiot' becomes 'There's something I've done that he doesn't perceive to be smart.' You tune in the part about what you can do better and tune out [the rest]."

NOT EVERY NHLER IS BLESSED WITH PENNER'S perspective, especially in an era when players tend to be more sensitive than their tooth-missing forefathers. Wayne Halliwell, a sports psychologist who works with Hockey Canada, says, "Players used to look in the mirror. Now they phone their agents."

The doghouse, as Murray says, "has undergone a lot of renovations. In my Washington days" – he coached the Capitals in the early 1990s – "you could easily send a guy to the minors. If you didn't agree with how a player was going about his job, often you could have that player traded. With long-term deals, a salary cap and no-movement clauses, you're often limited to knocking a guy down a few lines" or publicly criticizing him.

"Tomas Kaberle's a great example of [a reaction to public criticism]," Toronto's Wilson says of his thirty-one-year-old defenseman, who was second among Eastern Conference blue-liners with thirty-five points through Sunday. "Last year he was fat and out of shape. Fifteen percent body fat. Now he's at eight, and maybe the best offensive defenseman in the league. You can see him go, making plays at the end of games that he couldn't last year. [Burke, now the Leafs' G.M.] and I were blunt with him last season and went a little public with it. [Wilson also benched Kaberle in a December 2008 game.] That's presenting a message and him responding."

All of which proves that you can teach an older dog new tricks, something to which Hurricanes defenseman Aaron

Ward can attest. In his formative NHL seasons with the Red Wings in the late 1990s, Ward didn't need a Château Bow Wow so much as a kennel the size of Versailles. The joke in the Detroit dressing room was that Ward should have his name legally changed from Aaron to F——ing because that is the way he was generally referred to by Bowman, who once called him up from the minors but sent him back down after the morning skate. Ward presumes he had a bad morning skate.

"One time [the Red Wings] had played poorly on special teams and we were practicing the penalty kill," Ward says. "The puck comes to me, I stop for a second and then shoot it out of the zone. Scotty blows the whistle and starts screaming that I should get rid of the puck before I get it. There I am, wondering if that's even physically possible. Now we're doing a drill where the [defensemen] have to get the puck out of the zone off the face-off, and he's standing at the boards at the blue-line. For me to get it out, I'm going to have to wing it right at him. At this point I probably haven't been in the lineup for two weeks. Off the face-off the puck comes to me way too easy in the corner – you can see [centers] Steve Yzerman and Kris Draper grinning – so I fire it around the boards and *wham!* it hits Scotty in the head. He's bleeding. My career's over. He blows the whistle and screams, 'That's how you get the puck out of a zone.'

"You never knew. I was playing against Chicago, New Year's Eve. I'd been in the doghouse at that time, and I went down to block a shot on my second shift. My face is cut, lower lip to the nose. I'm off to the dressing room for repairs, and as I go by him, Scotty says, if you're not back in five minutes, you won't play another shift. There's an older doctor, not the fastest guy with stitches, and I'm trying to hurry him up. Glue, stitches, whatever. Let's go. I get ten stitches, I'm back on the bench quick, maybe four minutes. And Scotty still didn't play me another shift. Played five [defensemen] the rest of the game."

Bowman now recalls Ward as "very intelligent, just not someone who showed a lot of hockey sense. There were a lot of giveaways early in his career. I think he was nervous. The puck was like a hand grenade for him." Hmmm, you wonder why.

Now near the end of his career (last month he was put on waivers and went through unclaimed), Ward has generally been a dependable player, winning two Stanley Cups with Detroit and another with Carolina in 2006. He also kept himself clear of Julien's doghouse during two seasons in Boston. But a coach's mongrel treatment does not always yield a lasting benefit – Frolov, for example, has slipped back into Kibbles-'n-Bits territory, after his post-benching surge – and it can even be risky. "The response to the doghouse is based on the player," Penner says. "You can keep a player in there too long. And like baking a cake, if you keep it in the oven too long, you burn it. There's nothing you can do with it."

"If you have a player who's not playing well and you beat him, the player becomes insecure," says Thrashers coach and former NHL left wing John Anderson, who recalls being in Toronto coach Joe Crozier's bad books. "We always talk about confidence. When you strip that away, you're left with nothing."

If you are hardy like retired forward Scott Mellanby and can survive your early years under a taskmaster such as former Philadelphia coach Mike Keenan – "Keenan once personally skated Mellanby by himself after [the regular Saturday pregame skate] at the Montreal Forum, and you know how many people saw that," former Flyers teammate Dave Poulin says of the public humiliation – you might go on to a solid twenty-one-year NHL career. If you are not, well, then maybe no one can remember your name. "Those are the guys who just fade away," says Poulin, now the Maple Leafs' vice president of hockey operations. "In professional athletics, you really do need a thick skin." Without one, a dog may never have his day.

17. # I'M GLAD I WENT TO PRISON

Nearly seven years after he tried to arrange a murder, former NHL player
Mike Danton is studying psychology and finally piecing his life together

BY L. JON WERTHEIM 28/2/2011

A WATER MAIN HAS BURST NEAR ST. MARY'S
University, a small Catholic college a few blocks from downtown Halifax. This happens with some frequency, especially
during the harsh Nova Scotia winters, and means that students,
faculty, and the occasional nun must sidestep puddles as they
walk across the tree-lined campus. It also means that once again
the gym will lose its supply of hot water, so the skating rink
can't be flooded. As a result, the hockey team will have to cur-
tail its afternoon practice.

The news, delivered to the players as they prepare for the session, triggers a machine-gun spray of expletives in the Huskies'
dressing room, a cube as cramped as it is malodorous. It is
another perceived indignity to the team, the defending Canadian
college champs, whose home venue is far shabbier than the other
area rinks, including the ones in Cole Harbour where Sidney
Crosby developed his extravagant skills. The St. Mary's team
could use the ice time. It's winning games this season (the Huskies
finished 18–9–1 and earned a bye through the first round of the
Canadian Interuniversity playoffs, which began last week) but
winning ugly, with lines that still lack synergy.

The oldest player, though, is ambivalent about the session's
abrupt end. Mike Danton, a compactly built five-foot-nine forward, had hoped that a strong practice would help halt his
slump – "For whatever reason I can't find the back of the net," he
complains – and boost his conditioning, which slipped while he
battled a head cold. Then again, the sooner practice is over, the
sooner the thirty-year-old Danton can start studying.

PREVIOUS PAGE: Mike Danton as a St Mary's Huskie. His quiet
university life is a long way from the NHL, and an even longer way
from prison. (Photograph by Darren Carroll)

So it is that after briefly weaving up and down the soft ice with other members of his "shutdown" line, Danton showers, throws on a hoodie and a HOCKEY BOY ball cap and gathers a backpack so heavy it should be outfitted with a set of wheels. He's off to the Patrick Power Library, where, teammates joke, he spends so much time he should be paying rent. When it closes at 11:00 P.M. he will walk to the sparse off-campus apartment he shares with a teammate and, with eyes at half-mast, study some more.

Danton, a second-year student, is the Canadian equivalent of an Academic All-American. But that doesn't do justice to his scholastic record. He's taken eleven courses at St. Mary's. His lowest grade is an A–, and his GPA is a hair under 4.0. His course schedule in the previous semester included geography, research methods, social behavior, and memory. His grades, respectively: A, A–, A, A+. "If I'd done this ten years ago, I would have been partying and sliding by with teachers who were hockey fans – youth wasted on the young, you know," he says while sitting on a couch in the lobby of the library. "Now I've established a routine, and I've discovered that I really like the process of learning and thinking critically."

Danton's major is psychology. He's reading Jung, Piaget, and Freud – "I think Freud's the one who needed psychoanalysis," he says – studying the mysteries of the human mind. "It's amazing how important the brain is, how it controls so much," he says. "We do this because of that, that because of this. Just fascinating."

He entered school with vague ambitions of returning to his previous career, that of a grinding forward in the NHL. Although he still would one day like to play professional hockey again, now his long-term goal is to earn a Ph.D. in psychology. His professors say that's no pipe dream. "He's an absolutely out-standing student. He handed in a paper that I can freely say is one of the best I've gotten in my years of teaching," says St. Mary's psychology professor Lucie Kocum, who taught Danton's research methods course. "He has a self-exacting approach, but he brings this exuberance to class."

Is it too simplistic, Danton is asked, to assume that he's enthralled with psychology because of everything he's been through?

"Yeah," he says. "But if I were you, I'd put it in the story anyway. I mean, how can you not?"

MIKE DANTON RECALLS CLEARLY THE MOMENT HE hit rock bottom. In April 2004, the fourth-line center for the St. Louis Blues sat crying on the upper bunk of a Santa Clara (CA) County jail cell. He was twenty-three years old and had been charged with a felony less than two weeks earlier. The internal chaos born from his disjointed and dysfunctional child-hood had erupted in spectacular fashion. "And now I'm think-ing, I'm f——, I'm never going to be able to play hockey again. And then it's like, Who's going to give me a chance to be their husband, to get close to their family?"

On a wall opposite his bunk he scrawled the names of people he loved. Then he meticulously tore two-inch-wide strands from a towel he'd been given. He tied them into a noose, wreathed it around his neck and knotted the free end to the top of the bunk. Sobbing, he inhaled and jumped off the bed, figuring it was a better alternative to the bleak future now confronting him. It would be a brutally simple end to a story that had become impossibly complex.

Danton was born Mike Jefferson and grew up in the Toronto suburb of Brampton, the son of Steve and Sue Jefferson, who made their living operating a coffee concession at construction sites. Mike wasn't big, but he was a hell of a young hockey player, a rugged, energetic mucker who seemed to know where the puck was going before anyone else on the ice. From the time he was eleven, Danton's junior coach was David Frost.

Even before Mike's abundant talent was apparent, he had decided to devote his life to hockey. It was less what he did than who he was. The speed and the hitting were intoxicating, and he took particular pleasure in outskating (and later, outfighting) bigger opponents. Besides, he says, it beat being at home. Since his arrest Mike has repeatedly claimed that he was physically and emotionally abused, though there is no record he ever made such allegations before. It's a charge his parents have always vigorously denied, as they did to Sports Illustrated last week. By his early teen years Mike had left home and moved in with Frost and his wife, Bridget. He considered the couple to be his surrogate parents.

Frost's junior teams – led by Mike Jefferson; a second future NHL forward, Sheldon Keefe; and Joe Goodenow, son of former NHL Players' Association head Bob Goodenow – were cocky and combative, a reflection of their coach. In 1997, Frost pleaded guilty to a charge of hitting one of his own players. After a 2004 altercation between Frost and a Central A Junior Hockey League official at a game in Ottawa, the league's commissioner banned Frost and reportedly distributed his photo to arena personnel.

Frost, though, inspired fierce loyalty and closeness among his players, particularly Mike Jefferson, who sat with his coach on bus rides and communicated with him on the ice through an elaborate system of hand gestures. In the 2005 documentary *Rogue Agent*, aired by the Canadian Broadcasting Company, Frost is depicted as a manipulative Svengali who held his team's star under a spell. Sue Jefferson has claimed that Frost was so controlling he would permit her to see her son only for an hour on Christmas. Steve Jefferson later told the Toronto *Globe and Mail* that Frost "stole Michael from us, [and has taken] Michael's mind from him."

Apart from maintaining what some felt was an inappropriate closeness with Mike Jefferson, Frost was accused of hosting alcohol-fueled sex parties at a motel in Deseronto, Ontario. In a criminal case brought in 2006, he was charged with multiple counts of sexual exploitation stemming from several parties that occurred in 1996–97 while Danton was a member of the Junior A Quinte Hawks. According to the allegations, Frost encouraged, and then watched, sexual acts between his players and girls under the age of seventeen. (He was acquitted of all charges in 2008, in part because two of the former players appeared as witnesses for the defense and denied that any sexual exploitation had ever occurred.)

For all the dissonance in his life, Mike's hockey career was a steady progression of success. In May 2000 he led the Barrie Colts to the finals of the Memorial Cup, Canada's junior-hockey club championship. The Devils drafted him in the fifth round one month later. His agent of record: David Frost. It was around that time that Jefferson formally changed his surname to Danton – the name of a former teammate that Mike thought sounded "cool" – a further attempt to disassociate himself from his family. He reported to the Albany River Rats of the AHL and kept climbing hockey's org chart.

By the 2002–03 season Danton was in the NHL, making more than $500,000. In June 2003, he was traded to the Blues, one of the league's class organizations. "He had a smallish build, but he was strong, he had some speed, good hands, and we knew he'd battle," recalls Larry Pleau, then the general manager in St. Louis. "We knew there was some baggage – there were rumors about his agent – but we were happy to have him."

On the ice and in the dressing room Danton was fine. When he left the arena he was often miserable. "I had a big problem with being alone," he says. "I had no one I could count on and who cared for me the way I wanted them to." His solution was to avoid sleep. He'd go to strip clubs, drink immodestly, take up female companionship, and stay up until sunrise. He'd crash for a few hours and maybe steal a nap in the afternoon.

According to the complaint filed in the Southern District of Illinois on April 16, 2004, a figure later identified as an "individual from Canada" was, according to Danton, coming to St. Louis to murder him over money owed. Danton tried to have the man killed. On two separate occasions he offered $10,000 for the murder of the "individual from Canada," and asked that the crime be made to look like a botched robbery. An East St. Louis strip-club bouncer declined his offer; Danton next used an intermediary to approach another man about the job. The potential hit man, however, was Justin Levi Jones, a nineteen-year-old police dispatcher from Columbia, Illinois, who promptly notified the FBI.

On April 16, the night the Sharks eliminated St. Louis from the 2004 Stanley Cup playoffs, Danton was arrested by FBI agents at the San Jose airport, charged with what police documents termed a "murder-for-hire" plot. The person prosecutors contend he was accused of scheming to have killed? David Frost, who was then staying in Danton's apartment. (In the CBC documentary both men who were approached to carry out the killing confirmed Frost was the target.) "We were all just shocked," says Pleau. "I mean, shocked."

Danton refused to provide a motive or admit he was targeting Frost. (In 2009 he would tell Canada's national parole board that he was trying to murder his father, who he believed was trying to kill him.) But authorities released to the media a series of collect calls Danton made to Frost in the days after his arrest. In one, Frost told Danton to say that years of abuse by his parents had led him to commit the crime; in another Frost asked if there was any reason he should still fear for his safety – to which Danton replied no. When Frost pressed his protégé to explain why he wanted him dead, Danton rambled incoherently. "I don't know," he said. "Everything the same. I was just, I didn't know. I was just . . . obviously everything started coming down at the same time."

The most dramatic exchange came at the end of a call shortly after Danton was taken into custody.

"Do you love me?" Frost asked in a gravelly tone.

"Yes," Danton replied meekly.

"Say it."

"I love you."

"Do you?"

"Yeah."

Danton entered a plea agreement with the U.S. Attorney for the Southern District of Illinois in which he admitted to trying to arrange a murder and was sentenced to ninety months in federal prison. (*The Denver Post* would later reveal that the lawyer representing Danton was a convicted felon and never licensed to practice.) Even the judge felt compelled to remark at Danton's sentencing, "In over eighteen years on the bench I have [never] been faced with a case as bizarre as this one."

WHEN DANTON JUMPED OFF THAT JAILHOUSE BUNK bed with a terry-cloth noose around his neck, it was no half-hearted suicide attempt. "I absolutely wanted to die," he says.

But the strands of towel ripped, unable to support his 190 pounds. Danton landed on the ground and stared at the names he'd written on the wall, tears puddling next to him. He took his survival as a sign. "I'm not religious, but I realized that if I was supposed to die that day, I would have," he says. "From that moment on I was like, I have to better myself. I didn't like the person I was, and I had to be someone different."

The first step was intensive therapy. The NHLPA provided Danton with counseling services. Ron Dicker, a St. Louis–based psychologist, visited regularly when Danton was incarcerated in the Midwest, and assigned him readings and self-improvement exercises. As Danton moved from one federal facility to another, the psychotherapy continued by phone. Says Danton, "I'm simplifying a pretty complex situation, but it came down to this: You can't love others until you love yourself. You can't trust others until you trust yourself. You can't fully respect others until you respect yourself. He got me to understand myself."

It was a painful process, Danton stresses, made all the more difficult by his incarceration. But eventually Danton didn't merely get to know himself; he grew rather fond of that person.

He was transferred frequently among jails – not uncommon in the federal system – and in Fort Dix, New Jersey, he spent seven months in solitary confinement for, he says, abusing his library privileges. (The prison did not respond to calls seeking comment.) He struggled with being alone. Danton passed the time by reading ("everything from James Patterson to Fyodor Dostoyevsky") and writing and thinking. He also took correspondence courses through Queen's University in Ontario. He grew frustrated by his inability to ask questions or discuss the material with a professor. A decade after dropping out of school, he embraced learning.

"I know this is going to sound nuts, but I'm glad I went to prison," Danton says. "I don't like the length of time I went there for. But I'm fortunate for the opportunity, because the negative-slash-downward spiral that would have happened would have been ten times worse. It saved me in a way."

Danton spent his last few months of confinement in a Canadian jail, thanks to the country's transfer treaty with the United States. Canadian authorities reduced his sentence to sixty-five months. As his release date neared in the fall of 2009, he pondered his future. He was broke, lap dances and then legal fees having consumed his NHL money. He dreamed of returning to the league, but he hadn't skated in more than five years. Danton had nowhere to go. He was still estranged from his biological family – who recently announced a deal with Penguin to publish a book telling their side of the story – and had essentially cut ties with Frost, who, after so much unflattering media attention, had taken an alias and moved to California. (Though his family alleges Frost is still part of his life, Danton declines to elaborate on the record. "Nobody's business," he says.)

Danton did, though, have his newfound self-confidence and his newfound love of learning. His passion for hockey still blazed. And despite having played in the NHL, he was eligible to compete at a Canadian university. So at age twenty-eight, fresh off a prison sentence, he set about applying to college.

TREVOR STIENBURG THOUGHT IT WAS A JOKE. LIKE most Canadians he had followed Danton's rise and fall. Probably closer than most, in fact. Stienburg had been a first-round pick in the 1984 NHL draft, a dynamic winger with a swift slap shot and a commensurately quick temper. His body, unfortunately, was in a constant state of rebellion, and he played only seventy-one games over parts of four seasons for the Quebec Nordiques. Otherwise he lived a life out of *Slapshot*, pinballing around the minors. In 1997, three years after hanging up his skates, Stienburg landed the coaching job at St. Mary's. His take on Danton was, *How the hell could he scrap his way to the game's highest level and then, once inside the kingdom, piss away his career?*

Shortly after Stienburg got a letter from Danton in late 2009 expressing interest in joining the Huskies, he gathered his players. "I told them, 'You're never going to believe who wants to play here: Mike friggin' Danton,'" he says. "I laughed and sent them back on the ice."

But many of the players had already spoken to Danton, who had been seeking them out in an effort to learn about the St. Mary's program. The captain at the time, forward Marc Rancourt, drafted a letter to Stienburg, signed by the entire team. It read in part, "We have all made mistakes. Perhaps not to the extent of his, but still serious enough that we had to ask for forgiveness or a second chance. . . . We have a unique opportunity here to provide Mike with a second chance that he has not only earned, but is entitled to."

That echoed the message Stienburg was getting from his father, Malcolm, a prison chaplain and at one time a top-ranking officer on the national parole board. "My dad said, 'Remember how you were brought up, son,'" recalls the coach. "He was like, 'If you take this kid, cover up, because you'll take some shots. But if you don't take him, don't let him rehabilitate, you'll have second thoughts.'"

Stienburg explained to Danton that if he ever saw Frost in the arena, Danton would be off the team. Danton assured him that that would not happen. "He acknowledged very well that Frost can't be in his life," says Stienburg. "He does have a bit of an issue with the fact that as awful as [Frost] was in so many ways, he still gave the kid an upbringing. But Mike knows David is not good for him. He knows that."

Danton selected St. Mary's (enrollment: 8,500) mostly for hockey. But it didn't hurt that he would be getting away from Ontario – where he felt the Toronto media had often portrayed him unfavorably – and relocating to a more socially progressive Maritime province. Both the player and the coach were prepared for some blowback. Stienburg claims, though, that for every critical call, letter or e-mail he received there were ten that supported his decision. "People realized he didn't want a handout; he wanted to go back to school," says Stienburg, who soon mounted a sign in his office: IF YOU DON'T LIKE YOUR LIFE, CHANGE IT.

Skepticism ceased last season when Danton scored a goal in his first game and then helped the Huskies win their first

Canadian Interuniversity Sport title. Despite his NHL creden-
tials Danton served only as a defensive stopper. Still, he brought
savvy, industriousness and an infusion of energy. "O.K., maybe
he's not a twenty-five-goal scorer," says St. Mary's forward Cam
Fergus. "Still, if the puck goes into the corner, chances are he's
coming out with it." Teammates were surprised by his humility.
They once asked Danton how, having flown charter and skated
in the big arenas of the NHL, he could abide by the modest conditions of Canadian college hockey. "Trust me," he said, "this is
a lot closer to the NHL than it is to jail."

"Dants" was instantly popular in the locker room. He still gets
razzed about his age and his absence of hair and even, on occasion, his criminal past; he in turn dispenses grief over his teammates' zits and failings with coeds. Until January 22, Danton
was on parole, one provision of which prohibited him from con-
suming alcohol. At team functions he sipped Red Bull and water
while his teammates drank adult beverages. "I missed hockey,"
he says, "but I also just missed being on a team."

He quickly became a familiar face at St. Mary's, and concern
over his past dissipated. When Danton goes to the library's
atrium, he's greeted near the front desk by a girl wearing a
Muslim head scarf and then by a knot of guys in UFC shirts. He
organizes study groups. Other students say that the buzz on
campus quickly went from, *Pssst, there's Mike Danton*, to, *Hey,
what's up, Mike?*

When he talks about his childhood, his crime, even his prison
sentence, Danton speaks with a sort of clinical detachment,
almost as if describing another person. But he pauses to collect
himself when he talks about his classmates and the St. Mary's
community. "You hear so much negative about kids today,"

he says. "These people made a decision to accept me – a convicted felon [who] hired someone to kill another person. Why? Because they got to know me and realized I wasn't a monster. And they did it at age eighteen or nineteen. To me, that's amazing." He pauses and smiles, revealing a gap in his upper bridge. "Look at me, getting all gushy." Another pause. "Acceptance is a warm feeling."

With some clarity of mind and years of detachment what, finally, does he make of his bizarre saga? Conversant as Danton is with the vocabulary, he is reluctant to throw around terms like *suppression* and *repression* and *sublimation*. His more mundane explanation: "I was a dumbass." He believes that his unhappy childhood was a factor. "Do I wish I had more guidance, that things might have gone differently if the first ten years of my life were different? Yeah."

Ultimately, though, Danton resists playing the victim card. "I was the one who screwed up," he says. "I committed a crime, and I have no problem holding myself accountable. . . . There were a lot of psychological factors, and I just had a breakdown. Looking back, you see all the triggers, all the telltales. If it hadn't been [the murder plot], it would have been something else. I would have tried drugs or tried to kill myself. Yeah, I was messed up."

He tries not to talk about the Frost family, not least because "they have two kids, and they've been put through so much." But there's little doubt to whom he's referring when he says things like, "I couldn't make decisions for myself. I relied on other people. . . . I was a twenty-three-year-old infant who wasn't in the right mind frame to be an adult, much less an NHL player." Danton's take: That someone could have ended up dead speaks volumes about his mental instability.

Danton admits that his first thirty years could be a psychologist's lifework. "It's fascinating to me," he says. "I can understand why it's interesting [to outsiders]." But he's less interested in becoming a therapist and "dealing with darkness" than in working with athletes to help them elevate their performance when it matters most. "As humble as I can make this sound, I've played at the highest level; I made a pretty big mistake that cost me; I have a lot of knowledge of being an underdog and rising to the occasion," he says. "With some more knowledge and training, I think I can help other athletes."

He balances the hope of again playing high-level professional hockey with the reality. He's more concerned with keeping up his grade point average than his scoring average. Already he's torn between getting an advanced degree after graduation and getting a job. "I don't need much to live on," he says, "but I've basically had no income for seven years."

When he considers his future, he starts shaking his head, staring out the window of the library toward the ocean a few blocks away. "You know what I really want? To have a family, have kids, be a great dad," he says. "Just the usual, normal stuff, you know?"

18. ON AN ON AND ON AND . . .

...on. Gordie Howe is skating in his fifth decade, and while his legs are not what they used to be, his heart, head – and elbows – are

BY E. M. SWIFT 21/1/1980

GORDIE HOWE IS NOT A PHILOSOPHICAL MAN.
Philosophical men are forever brooding about things, mulling over the whys and wherefores of the six mad-scramble days of Creation, concocting philosophies that attempt to make order out of chaos so that they may cope. Gordie Howe does not brood. He has a philosophy, but he does not brood.

In that way he resembles, say, a farmer. Gordie Howe is not a farmer. He has never been a farmer, although before he was born his father did own a homestead in Saskatchewan and grew wheat – when anything grew at all. Still, there is something about Gordie that calls to mind that manner of man – horse sense, perhaps. Equilibrium. Farmers get it from the land, from weather that one year makes the crops fat and the next year brings a famine, from prices that fluctuate unpredictably, from things beyond a man's control. *No sense hollering about it. Make do.* Equilibrium. Who knows where Howe's comes from? But it is there. He is steady. And he has a down-to-earth way of speaking, so that the toddling grandson is "like a dog, examining every damn tree." Farmers say things like that.

One precept Howe lives by is this: Set your goals high, but not so high that you can't reach them. When you do, set new ones. The trouble is, he has attained so many that he is running out of goals to set. At age fifty-one, as a Hartford Whaler, he is in his fifth *decade* as a professional hockey player. "One of my goals was longevity; I guess I've pretty much got the lock on that," he says with Gordian understatement.

Five decades. The forties, the fifties, the sixties, the seventies,

PREVIOUS PAGE: **After twenty-four years in the NHL, Gordie Howe briefly retired, then returned to professional hockey to play seven more seasons, ending his career as a Hartford Whaler at age fifty-one.** *(Photograph by Walter Iooss Jr.)*

312

and the eighties. Old Gord has seen more decades in North America than the Volkswagen Beetle. You think he's old? Early in his third decade in the National Hockey League, 1961, the year Carl Yastrzemski broke into the major leagues – Yaz, the doddering ancient who this summer rapped his 400th homer and 3,000th hit – this magazine called Howe an "ageless one-man team." So, what is nineteen years beyond ageless? Eternal? And why shouldn't a hockey player set standards for longevity? Cannot mastodons be preserved in ice?

George Blanda kicked field goals until he was two years shy of the half-century mark. Hoyt Wilhelm threw a baffling knuckle-ball in the big leagues until he was forty-nine, and who knows how old Satchel Paige really was when he worked late innings of relief in the midnight of his career? Sam Snead, in his sixties, still plays competitively against the young golf pros on the tour; why, he even shot his age in a tournament last summer. But it is not necessary, or even desirable, to compare these geri-atric wonders. They endured. Endurance is a battle against time that no one can win indefinitely. We all wage it, and we all eventually lose, which is why these older athletes are so incred-ibly popular.

Howe has received stupendous ovations wherever he has played in this, his thirty-second season. The first round of applause is for his past, for what he has given the fans over the years in hockey artistry, for this man is the greatest player in the game's history. As Maurice (Rocket) Richard's scoring records receded further and further in the 1960s, people looked to other sports to find suitably sublime parallels for Howe. He was said to be as effortless as DiMaggio, as well-balanced and decep-tively fast as Jimmy Brown, as steady and soft-spoken as Gehrig.

A great to-do was made in 1969 when Howe scored his 715th goal, passing the home-run record of Babe Ruth. When, at forty-three, Howe retired for the first time, after twenty-five seasons as a Detroit Red Wing, NHL President Clarence Campbell gave him due credit for the robust good health of the league, which had recently expanded to fourteen teams. "When Gordie came into the NHL," Campbell said, "hockey was a Canadian game. He's converted it into a North American game."

As their hands warm to the occasion, fans applaud Howe for what he gives them *now*; for enduring. Suddenly there are two different games on the ice: the home team against the Whalers and Howe against Papa Time. So when, for instance, the Big Guy scored two goals his first time back in Maple Leaf Gardens since 1971, helping Hartford upset Toronto, the crowd cheered him as one of their own, and went home happy. Occasionally the two games will interfere with one another, which happened at the Montreal Forum when Howe, whose every move had been lustily hailed, high-sticked Guy Lafleur in the forehead, possibly by accident. For a moment there was a shocked silence as the 16,000 spectators collectively came to the same realiza-tion: *Why, the old bugger still has teeth!* Then they booed.

Clearly, Howe cannot stand to be too much loved in another team's building. On the night of November 27, 1965, in that same Forum, Howe scored his 600th goal, and Montrealers showed their appreciation for the unprecedented feat by standing, applauding and littering the ice for several minutes. They had barely settled back into their seats, however, when they were back on their feet, booing Howe as they had never booed him before. Exactly 2:26 after the historic goal, Howe was given a five-minute major penalty for elbowing and deliberately attempting to injure J.C. Tremblay, the Canadiens defenseman; Tremblay, in fact, suffered a broken cheekbone.

It would be absurd to suggest that now, in 1980, Gordie Howe is the player he used to be. He will be fifty-two in March, and is the grandfather of two. To compare a fifty-one-year-old man with the greatest player of all time is silly. But it is not silly to compare him with the players coming into the NHL, the twenty-year-olds who can skate and shoot and throw their bodies around but who cannot beat this man out of a job, or keep him from scoring. Howe has earned his position on the Whalers. He is not a continuing publicity stunt. The man can *play*.

"Players learn to play when they're young, and that's the way they play all their lives," says Maurice Richard. "There are a lot of skills this generation doesn't have. They know they don't have to stickhandle; just chase after the puck. It may be that today's game is faster, it may be there's more skating, but teams just throw the puck in and chase it. The game's become a foot-race. I guess that's another reason Gordie's still going."

Hockey, of course, was never meant to be a footrace, because the fastest skater in the world cannot outskate a pass, and because, for all its advantages, dumping a puck into the corner and chasing it proves little if, once regaining it, a man does not have the stickhandling skills to work it toward – and eventually into – the goal. Which is the point, after all. The art of stickhandling hasn't died; there are just fewer stickhandlers spread among more teams. And the great stickhandlers are still the great scorers: Lafleur, L.A.'s Marcel Dionne, young Wayne Gretzky of the Edmonton Oilers. Howe may now be the slowest forward in the league, but at last count he had eleven goals, which was sixth-best on the Whalers. There is so much more to the game than foot speed, or shot speed. There are men who point to the success of a fifty-one-year-old grandfather as proof positive of the sorry state of hockey today, but for those who love the sport, it is an affirmation of the game's subtleties that a man who has lost his youth and speed and recklessness can still succeed with strength and savvy and guile.

"Gordie has no set play for a given situation," says Don Blackburn, the Whalers' coach. "I never know what he'll do with the puck because there's no limit to his creativity." Says Jean Beliveau, who played center for the Montreal Canadiens for eighteen years and was even smoother than Howe, though not nearly so strong: "Gordie, he still has that instinct."

Time does not diminish instinct. Nor, surprisingly, does it necessarily erode strength. Howe is still tremendously strong, which is less of a surprise to his doctors than to the kids he plays against. Dr. Bob Bailey was the Michigan physician who gave Howe the go-ahead to come out of retirement the first time, at age forty-five, to play in Houston with his two sons. "I think if you looked at men who do comparable work, like farmers, you'd find similar musculature," Bailey says. "It's a matter of conditioning. What I found really incredible was his pulse rate, which was around forty-eight. That's almost the heart of a dolphin. A normal fifty-year-old man might have one around eighty."

When Howe had his physical before this season, the cardiologist said, "This man could run up Mount Everest." Howe, in fact, loathes running as far as up the driveway, although for the first time in his career he jogged some last summer. But his pulse rate and blood pressure remain those of a young man. "The stamina is there, the strength is there, it's the speed that goes," says Vincent

Turco, the Whalers' team doctor. "But age is kinder to hockey players, because skating is a little different than running."

It has been suggested that one of the reasons age has been kinder to Howe, specifically, is that none of the younger hockey players wants to be labeled as the guy who knocked the Old Man out of the game. Well, that simply isn't true. If players are staying away from Howe, they are doing so out of concern for their own skins, not his. Howe has spent more than thirty years playing what he calls "religious hockey" – it's better to give than to receive – and the woodwork crawls with horror stories of those who crossed him. *Tough men* who crossed him. Lou Fontinato, the Rangers' policeman, challenged Howe and took three uppercuts to the face – *thwap! thwap! thwap!* People who were there swear you could hear the sound of Fontinato's nose breaking all over Madison Square Garden. Jean Beliveau tells of seeing Howe release his stick following a wrist shot so that it slashed across Gilles Tremblay's forehead. Gristly John Ferguson, now general manager of the Winnipeg Jets, took over as Howe's shadow when Tremblay retired from the Canadiens. "He never scored on me," Ferguson says. "That's my claim to fame. Of course, he got a few when I was in the penalty box. And one night he stuck the blade of his stick into my mouth and hooked my tongue for nine stitches."

Colleen Howe, Gordie's wife and business manager, says "Gordie doesn't elbow somebody in the jaw out of anger; he does it to teach them a lesson, if they've embarrassed him on the ice. He's a tremendously prideful person."

It's a lesson that this generation of NHL players has largely accepted on faith. They may not be able to stickhandle, but they're no dummies. "Howe's still good with his elbows," says Blackhawk forward Cliff Koroll. "But he doesn't really have to use them much, because nobody comes near him."

It is obvious, too, that Howe has lost none of his subtlety. When he throws an elbow, he does not stop and fling one in anger, but incorporates it into his skating stride. So it is a rhythmic motion – left foot forward, right elbow back – barely noticeable. Except that the young pursuer is suddenly a stride behind and, now that you think about it, the natural rhythm of a skater does not call for elbows at ear level.

In a game against Winnipeg, Howe twice elbowed six-foot-three, 210-pound defenseman Scott Campbell in the third period. The second time, the twenty-two-year-old Campbell went after him, challenging Howe, until the linesmen stepped between them. After the game, an amused Howe shoved a powerful forearm into someone's collarbone, showing where he'd given Campbell his shots. "Those kind don't hurt too much," he said. "They don't count if they're not in the face."

But, as Beliveau suggests, "Let's remember Gordie Howe as a hockey player. Deep down he was – and is – a hockey player."

The Hartford Whalers – or, rather, the Springfield Whalers – were not supposed to be a very good team this year. Early in the season they beat Toronto (twice), Buffalo, and Atlanta, among the old-line clubs, and tied Montreal at the Forum. The Whalers' better-than-expected early showing was not so much a result of Howe's play as of the influence he had on the team. Who wouldn't become pumped up when crowd after crowd in stadium after stadium greets a teammate with prolonged standing ovations? Who wouldn't work that much harder to make a legend's return to the NHL a success? "The players are Gordie Howe fans," says Blackburn, forty-one, a thoughtful man who spent fifteen of his eighteen pro seasons playing minor league hockey and is in his first year as coach. "The *coach* is a Gordie Howe fan. He's so competitive. If you try to outdo him in a crossword puzzle, you've got a problem. So when you're twenty-two, and you see a fifty-one-year-old guy hacking guys and running over guys, how can you not go out and do the same thing?"

Yet for all his respect, Blackburn knows that his own job depends on the continued success of the team, and the Whalers have been in a miserable slump for the last six weeks, winning only two of their last twenty games. Howe, too, has slumped as a goal scorer; he had eleven goals through December 31, but has not scored since then. Compounding Howe's goal-scoring problems, he has had difficulty adjusting to Blackburn's unique defensive strategies. A right wing, Howe has spent his entire career covering his opposite wing in the defensive zone. But under Blackburn's system, his job is to cover the left defenseman at the point. "He forgets a lot," Blackburn says. "You just close your eyes and hope."

Says Mike Rogers, who centers Howe's line, "Gordie doesn't really know where he is defensively. He doesn't like standing in one place. So you let him go wherever he wants. He can't change. He might be out at the point, but then he might be hiding behind the net somewhere. Our line's not that great defensively."

Fortunately for the Whalers, the left wing on the line is a smallish, tough, brilliant player named Mark Howe, Gordie's second son. At twenty-four he is starting to come into his own, displaying flashes of the greatness that has been predicted for him. Already Mark is one of the finest defensive forwards in the NHL; smart, tireless, an honest back-checker who makes up for his dad's defensive hooky. The two Howes and Rogers make up Hartford's most productive line, but Blackburn is watching for signs that Gordie's legs can no longer put the hands and elbows and head in position to do the job. In the wings is a twenty-year-old speedster named Ray Allison, Hartford's top draft choice, who Blackburn believes would develop rapidly given a chance to play with Mark Howe and Rogers. "It's not an enviable position to be in – the greatest player in the history of the game and me a rookie coach," says Blackburn. "I dread what's coming."

THERE IS A LADY IN DETROIT WHO HEARD GORDIE Howe mention in an interview that his father's eighty-seventh birthday was coming up. She did not know Gordie, except as a fan, but took it upon herself to send his father a card. "Mr. Howe, Gordie's Father, Floral, Saskatchewan" was the way she addressed it. The card arrived, naturally – Gordie once received a letter addressed: "Mr. Hockey, Detroit, Michigan." The town of Floral no longer exists, having been swallowed up by booming Saskatoon, a sprawling transportation center in the heart of the prairie.

Ab Howe is somewhat brusque in his recollection of the boy Gordie. "He was clumsy and backward and bashful," he says. "That's why I never thought he'd amount to anything." The gentleness in Gordie's nature was a gift from his mother, Kathleen, who died at seventy-six, a woman who bore three of her nine children without help, while Ab was working the wheat fields. But the fierce pride, the toughness, the occasional meanness that show up on the ice come from Ab, who bequeathed a prairie philosophy to his big, backward son when he was sent home from the first team he tried out for: "Never take dirt from nobody, 'cause they'll keep throwing it at you."

Old Ab Howe never took any dirt from anyone. During the Depression he worked for the city of Saskatoon and earned 40¢ an hour – $4 a day to raise nine children, and lucky to have it – and every man in his construction crew wanted his job as foreman. "I had to set a few down," he says. "I fired this Frenchman, told him to collect his pay and get out of my sight, and he swung at me. I told him, 'You goddamn pea soup, you swung at the wrong man. I'll put you in the hospital.' Knocked him down and kicked him in the pants on his way out."

At eighty-seven, Ab is still square-shouldered and trim. His thick, mittlike hands are even bigger than Gordie's, which are size eleven, XXL in the catalogues. Genetically, Ab, whose own father died at ninety-four, can take a lot of credit for the way things have turned out for his clumsy son, the bashful, backward boy who flunked the third grade twice yet would sit up at night with a Sears catalogue and circle all the nice things his mother could use, promising, "When I'm famous . . ."; who would skate endlessly on the frozen sloughs between the wheat fields, a hockey stick in hand always, knowing the vehicle that would take him to fame, wanting nothing else, and in preparation for that day, practicing his autograph until his sister-in-law would ask:

"What the heck you doing, Gordon?"

"Which one do you like?"

"That one." She would point to one of four, and he would practice it.

Ab remembers, "When he joined the Wings, I told the wife, 'I hope that boy never fights. He's got a blow that can kill a man.'

He's both-handed, you know, like me. Worked on my crew two summers. Best man I ever had. Had him on the mixer with his brother Vern. He could pick up a cement bag in either hand – ninety pounds. Weren't the weight so much as you couldn't get a grip on them, the sacks were packed so tight. He'd pick them right up by the middle. His brother played out in two days, but Gordon, he liked that mixer.

"He was strong, all right. Fella came with some counterweights for a dragline in the back of his truck, and Gordon says, 'Mr. Driscoll, you want these off?' Well, it weren't a one-man job, but Driscoll, he winks at me and says, 'Sure, Gord, right over here.' Lifted 'em out of there like it was nothin.' Driscoll like to fall over. Oh, he was strong.

"That first night he played for Detroit, I put my feet up by the radio and listened to the game, and pretty soon Gordon was in a fight, all right. And he got in another. The wife was terrible upset, worrying he might kill someone. He got in fights about the first ten games, and after a bit Mr. Adams [Jack Adams, the Detroit general manager] calls him in and asks, 'Howe, you think you've got to beat up the entire league, player by player?'" Ab Howe stops here to grin. His eyes are beginning to pale on the outside of the irises, but in the center they are bright. He is clean-shaven and shiny bald on top.

"Gordon started to play hockey then. Mr. Adams, he treated Gordon like a son." Ab smiles; he is eighty-seven and he is going deer hunting in the morning. "Me, I could skate, but I never could shoot. I can't shoot them yet."

That first game was October 16, 1946. The Nuremberg trials were unveiling the full horror of World War II, and Detroit, whose automakers had long since stopped churning out Jeeps and tanks and amphibious trucks, was bloated with unemployed servicemen. Their sweethearts were on a different sort of production line, as the first of a generation of war babies were born. Doc Blanchard led Army to a rout of the University of Michigan, and Ted Williams, the American League's Most Valuable Player, saw his Red Sox fall in the seventh game to the Cardinals when Enos Slaughter scored from first base on a single.

Little notice was taken of a young country boy's debut in the National Hockey League, although Paul Chandler of the *Detroit News* recognized something of what was in store. "Gordon Howe is the squad's baby, eighteen years old," Chandler wrote in his account of the game. "But he was one of Detroit's most valuable men last night. In his first major league game, he scored a goal, skated tirelessly and had perfect poise. The goal came in the second period, and he literally powered his way through the players from the blue-line to the goalmouth."

"Power" would become Howe's nickname – the Whalers use it still when they are not calling him "Gramps." As a young man, with those giant hands and muscular back and low-slung shoulders that would be characterized hundreds of times in the next thirty-five years as "sloping," Howe might have been the prototype for the laborers in Thomas Hart Benton's murals. Yet his tireless skating was his most memorable trademark – excepting the elbows. Says Beliveau, "His stamina, maybe that's what you remember best when you've played against him. He just kept going and going and going."

The 1940s were Howe's decade of promise. He scored only six more goals that first season. In 1947–48 he added 16, and in 1948–49, when the Red Wings finished first, he scored 12 – hardly spectacular. But country boys keep promises. Beginning in 1949–50, Gordie Howe started a string in which for twenty consecutive years – two solid decades – he finished among the top five scorers of the NHL. So of course virtually every major scoring record became his. He was an institution, as stable in his field as ITT in the Fortune 500, year in, year out, from Truman to Nixon. For twenty years, he played at his peak.

Ted Lindsay was Howe's roommate in those early years, left wing on the Production Line with Sid Abel at center and Gordie at right wing. Lindsay and Howe worked the boards as no players had before them, throwing the puck into the opposite corner at just the angle to make it rebound back out front for the wing breaking in. "We were inseparable," Lindsay recalls. "He was always worried he couldn't make the team. Every year he was tough on left-wingers in training camp because of it. He lived to play the game, and nobody was going to get the job away from him. Genuinely, sincerely, he felt he had to worry about his position. He would say, 'Gee, I hope I make the team.' Or, 'That guy isn't going to get my job. He'll do it over my body.'"

Howe's prairie upbringing taught him that simply because it had been a good year last year didn't mean the rain would fall and the wheat would grow this year. Says Abel, now a Detroit broadcaster, "He'd practice with a bucket of pucks for a half hour by himself after the others were through, lifting the puck up to the top of the net. Once in Boston he skated in against the goaltender, feinted and deliberately tried to put the puck in the top of the net. He shot it right over the goal. But he went behind, dug it out, came back and gave the goaltender a different feint, then put it up top for the goal. He came over to Lindsay and me afterward and said, 'That's where the first one was supposed to be.'

"His peak, I think, was when he was about twenty-four, in 1952–53, the year he scored forty-nine goals. He did score his fiftieth, too, but didn't get credit for it. He tipped in a goal in Boston on a shot Red Kelly took from the blue-line, and they gave it to Kelly, Gordie didn't argue. He had a couple of games left to get his fiftieth."

At that time the fifty-goal mark was like sixty homers in baseball. It had been reached only once, by Maurice Richard in 1944–45, a war year. Much has been made of the fact that Richard scored his 50 goals in a 50-game season, but the fact is that over the entire 70-game schedule of 1952–53 fewer goals were scored (1,006) than in 1944–45 (1,103). In 1952–53 teams averaged a *total* of 4.8 goals per game, the lowest in modern hockey history. In 1944–45, when Richard set the mark, the average was 7.4 goals per game – the *highest* in modern hockey history. Howe's 49 actually represented a greater percentage of the total goals scored by the league than Richard's 50.

Despite all the goals he scored, critics contended that Howe didn't shoot often enough, that he was too unselfish. His first coach, Tommy Ivan, says, "I don't think Gordie realized what he could do with the puck. He could have scored more goals. But Lindsay and Abel were so darn great, and Howe handed the puck off because he realized how good they were."

With Howe, Lindsay, and goalie Terry Sawchuk in their prime, the Red Wings rattled off seven straight league championships between 1949 and 1955 – a feat still unmatched in the NHL – and won four Stanley Cups. Says Howe now, "You start off winning and you take it all for granted. My philosophy is never start talking about if, and, but or the past, because 90 percent of what follows will be negative. That's what I regret most, that I can never remember the good times with Abel and Lindsay. You're young and you take it all for granted."

They say one's personality is formed by age three. Gordie Howe, at three, did not think of himself as something very special, just another hungry mouth to feed. His whole life he has comported himself as if he were no more than that – one more hungry mouth forced upon the world. This feeling made him one of the world's worst negotiators. "I was sort of a pushover," he says with some understatement. "I used to come into Jack Adams' office and say, 'If I'm supposed to be the best player in the league, you can pay me accordingly.' He'd say he would, and that would be the end of it. Of course he never did. Later I found out there were three guys in the Detroit organization itself that were making more money than I was. The only time I ever brought anyone in to help me, it was Lindsay. We were going to negotiate together, but Adams negotiated with us with two words: 'Get out.'"

That was the Old School, when contracts were small, one year in duration and not guaranteed; when players kept mum about injuries for fear of being replaced by some hungry kid from the minors. Howe was a child of that school, and Adams was the principal. Fiery, gruff, tightfisted – so much like Ted Lindsay that the two stopped talking – Adams once called Colleen Howe's doctor to ask if he couldn't keep her in the hospital one more day with her firstborn; the Wings had a big game that night. (The doctor declined.) But Adams was something of a father figure for Howe, who has always gravitated toward strong-minded people – his wife, Lindsay, Adams – who do not mind making the off-ice decisions that Howe freely admits he prefers to avoid.

"I WAS A PALLBEARER FOR JACK," SAYS HOWE. "We were all in the limousine, on the way to the cemetery, and everyone was saying something nice, toasting him. Then finally one of the pallbearers said, 'I played for him, and he was a miserable sonofabitch. Now he's . . . a dead, miserable sonofabitch.' You could hate the bastard, but he was a good man. Deep down he had your best interests at heart.

"Bill Dineen [Howe's coach in Houston and Hartford and now a Whaler scout] has the greatest Jack Adams story. He was in there about a new contract, and Adams was all roses and honey, telling him he was just the type of player the Wings needed – a hard worker; that he wished he had seventeen more just like him. And at the end of all this – Bill feels pretty good, of course – Jack says, 'So I've decided to give you a $500 raise. Congratulations.' Well, after all those nice things, what could he say? He took it. Only later Bill found out the starting salary in the league had been raised from $5,500 to $6,000. Adams paid him the minimum wage two years in a row."

Years later, Dineen promoted Howe's return to hockey. Gordie retired at the end of the 1971 season, at forty-three, after the Red Wings had missed the playoffs for the fourth year in the last five; they have made them only once in the eight post-Howe years. He moved into the front office, leading a life he equated with that of a cultivated mushroom: "They kept me in the dark, and every once in a while opened the door to throw manure on me." For exercise, he worked on his golf game and played oldtimers' hockey – no checking, no slap shots.

The Howe story might have ended there had it not been for the birth of the World Hockey Association, which took the sport Howe had converted into a North American game and, in turn, transformed it into chaos. In the summer of 1973, as the WHA prepared for its second season, Dineen's Houston club selected Gordie's two oldest sons, Marty and Mark, in the amateur draft. Both had played the previous winter for the Toronto Marlboros, winners of the Memorial Cup, which goes to the junior champions of Canada, and Dineen called Howe to assure him that the Aeros were genuinely interested in signing the two boys, that they were not just capitalizing on the Howe name for publicity. Howe heard him out, then asked, "What would you think about having a third Howe?" Silence. "Bill? You still there? I asked what you thought – "

"I heard you," Dineen finally stammered. "I wanted to ask, but I had too much respect."

Playing on the same team with his sons had been one of those high goals Howe had set for himself. So, with his wife negotiating, he agreed to a one-year playing contract followed by three years in the front office. But after working himself back into shape – his playing weight today is 206 pounds, the same as when he broke in as a rookie thirty-four years ago – Howe proved himself too valuable to be shunted off to the front office. The man could play. Rejuvenated by his sons – what man wouldn't be? (Rocket Richard told a friend, "Isn't that something, playing with your own sons. I dreamed of that. For me that would be a dream come true") – Howe led the Aeros to the WHA championship, scored 100 points and was the league's Most Valuable Player. Mark was named Rookie of the Year. And, most appealing of all, a whole new wave of Gordie Howe stories appeared, this time relating how Papa would come to the defense of the kids. Marty tells of the time one of the WHA thugs was on top of Mark, and Gordie asked him once, politely, to let Mark up. "When he didn't, Gordie reached down, stuck his fingers into his nostrils and pulled him up off the ice. The guy's nose must have stretched half a foot."

"If I'd failed badly," Howe says, "people would have remembered me more for trying to make a stupid comeback at forty-five than for all the other things I did in hockey." Because that's how *he* would have remembered himself. When the land has been fruitful for twenty-five years, it counts not if now, with the drought, the farm must be sold. The man lives in the present. To Howe, the only negative aspect of his experience in the WHA was the destruction of his friendship with Lindsay, who – in the brusque Jack Adams style – could say nothing kinder about the return of his old line-mate than that it showed what a sorry league he was playing in if a forty-six-year-old man could score 100 points. Howe took the remark as a personal affront, and three years later, when the Houston club was going under and the Howe family was attempting to relocate, the rift widened. By this time Lindsay was general manager of the Red Wings, a job that Howe had been in the running for, and he criticized the Howes for demanding to be paid by Houston when some of their Aero teammates were being left out in the cold. Lindsay was clearly out of line commenting on a situation he knew little about. Later, when there were reports that all three Howes would like to play in Detroit, Lindsay said he would not give Boston a first-round draft choice for the negotiating rights to Mark Howe. "Can you imagine that?" Howe says, still bitter. "Not giving up a draft choice for Mark?"

So the Howe family moved to Hartford in 1977.

Howe's final aim in hockey, for now anyway, is one that probably will never be realized. His oldest son, Marty – the one who kept Colleen in the hospital one day less than Jack Adams would have liked – was sent down to the Springfield Indians, the Whalers' top farm club, before the start of the season. He has since broken his wrist and will miss most of the season. If, and when, Marty makes it back up, Gordie will probably be in the front office for good.

"It really hurt Dad when Marty was cut," Mark says. "I thought he was going to quit. He almost did."

Gordie now says he wished the Whalers had let Marty play at least one game in the NHL before they sent him down, to fulfill that one final goal. Bill Veeck, perhaps, would have done it that way. But there has been nothing promotional or phony about the Big Guy's final year. No "Nights." No farewell tour. Howe's team has come first. Marty was his single blind spot. On Howe's return to the Forum last month, the Montreal fans applauded his every shift, the routine plays and the occasional surprise, and they looked away when he turned over the puck. Afterward, generally hard-boiled reporters complimented him on a nice game; but it was son Mark, who scored the tying goal, whom they selected as the game's first star. With three minutes left, Mark came gliding effortlessly down the left wing and rifled a shot over the goalie's right shoulder to get the Whalers a tie; he also had killed penalties and assisted on a power-play goal. None of which was lost on Coach Blackburn, the man in the not-so-enviable position should Gordie's magic suddenly be gone. "They came to see Gordie," Blackburn said. "Well, instead of seeing Gordie at thirty, they saw Mark at twenty-four. They saw the heritage. A different Howe era."

Which would suit the Old Man just fine. That night, he stood outside the Forum signing the very autograph his sister-in-law had chosen for him so many years back. His son and teammates were off to Crescent Street to celebrate the tie. You cannot imagine what it does for an expansion team to get a tie its first time into the Forum. It was cold, and Gordie's hair was wet. A young boy handed him a program, and Howe signed it over the picture of his son.

"That's not you," the boy protested.

"No, but that's my *work*."

Howe has always been good with children. He chides and kids remorselessly, and who can guess what must go through their minds? They worship him. He takes a giant hand now, and musses up the boy's hair, a great blond shock. "Look at you with all that hair, and me with so little. That's not very fair."

The boy blushes. Ah, that he, and his hair, might endure so well.